STOKED

A Spiritual Journey
from Employee
to Lifestyle
Entrepreneur

STOKED

A Spiritual Journey
from Employee
to Lifestyle
Entrepreneur

GREG REX

MERACK PUBLISHING

Published and distributed by Merack Publishing

Library of Congress Control Number

Rex, Greg, 1964 -

ISBN 978-1-949635-21-8 (hc) / 978-1-949635-22-5 (pb)

Text set in Georgia

Cover Design by Yvonne Parks

Illustrations by Greg Rex

Printed in the United States of America

DEDICATION

This book is dedicated to the crazy, courageous entrepreneurs who are willing to risk failure, break away from the pack and follow their inner voice. To the ones willing to take responsibility for their life, their lifestyle and their total wellbeing. May you experience the joys and challenges of becoming a lifestyle entrepreneur.

The minute you begin to do what you want to do, it's a different kind of life.

—R. Buckminster Fuller

CONTENTS

∞

INTRODUCTION

Unity is plural, at minimum two.

—R. Buckminster Fuller

At age thirteen, my best friends Rusty and Kenny were stoked to get our first surfboards for $12.00 at a garage sale. Kenny's dad, Ken Sr., gave us a quick lesson, and we paddled out at La Jolla Shores. It was "radical", so fun! Completely head-over-heels, "in love" with surfing and the ocean herself.

Decades later, the rush, the tingling feeling of weightlessness that comes from standing up and dropping in on your first wave is addictive. The new goal in life ... to figure out how to get to the beach when the waves are good.

By age fifteen, going crazy having to rely on mom for a ride... or worse having to waste an hour of daylight both ways on the bus to the beach—Gotta get my own wheels. My plan was to get a paper route, save my money, and buy a car.

My parents taught me "Work hard' and "follow your heart" and you will be successful at anything you chose."

Intuitively, I figured if I wanted to be good at something, I could find an expert— someone who'd already done it—and learn from them. Why reinvent the wheel?

So instead of grabbing the first available route, I started interviewing the local paperboys to find out who had the best route with fewest hills and the most paying accounts. Once I found the right paperboy with the right route, I offered to apprentice and substitute for him whenever he needed a day off, with the agreement that when he retired I would inherit the route. Even though I had to wait over a year and pay the price on those cold, rainy Sunday mornings, bagging and delivering monster three-inch thick newspapers, this was my first taste of being an entrepreneur and I learned so much. It taught me a key lesson that is at the heart of this book: Mastery through Mentorship.

My formula for success became:

1. Decide what I want to master
2. Find / befriend the best people in the field and become the "Eager Apprentice"
3. Work my ass off to model them and duplicate their level of mastery
4. Then become the "Humble Mentor," paying it forward to the next generation always remembering mastery is a practice—not a destination

There is something sacred and timeless about this method of passing down principles, practices, and knowledge. From the conscious, humble mentor and the eager, coachable apprentice I've learned to appreciate the integrity and harmony of these two sides of the same coin. Like the yin yang symbol, there is a polar opposite—yet inseparable—connection between dichotomies.

As I learned to honor the dynamic flow and relationship between "opposites" such as north and south, masculine and feminine, giving and receiving, shadow and medicine, learning and teaching, leading and following, mentoring and being mentored, I have learned to enter my flow state more easily.

This synergistic energy exchange between the "eager apprentice" and the "humble mentor" seems to generate and amplify intrinsic motivation for both. And when the master is humble and open-minded, they too benefit from the reciprocal learning that is inherent in teaching.

This book pays homage to many of my amazing teachers and mentors. Some of these mentors I've worked for or with. Some came in the form of books and audiotapes. Others came when I invested in myself and attended their seminars and courses. I am blessed to say several have become my best friends. Having an ongoing, mutually respectful relationship magnifies the impact we have on each other.

One thing that makes a great mentor is the ability to ask the right questions at the right times. One of my best friends and mentors is business coach, entrepreneur, and best-selling author John Assaraf. He asked me, "So who are you writing this book for? Who's your audience?" My answer came quickly: "Myself... 25 years ago. Maybe by sharing some of my lessons and "mis-takes" I can help some young ambitious entrepreneurs have the life of their dreams and do something amazing."

STOKED is a fictional story, loosely based on my life but more so on the lessons I've learned on my spiritual and entrepreneurial journey starting and building more than ten companies (not including the paper route, lol).

All but a few of the characters, names, and events are fictitious. My intention is to give credit to and recognize the many mentors who I learned from directly whenever possible, however, so you will notice I recommend many of their books (*See Appendix – Recommended Reading). Like most entrepreneurs, I learned many lessons from the school of hard knocks, however, it has been through my relationships with mentors that helped transform my so-called "failures" into key distinctions and invaluable experience.

Failure has also proven to be a profound teacher. In many ways more than my successes. At thirty-seven years old, I had a breakdown / breakthrough. Working with a myopic focus on my career and financial success, I had a mid-life crisis. Working for Tony Robbins in my mid-twenties I learned the mindset to "do whatever it takes" to reach my goal of "being a millionaire"—first by age thirty, then thirty-five. But what I was doing wasn't working, and it was clearly unsustainable. There I was, fifty-plus pounds overweight, burned out in an unfulfilling sixty hour per week, life-sucking corporate job plus twenty hours per week coaching with no time to help myself find balance. I was living way beyond my means trying to look good and keep up with my peers. I had $100,000 in high-interest debt and school loans, I was faltering in my relationships with family and friends, and no time for my passions or my health.

Seeing the writing on the wall about my corporate job and craving the freedom I had when I was an entrepreneur, I decided to add another plate to spin. My best friend, Jim Bunch, and I co-founded a coaching business called Happy Healthy Wealthy Enterprises focusing on those three areas we call the Trilogy: Healthy Body, Healthy Mind and Healthy Finances. Although I had a modicum of "success" in helping others simplify and reorganize their lives, I felt totally incongruent teaching these principles while being overweight, stressed out, and broke myself.

My "rock bottom" coincided with the nation's trauma of 9/11—all of my stocks and investments tanked and I was laid off. My sweetheart at the time, Whitney Kell, and I took a sabbatical to Costa Rica. I needed to figure out my next move. Being so out of shape I could barely surf the most amazing waves I'd ever seen was the straw that broke my back. This made me feel like even more of a failure.

In my heart, I knew there had to be a better way. I yearned for nature, to slow down and simplify my hectic life. I remember walking down a path in one of the most amazing rainforests in the world, praying and asking for guidance. I knew I couldn't go back to the corporate grind. I looked up and saw a Tico (Costa Rican man) raking his colorful, tropical front yard. There were a few pigs, chickens, papaya, banana and coconut trees in his simple house with a thatched roof. He smiled beamingly, threw me the shaka sign and said "Pura Vida!" which translates to "pure life", but is more like "hello" or their version of aloha. I replied and waved back and thought to myself, I want his life! Simple, stress free, abundant, connected to nature and happy & healthy...But how am I going to make a living? I realized I had been earning (and spending) more than $100,000 per year since starting with Robbins at age 26. There were hundreds of companies and different careers I could choose.

I thought, I can't go back to the corporate rat race and concrete jungle. I needed to simplify and change my entire life and alter my definition of success. As I looked around I was in awe of this jungle. I sat there and realized how perfect the ecosystem was. How everything was connected. Food chain, how water, earth, wind and fire all come together in harmony to sustain life. One of my natural abilities is to recognize patterns. This was refined even more by learning about "modeling" while I was working with Tony Robbins. What is working, what is not working? What patterns do my role models practice?

I started to notice a pattern of three's. Three poisonous, colorful frogs. Three birds. Three types of monkeys. Three stones. Everywhere the trilogy. I took this as a sign spirit was directing me to focus on my coaching business with Jim.

My new definition of success was more about "being" then "achieving." I decided I was going to focus on creating balance and harmony in three key areas of optimal health: Healthy Body, Healthy Mind, and Healthy Finances.

I knew being an entrepreneur was better suited for me than working for "The Man." But I wanted to make sure no matter what I did, there would still be time for my passions. So I set out on a journey to become a lifestyle entrepreneur. One who decides what their optimal lifestyle is FIRST, then creates a business that allows them to work doing what they are passionate about, using their unique gifts and talents, with a profitable business model that supports it all.

It was March 5, 2002 when I met my ultimate health mentor, Dr. Wayne Andersen, a pioneer in Health and Wellness. He had left critical care and allopathic medicine to move into prevention and wellness. Our visions were aligned, so for the last 17 years we have partnered to create what has now become an international movement.

Today, in my fifties, I'm at my optimal weight, with less than fifteen percent body fat and can do things some twenty-five-year-olds can't. I've identified my passions, gifts, and talents and helped build a conscious business called OPTAVIA™, which has become one of America's most successful transformational health coaching businesses. Through this business, we've helped more than 1,000,000 people transform their lives. Since my work can be completed virtually, I can run my business from anywhere in the world. This gives me a lot of freedom. I've gotten my finances in order and now have zero "bad debt". I own my dream cabin on forty acres in the mountains of Lake Tahoe, and have a beach house in San Diego. I can surf and snowboard right outside my two front doors! With this balance, I finally have time for the amazing people in my life. I feel very blessed to have created my optimal lifestyle, and now my goal is to help others do the same.

As you read the story and learn the principles in this book, my hope is you ask yourself, "How can I apply these to my career and to my life? How can I build a life of meaning and purpose while contributing to the greater good?"

I believe in taking a holistic, integrated approach to life and learning. Because of that, this is a book about well-being and life integration, covering a lot of ground: business and social entrepreneurship, surfing, love, relationships, the environment, health, and spirituality.

You'll notice at the beginning of each chapter, there's a quote by Buckminster Fuller, aka "Bucky." Bucky was one of the most influential mentors I never met. He was the "Gentle Genius," a humanitarian who dedicated his life to making the world work for 100 percent of humanity by identifying, applying, and teaching the immutable laws he called Generalized Principles. The criteria for these principles are:

1. Eternal, with no exceptions
2. Inter-accommodative to other Generalized Principles
3. So predictable they can be demonstrated mathematically

Bucky was said to have believed there were hundreds of Generalized Principles. This book introduces a powerful few: Integrity, synergy, leverage, and precision. Through my time with Marshall Thurber, who personally studied with Bucky for a decade until

Bucky's passing, and by reading Bucky's books, I learned how critical these principles are for sustainable success. I also realized there could be harmony between science and nature, between finances and spirituality, and between enterprise and humanity.

Nature is a totally efficient, self-regenerating system.
If we discover the laws that govern this system
and live synergistically within them, sustainability will
follow and humankind will be a success.

—R. Buckminster Fuller

A socially conscious entrepreneur who builds a business with a higher moral purpose can have not only impact, but also create a sustainable and profitable for-benefit business. By "for-benefit" I mean a business that is established with the primary mission of having a positive impact on society. Its shareholders understand that there is a need to make enough profit to execute the mission, but they're not in business primarily to make a profit for themselves—they're in business primarily for the benefit of society.

I wrote this book for the ambitious, courageous entrepreneur who wants to make a difference in this world but doesn't want to exhaust themselves in the process. Success doesn't mean giving up everything that's important to you in order to meet someone else's goals.

While writing this book with my amazing writing coach, editor, and friend Rebecca L. McCarthy, we realized there was more information I wanted to share than I could possibly fit into this one story. For those of you who want to go deeper into the journey of creating optimal health, becoming a lifestyle entrepreneur, and joining part of a community of like-minded people, I've created a mobile app and online community. STOKED, a free mobile app, will provide challenges, exercises, worksheets, video trainings, and an interactive community to support you as you design your ideal life. To get a free copy of the app, search "STOKED" in the app store and look for this icon to download it and join the community.

Everyone will get something different out of this book. Not everything will resonate with everyone. Take and leave what you will. My intention is to pass along a few principles and strategies that were passed down to me from my mentors and hopefully they work for you as well as they have worked for me. If you are ready to become a "lifestyle entrepreneur" and use these principles and strategies to identify your passions, gifts, and talents, and then explore careers in business models that allow you to express those gifts in service of humanity, I applaud you and hope you enjoy the journey.

And just as important, my hope is something in this book touches you and reminds you that you are the writer, director, and actor of this movie called "Life." Are you ready to take responsibility for your creation and begin to organize your life around what matters most to you?

Then alright, let's go!

With love and respect,

CHAPTER 1

LANDLOCKED

*People should think things out fresh
and not just accept conventional terms and the
conventional way of doing things.*

—R. Buckminster Fuller

Mitch Springer stood by the lobby window on the seventeenth floor of Reynolds Pharmaceuticals with an energy drink in his hand. He stared out beyond the medical center, beyond the busy streets of Los Angeles, to the thin blue horizon that allowed the company recruiters to boast "ocean views." The only sound was the occasional soft chime of the elevator, and the musical, soft tone of the receptionist answering the phone behind him, "Reynolds Pharmaceuticals..."

Through LA's thick morning smog, he caught a glimpse of a distant sailboat across the horizon, which reminded him of his trips to the beach when he was a kid. It was just Mitch, his mom, his best friend Dusty, and his little brother and sister. There was nothing like the thrill of catching his first wave, feeling the power of the ocean as it picked him up and carried him all the way to shore. He closed his blue eyes and took a deep breath.

He saw himself push the nose of his surfboard underwater just before the lip of a seven-foot wave started to pitch. He executed a perfect duck-dive, while the breaking wave rolled by harmlessly. The buoyancy of the surfboard pulled him back to the surface, and he came up smiling.

Just then, in his pocket, his cell phone vibrated. Mitch blinked and shook his head, almost spilling his energy drink. "Urgent text" from Mr. Gordon. He pressed the "Ignore" button with one chubby finger and put it away.

As 8 a.m. approached, the phone began to ring and the elevators began to ding. The interns arrived first, carrying trays of hot coffee for their bosses. Then the associates from the legal department rushed in—that is, the associates who'd actually gone home the night before. At Reynolds, some employees worked so late they found it easier to sleep in their offices than to make the long commute home and fight traffic again in the morning. This occurred with enough frequency that Reynolds actually equipped the offices in the legal department with "recharging pods," basically a fancy word for cots.

Mitch bent forward to pick up his Cucinelli leather portfolio on the floor. He rubbed his eyes, yawned and thought, *Maybe I should get a cot*. Then he felt a sharp pinch from his belt buckle pinching his belly-fat. He stood up straight and tried to loosen it a bit, but saw that it was already on the last notch. He sucked in his stomach to try to create some space, but even that didn't work.

"Hey, you know you can take a pill for that," Mitch heard a man's voice suddenly. He wheeled around to see Matt O'Reilly, a fellow sales rep, snickering as he paraded briskly across the lobby toward the executive offices. Matt was a burly man in his mid-thirties with black hair and thick eyebrows. Matt and Mitch traded barbs a lot, but for some reason this morning, Mitch just wasn't on his game.

"Oh, I . . . " Mitch stammered, but he couldn't think of a clever comeback before Matt disappeared down the hallway.

Looking back down at his belly, Mitch thought, Maybe I should try the pills. Reynolds was a wholesaler and distributor of pharmaceutical drugs to large medical institutions like hospitals, pharmacies, and medical centers, so he certainly had access. In fashion-and-image-crazed Los Angeles, his three best sellers were Meridical, an appetite suppressant to help people lose weight; Fotox, a muscle relaxant to reduce wrinkles; and Triphanolin, a cholesterol-lowering drug most commonly consumed after a double bacon cheeseburger.

Mitch considered making a call to one of the doctors he knew to see if he could get a prescription for Meridical, but then thought better of it. *I probably only need to lose about twenty pounds, he thought. I'll start my diet next week.*

He glanced at his silver-and-black Rolex and quickly gulped down the last of his energy drink. He crushed the can against his hip, tossed it in the recycling bin nearby, and in the last quiet moments of the early morning, turned to take one last look out the window.

As soon as I close this deal, I'm gonna book an epic tropical surf trip, he thought as he adjusted his striped silk necktie and strode down the hall toward his cubicle.

Mitch passed the 'Wall of Fame' that featured engraved name-plates of every top producer of the month for the past fifteen years. His name dominated the last column, which was this year, and he had a nice presence on the column to the left, which was the previous year—his first at Reynolds—when he won Rookie of the Year.

Mitch was an easy hire for Reynolds recruiters because of his job performance at previous companies and his pedigree: he was in his late twenties with a college degree and was an ambitious, good-looking, competitive achiever with great people skills. The recruiters had told him all about life in Westwood.

"It borders Bel Air and Beverly Hills," they said. "Reynolds is right near UCLA Medical Center, LA General, and Cedars-Sinai Medical Center, and it's only eleven miles to the beach!"

Mitch envisioned himself cruising along Pacific Coast Highway in a convertible with his surfboard in the back seat, wearing designer suits, eating at all the best restaurants, having a beautiful woman on his arm, and taking exotic surf vacations. When they offered him a near-six-figure salary plus commissions and bonuses, he signed right away. What more could an employee want?

Mitch always felt a combination of pride and anxiety as he walked by that Wall of Fame. Pride because his hard work had paid off, and anxiety because there was always the next month to prove. Mitch approached the main office area and put on his game face.

He walked briskly through the sea of cubicles, and a wave of office sounds rolled toward him—clacking keyboards, beeping cell phones, rustling papers, and the rhythmic hum of photocopiers.

"Hey Mitch!" called out Jeremy, one of the newer sales reps, as he headed into the break room on the left.

"Hey guy," Mitch said smoothly, flashing a smile as he walked toward his cubicle in the back. He nodded at his coworkers as he passed, while they talked on the phone or checked email. They gave him chin raises and thumbs-up in return.

Mitch slid into his swivel chair and booted up his computer. He grinned as he looked over the figurines on his desk—a miniature model VW van with a surfboard on the roof and a bobblehead hula dancer playing a ukulele under a palm tree. The monitor lit up and he opened his inbox, which was flooded with dozens of unopened emails. He deleted the spam, skipped over the business emails he wasn't interested in, but stopped when his eye caught a subject line that read, "Dude!" from "dustinthewnd79@gmail.com". A smile lit up Mitch's face and his eyebrows popped up. He clicked on the message:

```
Dude, meet me down in Mex. There's a
big swell coming in and I found this
killer little campground with a perfect
left-point break. Hardly anyone out. And
there's these two hot Canadian chicks.
I need a wingman! Why don't you drive
down for the weekend? Let's get some
waves. -Dusty
```

Mitch could visualize Dusty, tall and lanky with shaggy, sun-bleached hair, hanging out on beach chairs with two gorgeous women, a Corona in each hand—one for himself, one for Mitch. Ah, that would be *so killer*, he thought, and reached up to loosen his tie, which suddenly felt like a noose around his neck.

But Mitch also remembered that Dusty had no job, no career,

and no money. He did odd construction gigs for a few dollars here and there, but essentially, he was homeless. All play and no work. Mitch loved him but had to stay focused on his career.

He wrung his hands together, shook his head, and sighed. Saying no to this invitation was really going to hurt, but it had to be done. Mitch hit "Reply" and typed:

```
Dude, it sounds awesome. I so wish I
could be down there with you and be
your wingman, but I've got this big deal
getting ready to close and our annual
sales conference is next week. There's
no way I can get away, even for the
weekend. But after I close this deal, I'll
come down for sure and hang out with
you for a whole week. Later, Mitch
```

Mitch growled audibly as he hit "Send" but he looked up at the sales calendar pinned to the wall behind his computer and knew he had made the right choice. The close of the fiscal year was coming up and there was a $50,000 bonus up for grabs. Mitch was currently the front-runner, but Joe Weiss, whose name dominated the winner board in the years prior to Mitch's arrival, was a too-close-for-comfort second. *This is what I've gotta do, Mitch thought. I've gotta close the deal, win the bonus, go on a diet, work out hard for a month, and then . . . Mexico, here I come.*

"Uuunnnhhhh . . . " Mitch heard from across the room. Joe Weiss was standing up—it always took a while and happened with a groan. Joe was only fifty-nine years old but looked much older, and lately he'd been having some trouble with his back.

"What's going on, Joe?" Mitch asked. "Waking up from a nap?"

Joe chuckled, placed his hand on his lower back, and walked over to Mitch's cubicle.

"I've only got eight more months in this rat race."

"Yeah, lookin' forward to retirement?" Mitch asked.

"Oh yeah. I'm already planning my first golf vacation."

"Really! Where you going?"

"Well, I know where—Cabobut I'm not sure when. Turns out I need to have knee-replacement surgery." Joe rested his elbow on top of Mitch's cubicle wall and sighed as he leaned onto it. "But as soon as I have my surgery and finish my recovery, Cabo, here I come."

Mitch froze for an instant as it occurred to him that he might be staring at a future version of himself. The screen saver took over Mitch's computer and distracted him from the thought. It was a collage he had made from a surf trip back in college.

"Is that you?" Joe asked, noticing the surf pictures. In one photo, Mitch stood tall, his shoulder-length brown hair swept off to the side and behind his tanned shoulders. His athletic build showed off his chiseled abs and rock-solid biceps, aka "the gun show." His left arm was wrapped with pride around his new Thruster surfboard, and his right hand flashed a shaka brah, or "hang loose" sign.

"Yeah, that was like, ten years ago," Mitch said.

"I bet you kids are out there surfing every weekend," Joe said with a wink.

"Every weekend?" Mitch laughed, "I wish. These days I'm lucky if I get to go a couple times a year. I'm planning to go to Mexico in a month or so, though!"

"Mmhmm," Joe nodded. "Yes, well, work comes first."

"Yep!" Mitch agreed.

"See you later," Joe sighed and strained as he hobbled back to his desk. "I've got a doctor's appointment this morning. Oh hey…" Joe said as he noticed something on his desk. He picked up a thick, gray book and brought it over to Mitch. "Do you want this? My nephew sent it to me from college. Says it's gonna make me 'more successful.'"

Mitch glanced briefly at the title, Toxic Success: How to Stop Striving and Start Thriving, by Paul Pearsall.

"Nah, I don't have much time for reading," Mitch replied. "Thanks though."

"What bothers me is that the little shit thinks I need to be more successful," said Joe, frowning at the jacket copy. "These millennials are so entitled. They have no idea what it takes to be successful."

"Absolutely!" said Mitch supportively. "You've worked hard every day of your life, late nights and long weekends. You've been killing it for years with bonuses, a strong six figure income and don't you own like three houses? Two rental properties in Vegas, and one here in La Jolla?"

Joe nodded.

"Well if that's not success," Mitch pounded his open palm on his desk, "then I don't know what is." He picked up the wastebasket under his desk and held it out toward Joe. With an assertive grunt, Joe slam-dunked the book in the trash. The two high-fived, and Joe chuckled and turned away. Mitch watched as Joe stiffly put on his jacket and shuffled toward the door.

Suddenly remembering all the emails that needed his attention, Mitch reached into the top drawer of his desk, grabbed his earbuds, and put on some Bob Marley. Appointment confirmed, invoice approved, contract-signing date set, question answered, did so-and-so ever get in contact with you about such-and-such? Yes, I spoke with so-and-so last week, thanks.

"Mitch!" a voice barked from the front of the office. Mitch could hear it—even through his earbuds. He felt footsteps vibrating on the floor, coming toward him. Without missing a beat, he yanked out the earbuds and put his cell phone to his ear.

"Yes, of course, I'll get that over to you right away," Mitch said to no one. Then he looked up and saw Mr. Gordon's light brown, almost yellow eyes and unusually pointed nose looming over him from the side of the cubicle wall. His face was quite pale and white, with orange rust-colored hair. One could not help but feel startled for just a moment every time he entered the room.

"Didn't you get my text?"

Mitch held up one finger and said into the phone, "All right, great! I'll follow up with you tomorrow. Bye-bye." He tapped the screen with his thumb, pretending to end the call and gave his boss a you-know-how-it-is look.

"Sorry, that was Dr. Hahn. What's going on?" Mitch asked innocently.

Mr. Gordon waved a copy of the LA Times in Mitch's face and slapped it on his desk. The headline of the second article on the front page read, "Hospital Bans Controversial Weight-Loss Drug Meridical."

Mr. Gordon spoke while Mitch began to read.

"Look, I need you to fix this. It's your account. Cedars-Sinai just called to say they're talking about backing out. We're supposed to sign the contract next week!"

"High blood pressure, arrhythmias, twenty-eight percent increased risk of heart attack, and thirty-six percent increased risk of stroke," Mitch read aloud, then looked up. "These are the side effects of Meridical?"

"Eh, it's bullshit!" Mr. Gordon puffed. "The Public Citizen's Health Advocacy Group isn't even made up of doctors. They get these quacks to do bogus research and get everyone freaked out over nothing."

Mitch listened while reading and rubbed his neck. "Yeah, but, heart attacks and strokes—these are serious complications."

"It's all rumors! It's all hearsay. All the research they cite is from some European study. This has got the legal standing of an op-ed, for God's sake!" Mr. Gordon yapped while pacing the floor.

Mitch continued to read, fixated on the newspaper, which Mr. Gordon then snatched away. Mitch looked up, startled.

"Listen," said Mr. Gordon, leaning in, his yellowish brown eyes fixed on Mitch's. "The details are not our concern. Let the scientists fight it out. We're businessmen. We do the numbers. Corporate has been breathing down my neck to increase profitability. We're over budget on our marketing, the stock price is down, and this is not going to help. We need to focus on saving your deal. Worry about that, okay?"

Mitch looked down at the newspaper now crumpled under Mr. Gordon's arm.

Suddenly, Mr. Gordon stood upright and said nonchalantly, "By the way, don't forget that Joe Weiss is close to closing that UCLA deal. If you lose Cedars-Sinai, there goes your bonus. Gee, I'd hate to see you lose in the home stretch..."

Mitch glanced at the VW van and hula bobblehead on his desk. He shifted his belt buckle and sat up straight. He took out a yellow legal pad and pen from the side drawer of his desk.

"What do we need to do?" he asked faintly.

Mr. Gordon grinned and proceeded to give instructions while pacing back and forth. "We need a credible doctor to write up a report that counters the findings of these bogus European studies. That'll keep everyone busy for a while. One good doctor's word against another. Your job is to find our doctor. Who is the biggest prescriber of Meridical?"

Mitch scribbled notes on the legal pad, then opened his contact database on his computer. He turned away from Mr. Gordon and surveyed the list of names on the computer screen. "Don't worry, I'll take care of it," he muttered as he scrolled down the list.

Mr. Gordon nodded, tapped the newspaper against the wall, and strode out of the cubicle. He scanned the room as he headed back to his office, his head turning left, then right, then left again, like a fox sniffing for its dinner. Everyone in the room seemed to be on the phone, working hard.

* * *

One week later, Mitch sat with his coworkers at one of twenty round tables in the grand ballroom of the W Hotel in Beverly Hills. Almost two hundred people attended Reynolds Pharmaceuticals' sales rally and awards banquet, and the company spared no expense. The theme was Asian Fusion, and each table featured a floral center-piece on top of a tall, solid-gold base. Tassels dangled from colorful lanterns strewn about the banquet hall. Red satin tablecloths glowed from the tea lights carefully arranged around the gold centerpieces, and each place setting featured a small fortune cookie next to a tea-cup bearing the Reynolds logo.

Mitch sipped champagne, laughed, and shook hands with every-one around him—those he knew and those he didn't. They talked about the weather, the stock market, the movies, and of course, Mitch's big win. Even Joe Weiss, who came in second, came up to Mitch to shake his hand.

"Congratulations, kid," he said, barely audible above the music blaring from the speakers in the DJ's corner—a contemporary ver-sion of Sinatra's "Come Fly With Me."

Mitch shook Joe's hand with both of his. "Aw thanks, Joe. Hey, you really gave me a run for my money, that's for sure."

"Heh?" Joe said, squinting and leaning in.

Mitch paused, then just shouted, "Thank you!"

"Oh. Say, where's that cute girlfriend of yours? The one we met at the company barbecue last June."

Mitch hesitated, genuinely having no idea whom Joe was talking about. Then suddenly he remembered, "Oh right! I . . . no, she's not my girlfriend anymore. I have a new girlfriend now."

"Okay, and where is she?"

"She's working late," Mitch explained. "I'm gonna meet up with her after." Mitch made a mental note: Don't forget to text Gina to meet us for the after-party.

"Good boy," Joe said, then tilted his head to raise his ear to the ceiling. He began to snap his fingers in time to the music and stepped rhythmically from side to side. He said to Mitch, "Say, do you know how to foxtrot? I always wanted to learn to foxtrot." Mitch shook his head and wondered, What the heck is foxtrot?

Suddenly, Joe winced and he hunched over to clutch his thighs. His eyes darted about until they spotted a nearby table and chairs, and he hobbled quickly toward them. Mitch followed, asking, "Are you okay?" Joe didn't answer—just kept walking until he was able to sink into one of the chairs. He breathed deeply and rubbed his knees while Mitch flagged down one of the cocktail servers and asked for a glass of ice water, but Joe raised his arm and said, "Ice water ain't gonna cut it! Make that a scotch." Mitch did a double-take, but then shrugged at the cocktail server as if to say, "Give him what he wants."

The lights dimmed and the music stopped, signaling everyone to find their seats. Mitch patted Joe on the shoulder and then walked across the room to his assigned seat at table six, next to his crew of all the younger sales reps.

"Welcome everyone," blasted a nasally voice through the loud-speaker. "Please take your seats. I have some very exciting announcements." Mitch looked up at the podium to see Mr. Gordon, dressed to the nines in a black Armani tuxedo. He leaned into the microphone and said, "Shhhh," and gestured, as if pressing his hands down onto an imaginary pillow. Mitch exchanged glances with his colleagues and they all pressed the imaginary pillow as well. "Shhhhh," they joked. "Exciting announcements. Important announcements. Shhhh..."

"I know everyone is eager to get to their wontons and spare ribs so I'll get right to it," Mr. Gordon continued.

Conversations wound down and eventually the room was quiet.

"Well," said Mr. Gordon, like a parent about to reveal a Christmas surprise to his five-year-old, "We made our fourth-quarter earnings!"

The audience erupted in applause, hoots and whoops, high-fiving each other and patting backs. Making numbers meant corporate gifts and bonuses for everybody. Last quarter they all got new iPhones. The quarter before, there were Dodgers tickets.

"A big part of that is from our Salesperson of the Year," said Mr. Gordon, as Mitch straightened his tie. "I'm going to bring him up right now. Mitch Springer, where are you? Come on up here."

Everyone applauded as Mitch rose and strode across the floor and up the stairs to the podium.

"Mitch! Mitch! Mitch! Mitch!" they chanted, like kids cheering for their star Little League player. Mitch waved and grinned as he trotted to the stage. Once he got there, he looked back and tried not to laugh as he saw his colleagues back at the table pressing their hands down on the imaginary pillow and shushing each other.

Mitch took his place next to Mr. Gordon, who then raised his arm around Mitch's back and firmly shook him by the scruff of his neck.

"Everyone knows there's been some controversy over that horse-shit report in the Times," started Mr. Gordon. "The day it hit, Mitch and I were talking and I came up with an idea and thought: What better way to fight fire than with fire? They're writing bad press about us, and I thought, let's get some good press about us!"

Mitch stiffened as Mr. Gordon continued, "I asked Mitch who the most credible doctors are that he knows that really believe in Meridical." Mr. Gordon paused, as if expecting Mitch to say something. Mitch stood paralyzed, a plastic smile on his face.

"And so we called 'em up to the plate," Mr. Gordon said, pointing a finger in the air. "And one of those was Dr. Watson."

Mitch could hardly breathe.

"And because of his white paper, now all of us have the ability to get out there to protect and defend one of our biggest and most profitable brands. What does this mean? Increased sales!" After brief applause, Mr. Gordon clenched his fist, waved it in the air and barked, "And just wait until you see the new national TV ads we're launching next month. We expect a significant increase in market share!"

More applause, hoots, and whoops. Mr. Gordon let go of Mitch's neck and Mitch exhaled, smiling and clapping along with everyone else. Suddenly, a blonde bombshell in a sparkling silver mini-dress strutted out from the side of the stage carrying an oversized check. It was written out to Mitch in the amount of $50,000. Mitch's eyes practically jumped out of their sockets as he read the number. As the showgirl handed him the check and kissed him on the cheek, his whole face brightened. He looked at the giant check, lifted it over his head like a trophy, and nodded at his table of cronies, making sure they took a picture of him with the oversized check and hot chick. He had worked so hard, for so long, and now he had won.

I can live like a king down in Mexico on this! he thought. Confetti fell from the ceiling and Kool and the Gang's "Celebration" blasted from the DJ booth. The lights went up and the whole room started dancing and singing.

Mitch shook hands with the corporate executives and members of the board of directors as he made his way back to his table. They each thanked him for a job well done.

"You're one of our best success stories, Mitch," said one.

"We can't wait to see what kind of numbers you put up next year!" said another.

"That white paper strategy was genius. Way to go, kiddo!"

Mitch couldn't even hear, let alone process, what people said to him as he carried the check back to his table. After a few more boring announcements he found himself grabbing his group of cronies and saying, "Let's go to Sky Bar. Drinks on me!"

Eventually, he remembered to text his girlfriend, Gina.

`Going to Sky Bar now. See you there?`

Within seconds, a message came back:

`Sure, baby! I'm just wrapping up.`

Mitch didn't particularly like it when she called him "baby," but he didn't make a big deal about it. The relationship was casual enough, and he didn't see a need to get into it about things like that.

Later that night at Sky Bar, Mitch talked with Adam, one of his coworkers, at the posh lounge, the bar lit up in blue from the inside. Suddenly, Gina ran up behind Mitch and crashed into him with a huge bear hug, causing him to spill his cocktail. He wasn't fond of that habit, either.

"Oh I'm sorry, baby!" Gina gushed. "Are you okay?" She took

some cocktail napkins off the bar and started blotting Mitch's hands. He asked the bartender for some paper towels.

"It's okay," he said to Gina. "We're celebrating. I'll get us another round. What would you like?"

"Ummm, I'll have a Cosmo, please. And do you think we can see a menu?" she said in her poutiest baby voice, "I wowked aww night and didn't get a chance to eat anyfing!" She crossed her arms behind her back as she pouted, accentuating the curves that men always appreciate. Whatever Gina lacked in terms of her compatibility with Mitch, she made up for in looks and sex appeal. She was, by anyone's standards, hot. Without taking his eyes off her thick, shiny red hair and green eyes, Mitch reached behind him and grabbed a menu.

A shrill female voice interrupted them, followed by the appearance of a tall brunette with arms outstretched and head tilted to the side. "Ginaaaaa! Ohmygosh! I haven't seen you in forever!" It was Kathleen from the Reynolds' Marketing Department.

"Kathleeeeeeeen! Ohmygosh!" Gina responded with a hug. Mitch and Adam exchanged an amused glance.

"You look so cute and I love your purse. Is that Gucci?" Kathleen asked Gina.

"Prada. There's a new shop that has all the high-end brands. It just opened near my office, right next door to the best French bistro ever," Gina replied.

"Really?" Kathleen said effusively.

"So amazing, and I'm not even kidding you. Mitch, isn't that new French bistro so amazing?"

"It's pretty amazing," Mitch agreed. In fact, it was so amazing he had eaten entirely too much of it over the course of the past few months. Mitch suddenly became aware of his belly again and tried to sit up a little taller on the bar stool.

"We saw Beyoncé there, too, once. Last month, right?" he added. Gina locked eyes with Kathleen and nodded in a very serious way.

Kathleen grasped her long pearl necklace and smacked them

playfully at Adam's chest. "Ohmygosh. Adam, why haven't we been there? Promise to take me?"

Just then a burly man with a ruddy face, holding a beer mug, came barreling over to the group. Mitch looked up and saw Matt O'Reilly.

"Here's to the big man!" said Matt, raising his mug to Mitch, who raised his glass in return. Matt O'Reilly came in third in the race for the bonus, right behind Mitch and Joe Weiss. "Whatcha gonna do with that bonus check, big guy?"

Mitch shrugged humbly.

Matt raised his elbow to lean against the red brick wall, but it slid right off and he almost stumbled into Gina. Gina stepped closer to Mitch and wrapped herself up in his arms.

"A buddy of mine is making a killing on this new cryptocurrency," Matt slurred. "If you want, I'll give you his name."

Mitch shook his head. "Nah, I'm good, man. I've been investing in Reynolds for the last two years since I started. I take all the employee stock savings plan that they offer with the matching funds."

"But you gotta diversify."

Mitch raised his eyebrows, wondering if Matt even knew what "diversify" meant.

"Man, you got this fifty grand just handed to you. You should turn it into something," Matt insisted.

"You want to see what I did with my bonus?" Mitch said, as if accepting a dare. "I'll show you. Come on Gina, Matt, everybody—let's go outside. I have a surprise."

Mitch handed a ticket to the valet and waited with his hands in his pockets. A few minutes later, a brand-new black BMW drove up, and the valet stepped out. Mitch tipped him with a twenty-dollar bill.

"Whoa!" said Adam, raising his hand to Mitch for a high five. "The new six series! Awesome!"

"Yep. Leather seats, Adaptive LED headlights, surround-view camera system, night vision, 3D projected windshield display. This mother is badass."

Gina squealed, "Ooooh, I can't wait to ride in it. You're taking me home, right?"

Mitch put his arm around her and grinned at Matt, who bent over, clutched his belly and drooled a little bit. "I feel sick," Matt mumbled.

Mitch cocked his head to the side and joked, "Hey, you know you can take a pill for that."

Matt attempted to laugh, but only half of his face worked. Eyes half closed, he stumbled back inside the lounge.

* * *

The glow of the full-color, head-up display illuminated the interior of the car as Mitch drove Gina back to her apartment. She rifled through her purse looking for her lipstick while he punched it, with one hand on the gear shift, even though it was an automatic.

"I can't wait for Mary Anne's wedding next weekend. You and me, driving up in this car, ohmygosh so hot!"

Mitch slowed down. "Mary Anne's wedding...?" His face changed from one of delight to one of stone-cold zombie horror.

"Yes. Mary Anne's wedding," Gina repeated. There was silence. "You forgot!" she exclaimed.

"Well...I..." Mitch stammered.

"I can't believe it," she said bitterly.

"No, but...it's that we hardly even know her," Mitch pleaded. "So why are we even going to this thing?"

"It's at the Mirage. Everyone will be there."

"Okay, but why are we going?"

"Because it's at the Mirage and everyone will be there."

"You don't even like Mary Anne."

"So?"

Mitch snorted derisively and shook his head.

Gina shifted in her seat to look at him squarely. "Listen. We need to talk."

Mitch clutched the steering wheel with frozen fingers. In his mind's eye he envisioned himself running with a surfboard toward the ocean, but somehow the faster he ran, the farther away he got from the water's edge. Some sort of invisible harness kept him moving in slow motion, and the water seemed to be unreachable.

Gina asked, "Where is this relationship going?"

The words hung in the air like thunderclouds. Mitch swallowed hard.

"It's going...great," he said. "We're having fun. We're hanging out and...doing stuff."

"We've been together for eleven months," Gina said, like a lawyer presenting the evidence. "I'm going to this wedding, and I expect you to go with me. Everyone will be there and everyone expects to see us there. All my friends are getting engaged or married, Mitch. Now that you're finally doing so well at work, I just thought...I mean, I gave up that job offer in New York..."

Mitch started to speak and then stopped. He tried again but couldn't. He really didn't know what to say.

"And how is 'what's-her-name'? That girl in your accounting department?" Gina said in a tone that shot poison darts in all directions.

"Huh? Who?" Mitch asked.

"Muffy. Millie. M-something. That woman you're working with on that big hospital deal?" With each passing moment, Gina grew more upset.

"Oh, Misty. No. She's just a coworker. We've worked on some projects together, and she takes care of major contracts and invoices, but that's all."

"Mmm. Projects. Is that what you call it?"

"What? Gina, you're acting really..."

"I'm acting *what*? You work all the time. Taking clients out at night, I mean. When I hear you say you're working late at the office on a project with Misty, what am I supposed to think? Misty is such a bimbo name. What is it—short for 'mistress'?"

Mitch sighed. "No, there is nothing going on between me and Misty."

The next five minutes were deadly silent. Gina turned and sat with her arms folded across her chest, head leaned up against the window.

"Hey," Mitch said playfully. He reached out to tickle her leg. "Hey, you okay?"

"I'm fine."

"Oh. I know I'm a just a guy, but even I know that 'fine' means 'not fine.' So what's wrong?"

"Nothing. Just drop me off here at the next corner. I think I'll walk home."

"Come on. Look, how about we talk about this tomorrow, all right? Can we just take a little bit of time to cool down? It's been a heck of a night, I'm so tired, and I just really can't focus right now. Can I call you tomorrow?"

Gina sighed, and her face softened. "Okay."

Within minutes they arrived at her apartment building. Mitch kissed her goodnight and she smiled weakly at him as she exited the car. She walked up the stairs to her front door, fumbled for her keys, and walked inside. Once she was out of sight, Mitch leaned forward, rested his forehead on the top of the steering wheel, and took a moment to appreciate the quiet. Then he sat up, threw the car into gear, and sped home.

CHAPTER 2:

GETTING HAMMERED

*If humanity does not opt for integrity we
are through completely. It is absolutely touch and go.
Each one of us could make the difference.*

—R. Buckminster Fuller

On Monday morning, Mitch stood by the window in the lobby on the seventeenth floor of Reynolds Pharmaceuticals once again, energy drink in hand. Usually by this time, he was lost in ocean daydreams or memories of past surf vacations, imagining them so intently that he could practically taste the salt water on his tongue.

But not today.

He kept seeing Gina's pouty face every time he dared to think about surfing. He kept hearing the office—yes, the office itself—castigating him for planning to take time off. When the receptionist picked up the phone and said, "Reynolds Pharmaceuticals . . . " Mitch actually thought he heard, "Get back to your cubicles..."

As he walked past the Wall of Fame, Mitch heard muffled whispers and slamming doors—not the lively bee-like hum of activity he was used to. He stepped through the double-doors to the open office floor and couldn't believe what he saw. People looked positively green, as though they had just been attacked by zombies and were now undergoing transformation. They moved slowly and cried out to Mitch with their eyes. An image appeared in his head for a moment of the whole office full of undead employees, gnashing their teeth into cell phones and bashing their heads into computer screens.

Mitch scanned the room and saw one person who appeared to be unaffected, and that was Jeremy over by the water cooler, replacing the jug. Mitch cleared his throat to catch his attention. Jeremy turned to see Mitch, and raised his hand weakly as if to say, "Good morning, sort of. " Mitch responded with his palms open and an inquisitive glance. Jeremy nodded toward a newspaper on the corner of someone's desk nearby, and Mitch picked it up. He looked down and read the headline: "FDA Confirms Dangers of Weight-Loss Drug Meridical."

"Oh shit," Mitch said out loud. All of the zombies looked up at him, wondering if another victim would enter their fold. Indeed, as Mitch started to read the full article, the color began to drain from his face. Reynolds investors fled as their most popular drug fell under investigation by the FDA.

"MITCH!" Mr. Gordon barked, poking his head out of the doorway to his office. "Get in here!" Mitch walked forward, his feet feeling like cement blocks.

Mr. Gordon's office had no windows, and to Mitch it seemed small for such a high-level executive. Mitch always flinched at the musky scent upon entering and wished Mr. Gordon would at least let him keep the door open.

"Close the door behind you," Mr. Gordon said from his leather swivel chair. He sat behind a pile of newspapers, take-out cartons, three computer monitors, and a keyboard buried under folders on his desk. As Mitch turned and gently pushed the door closed, Mr. Gordon's phone rang. He quickly picked it up and Mitch stood by.

"Whaddya got?" Mr. Gordon said into the phone. "Mmhmm . . . mmhmm . . ."

Mitch glanced back down at the newspaper in his hands and tried to read more of the article.

More than 3,000,000 people have been pre-
scribed Meridical since 2002. It was tak-
en off the market in January in Europe,
and now the FDA recommends pulling it
from the American market as well. The FDA
just made an announcement advising all
patients to stop taking Meridical, and to
talk to their health care professionals
about alternative weight-loss programs.

"The fact that it showed no measurable
benefit compared to lifestyle changes
but actually did harm was important information for the investigators," medical
risk specialist, Dr. McConnell said. "When
we started reviewing this data, we realized that all patients using this drug
are at risk of those events. The risks
far outweigh the benefits."

Mr. Gordon stood and began to pace, his back to Mitch. "Look,
I'm not a scientist. My job is to sell these pills—not prove that they're
safe."

Reynolds stock price slides as investors
react to the negative publicity.

Mitch read while Mr. Gordon continued.

"We closed the deal! We got the PR that we needed! We did our
job, now you do your job!" Mr. Gordon slammed the phone back
onto the receiver and then looked up at Mitch. He made a motion
with his hands as if wringing someone's neck. Mitch tried to smile
but felt awfully weak.

"Cedars-Sinai cancelled their contract, buddy," Mr. Gordon said.
Mitch shuddered at the thought that they could be buddies. "The
hospital lawyers have filed a lawsuit. They want all their money back.
So, you know, I hate to do this to you, but we don't have a choice. No

order, no contract, no top-producer bonus. Accounting has voided your bonus check."

The words echoed in Mitch's ears. The ocean zoomed a million miles away. He envisioned his new car being towed to the dealership. His chest tightened.

"You're gonna be alright." Mr. Gordon said, with no real concern. "Hey, I know it's rough news but you've got to understand our position. You get paid when the company gets paid. If the company doesn't get paid, then, well…" He shrugged.

Mitch stood motionless.

"Hey, on the bright side: layoffs start tomorrow, and you're not on the list." Mitch's eyes met Mr. Gordon's. "We have to stay profitable for our board and shareholders. That means you can either make more or spend less. Reynolds is going to spend less. This is a tough time for all of us. Nothing personal."

"Nothing here is personal," he mumbled.

"What's that, buddy?" Mr. Gordon said vacuously.

"Nothing," Mitch said with a sigh and turned toward the door. As he stepped out, he considered the beige carpet, the stark white fluorescent lighting, and the gray cubicle walls. They seemed to close in on him as he contemplated that it might be another year before a sales bonus became available again, assuming Reynolds could survive and bounce back from the current situation.

Layoffs. Who would be the first to go? he wondered. Maybe he's right. Look at the bright side, at least I'm not on the list. And who'll take the positions of the people who are let go? Will there be promotions? Maybe I'll get promoted to regional director? The current regional director once said he was thinking of retiring early, so maybe if they let him go, I could just take his place.

"Uunnnhhhh…" Mitch heard from behind a wall to the right. He stopped at Joe Weiss's desk and watched him stretch. Joe looked up. "You ready, kid?"

Mitch looked at Joe out of the corner of his eye. "Ready for what?"

Joe took his jacket off and placed it on the back of his chair. As he adjusted his cufflinks he said, "Don't play games. You know damn well ready for what."

Quickly, Mitch stepped across the aisle to his desk, grabbed his chair, and rolled it over to Joe's cubicle. He sat close and leaned in. "So how does it work?" Mitch whispered.

"They call in a guy from headquarters," Joe explained in a low mutter. "Someone from HR in New York. He's like the clean-up guy from Pulp Fiction. He'll come in, set up shop in one of our empty rooms, and start calling people in, one by one. It'll be fast. People will get their paperwork, clean out their desks, and security will escort them out."

Mitch shook his head.

"This is the third time in my career at Reynolds that I've seen this," Joe said. "Last time, they were merciful and called people in groups. It's less humiliating that way. We'll see what we get this time."

Mitch noticed that Joe didn't seem nervous in the slightest. He was lying low and speaking softly, but didn't exude the same morose, fearful energy as everyone else around the office.

"Aren't you worried at all?" Mitch asked.

"Nah," Joe answered. "They don't need to let me go. I'm gone in a few weeks anyway." Mitch wished he could be as blasé.

"They took my bonus back," Mitch confessed.

Joe looked down and placed his hand on Mitch's shoulder. Of all people, Joe knew how hard and long Mitch had worked to earn that bonus. He knew it meant everything.

"Well, on the bright side maybe," Joe said, "once the rounds are done, they're going to have to reorganize the teams and put in new leaders. Either they'll bring in people from New York to start fresh, or they'll hire from within. I can't predict the future, but for sure you're a candidate to be a team leader of some kind. District Manager, possibly even Regional Manager. O'Reilly's got more seniority than you, but you've been outperforming him the last couple of years. Also, he's an asshole."

Mitch chuckled out loud but then swallowed it, looking up to make sure he didn't draw any attention to their conversation. The two continued to play fantasy football with the lives of everyone in the office until they had analyzed the odds, pros, and cons of every possible outcome once the layoffs started. They did not foresee, however, the kickoff that would set the whole game in motion in the first place.

"Gordon?" said the man in the navy-blue suit. Mitch thought if he just added a pair of sunglasses, he would look exactly like Agent Smith from The Matrix. The man in the navy-blue suit worked alone—no team, no office furniture. The only items on his desk were a laptop and a stack of forms. "Jack Gordon?" he said again, waiting for someone in the office to respond. Mr. Gordon peeped out of his foxhole, clearly not expecting the interruption in his workday. He stepped out, muttering something about how if the Yankee wants coffee he can always ask the receptionist where the breakroom is.

Everybody, including Mitch, kept their head down. Once Mr. Gordon went back in the office and shut the door, heads popped up over cubicle walls like a giant game of office whack-a-mole. People exchanged glances, shrugged, and raised questioning eyebrows. No one made a sound. Collectively, they knew that if they were quiet enough, they might be able to catch a sound bite from inside. Then suddenly...

"WHAT?!" boomed Mr. Gordon's voice. Everyone gasped.

"That's bullshit!" he shouted again. "I did my job! I was the only one who did my job. It's the guys in R&D you should be canning. They're the ones who approve our inventory! What the hell are you firing me for?"

Everyone in the office heard. Some people stood up to get a better view. Even though Gordon was behind closed doors, they still wanted a front-row seat.

"You guys are so full of shit!" Gordon continued. "I. Did. My. Job. I got the PR. I closed the deals. I'm the only one making money around here while all your other departments burn it, so don't even think about blaming me!"

Just then two security guards marched rapidly down the hallway and opened the door, linked arms with him and began to escort him out.

"Are you fucking kidding me?!?" Mr. Gordon shouted even louder, having lost total control.

"This is not personal. Don't make this hard on yourself," Agent Smith said. He acknowledged the staring faces of everyone in the room and shut the door.

Mr. Gordon resisted and shoved the two security escorts, which made them strong-arm him all the more. As he was taken into the elevator, he could be heard shouting, "I always made my numbers no matter what! I always made my numbers!"

A shock wave rippled throughout Reynolds as it sank in that Mr. Gordon had just been fired. One woman at the front of the room turned to face everyone, and her jaw dropped into a wildly amused smile. Everyone broke into smiles as well, but awareness of the agent behind the door never faded.

Mitch turned to Joe Weiss and mouthed the words, "Oh my God!"

Joe shook his head and mouthed, "Whoa."

* * *

The next two days swept through like a tornado. First, the FDA found Meridical guilty of submitting falsified data during early-stage trials and issued a citation as well as a heavy fine. The headline of the LA Times read, "Meridical Fined $200 Million for Drug Pulled off the Market." Sales came to a halt. Instead, hospitals began demanding refunds and returning all inventory. This was their top selling drug. Reynolds Pharmaceuticals' stock price plummeted from $80 to $40 the first day, then settled at $25 a share. Mitch was at his desk when he heard, from Matt O'Reilly no less, about the stock.

"I told you, you gotta diversify," he said, taking sick pleasure in

Mitch's pained expression. There was still no replacement appointed for Mr. Gordon's position. Mitch had to come to grips with the fact that Reynolds was in dire straits. Even if he got promoted, it likely wouldn't mean an increase in salary with all the pending lawsuits.

Not only that, but one by one, employees were called into Agent Smith's office to undergo the discharge process. The mood on the floor, so celebratory on Monday, sank into a deep blue funk by Thursday. Smith called names, the employees marched knowingly to their termination, signed some forms and received their final paycheck. Security then accompanied them to their desk and to the elevator.

Mitch felt some relief knowing he was safe from this, having put in so many hours, so many late nights and being the "top producer." He felt he was indispensable to the company. Just like his father said, "If you work hard and go the extra mile, you'll have job security for life."

After a brief lull in call-ins, he felt a bit of excitement when the office talk seemed to suggest that the layoffs were over, and now all the new managers would be appointed. He felt confident that he would be among the first employees to be promoted and asked to lead a team. He really looked forward to it.

Just then, Agent Smith poked his head out from his office door with a clipboard and called out, "Mitch Springer?" Mitch turned his head to see him duck back inside his office, the door slightly ajar.

Finally! Mitch thought. He grabbed a notepad and pen before walking in, ready to ask questions and step into his new role.

As he watched the man in the navy-blue suit arrange the forms on his desk, Mitch was suddenly overcome by a feeling of uncertainty.

The man didn't look up or introduce himself. "Mr. Springer, I'm sure you're aware of the adversity we're facing now as a result of the recent removal of Meridical from the market. As a result, your position is no longer... "

"What?" Mitch interrupted, just at the same time the man said, "needed."

The man looked up at Mitch and repeated, "Your position is no longer needed."

Shocked, Mitch searched for answers in the man's face, but he just stared back with indifference. "But why?" he asked softly.

"I'm sure you're aware of the adversity we're facing now as a result of the recent..."

"Yes, I know. But why me? Don't you know I'm your top producer? Check your files, check the Wall of Fame. I just won Top Producer of the Year. And Rookie of the Year last year."

The man in the dark suit looked back up at Mitch. "As a result of the recent removal of Meridical from the market, your position is no longer needed."

"Sales are no longer needed?" Mitch snapped.

The man stared at him. Mitch stared back, resolved not to leave until he got a straight answer. As he looked into the cold, soulless eyes of the man in the dark blue suit, the answer suddenly occurred to him. It's my connection to Gordon. It was the white paper. They don't want anyone around who knows about it while they're under investigation by the FDA. Mitch felt fear in a wholly different way.

"But I was just following orders," he said sheepishly. "I did what my boss told me to do. That's what you want us to do, isn't it?"

The door swung open and two security guards appeared, at which point Mitch backed down. Emotionally, he wanted to fight, but intellectually, he knew it was useless.

The guards led him to his desk and carelessly held a cardboard box while he chucked his bobblehead hula dancer, miniature VW van, and various other items into it. Mitch thought he might die from humiliation. He looked over at Joe Weiss to try to catch his eye, to beg him to intervene on his behalf, to stand up and say something, but Joe's head was down at his cubicle. He seemed to be on the phone, working hard.

It was barely four o'clock, and this was the earliest he'd ever come home on a weekday. On the bright side, he said to himself, no more brutal commutes through rush-hour traffic.

After he left Reynolds, he drove directly to the car dealership where he bought his BMW and turned it in. He took a bus the rest of the way home. Mitch fiddled with the keys to his luxury apartment in Huntington Beach with one hand while he held his cardboard box of belongings with the other. On top of the box, he balanced a bag of fast food. If ever there was an excuse to say, "Screw it!" and eat a large order of fries, a burger, and a shake, this was it.

Mitch pushed open the door and let everything drop onto the sand-colored quartz countertop in the kitchen. He grabbed the now cold bag of fast food and walked over to the black leather reclining sofa in the TV room. He dropped his shake into the lighted drink holder and looked at the bills and statements strewn about his glass-top coffee table. The thought of opening the envelopes and looking at them filled him with dread. He ate a couple of french fries.

First, he opened a student loan bill. Ugh, he thought, get to that one later.

Then he opened the utility bills. Okay I have to pay that one now.

Cable bill. Have to pay that one now.

BMW statement. Mitch felt a knot in his stomach. He ate a couple more french fries and threw the statement into the do-not-pay pile.

Next, he opened his visa credit card bill, which, because he missed a couple of payments, now carried a twenty-five percent interest rate. Gotta pay the minimum on that one, Mitch thought and threw it onto the pay-the-minimum pile.

Oooooh! Mitch felt a surge of excitement as he picked up the next envelope. On the back it read, "You may be eligible for a $10,000 line of credit." He thought perhaps this could be his cushion. If I can apply and get approved before they find out I don't have a job, maybe I can get $10,000 and still go on my surf trip. He opened the envelope quickly to see if there was one of those write-yourself-a-check offers inside. There wasn't, but he kept the paperwork in the pile for later.

Next there was a car insurance bill, and he wasn't sure he if he needed to pay that one or not, because he didn't have a car anymore. He rubbed his neck and threw it onto the do-not-pay pile.

Pay-now, pay-later, pay-the-minimum, do-not-pay—eventually they were all sorted. The last bill he opened was from the furniture store where he had bought everything for his luxury apartment. He was still paying down an $11,000 balance on that one. Pay-the-minimum.

Mitch sipped his shake and shifted his attention to the statements. All the news was bad. His Merrill Lynch statement was entirely in the red. His portfolio, which consisted of almost all Reynolds stock and worth $150,000 just one month ago, was now worth about $34,000. His checking account balance was just above $8,000, and his savings account balance was still only $200, the amount he opened the account with.

He stood and started to pace briskly about the apartment. He didn't have anywhere to go, but he wanted to get away from the bills. He wanted to not see them anymore and for this nightmare to end. He looked over at his small cardboard box from Reynolds. He imagined grabbing a baseball bat, bashing the side of the box, and letting out a savage scream as he released his anger on the miniature VW van figurine. He had worked so hard! He had done everything right! How could this happen?

He picked up the phone and called Gina, which he didn't think he'd ever do again, but the truth was, he didn't have anyone else to call.

As he shared his woeful story, Gina gushed, "Oh baby, I'm so sorry. How can they just do that? You did everything for them!"

"I know!" Mitch agreed. "I gave them all my time, all my energy. I worked so hard."

"You did. You're the hardest worker I know. But you know what, everything will work out just fine. Maybe this is a sign."

"And now how am I gonna find a job?" Mitch continued, starting to whine a little bit. He couldn't help it—Gina made it so easy. "Now I'll have this stain on my résumé because of Reynolds. I'm running out of money. I'm in debt. I have to figure out how to pay my rent. I have to figure out my car situation. I'm so screwed."

"What car situation?" Gina asked. "I thought you bought the

BMW with your bonus."

"Yeah, more great news, I had to return it. It was an eighty-thousand-dollar lease, and I know my bonus was only fifty thousand dollars, but I figured I could afford it because I only needed the down payment. So I put eighteen thousand dollars down, and worked out a deal where I owed only one thousand dollars a month. But then once Reynolds took back my bonus and fired me, I had to return it and break the lease. So I lost my down payment, I had to pay a fat penalty for breaking the lease, and then the dealer bought back the car for a fraction of what I paid for it! When the smoke cleared, I ended up paying over $25,000 for a car I had only three weeks! I can't believe what crooks those guys are!"

"Aw, baby!"

"I know!" Mitch walked back to the sofa and collapsed onto it. Sympathy was just what he needed, like ice cream on a hot summer day.

"You poor thing!" she said, then, "Hey, I have an idea. I think I know a way you can save money. What if we move in together?"

Mitch almost swallowed some air. "Huh?"

"Well," she continued, "do you need to save money? Yes. Do you need a place to live? Yes. Do you love me?"

Mitch stammered, "I...it's...it's not a question of love, it's just that I have so much going on right now."

"Ohmygod!" Gina exploded. "Are you serious? You can't even say 'yes' or 'no.' Do you love me?"

"Hey, wait a second," Mitch sat up.

"Okay, that's it. That's all the answer I need," she said.

"But honey..."

"But nothing! I'm so sick and tired of your fear of commitment. I deserve a man who's gonna love me and not be afraid to say it. You don't want to move in together? Okay fine. But then, I'm sorry, I can't sit around here waiting for you anymore. Geez, the last time

I saw you, you said you would call me the next day, and now you go and call me like two days later and don't even say you're sorry. All you do is make me wait. Well, I'm not waiting anymore. We're done! Good-bye!"

Mitch sat stunned as the phone went silent. Did that just happen? he thought. Did she just ask to move in together and then ten seconds later tell me off and hang up on me?

The experience was familiar, actually. His previous girlfriends had broken up with him for similar reasons and in much the same way. It's not that he was heartbroken—the feeling was much more like relief—but still, he didn't understand how or why it kept happening. Do I have a sign on my forehead? "Girlfriend wanted. Must be beautiful, high maintenance, and hell-bent on marriage. Fall in love and then tell me I'm the biggest jerk alive. Inquire within."

Mitch shook his head, put the phone down, and combed his fingers through his hair, as if trying to pull the headache out. He grabbed the remote control and turned on the TV.

"Surf advisory in effect one more day," said the weather reporter on channel four. Mitch turned up the volume. "Conditions are clean with twelve-to-fifteen-foot waves." Mitch checked the time: only five o'clock. He could make it. He had nothing to lose. It's not like he had to wake up early for work the next day, and there was so much stress to burn. So for the first time in six months, he put on his board shorts and got ready to go surfing.

* * *

Mitch went downstairs to the garage in his building and pulled his biggest board, his six-ten Thruster, his leash, and a two-millimeter rash guard from his storage closet. But then he looked around and remembered his car wasn't there. He saw his old skateboard in the corner of the closet. He hadn't touched it since he started at Reynolds, but desperate times called for desperate measures. The beach is only a mile away, he thought. I can do it.

He dropped the skateboard on the sidewalk and started off, holding his board under one arm and gear in the other. The good news was that muscle memory kicked right in and he was able to skate just fine. The bad news was that after only a few blocks, his legs started to burn and it became difficult to breathe. He persevered and eventually made it to the beach, but he was so tired already, he worried he might not have anything left for the water. Mitch hid the skateboard in some bushes, caught his breath, and walked down toward the shoreline.

As he got close enough to see the ocean, Mitch was so excited and focused on the huge sets rolling in that he accidentally whacked a few passersby as he marched down from the boardwalk. He didn't mean to—he just didn't account for the rotation of the surfboard as he wove through the crowd.

"Sorry! Oops!" he called out as he walked quickly by.

"Watch it, buddy!" someone called out after him.

He trotted down the stairs and past the concession stands, where the air smelled like chili-cheese fries and hot dogs. Then he passed the bathrooms, and finally Jake's Surf Hut, which looked like something straight out of Gilligan's Island. The bamboo-style hut with a roof covered by palm fronds featured two large wooden, carved tikis at each side of the front entrance.

Mitch walked past Jake's Surf Hut, and then continued toward the ocean. He noticed two people seated on lawn chairs on the sand near the back patio as he walked past. First, there was a man with long, silver-streaked hair wearing nothing but board shorts and a tank top, watching a handful of surfers out in the water and drinking water from a gallon jug. Mitch wondered if he was one of the many homeless surf bums that hung out on the beaches in Southern California. That bum better not leave that bottle on the beach, thought Mitch. Nothing riled him worse than litter on the beach. It was like litter on his childhood.

In the other chair, a woman nursed a tropical drink of some kind. Mitch could see a flower in the glass as she held it out to the side. Other than that, he noticed only her long, dark hair that hung like silk behind the back of her chair and the orange sarong that covered her slender legs in front. Nice skirt, but I'm done with skirts, he thought, and walked faster toward the shoreline.

The moment Mitch set foot on the sand, he felt a rush of energy. *I can't believe I'm finally going to paddle out!* He charged into the water, heading toward the south side of the pier, straight past a red warning flag with a sign attached to it.

I'm not in doubt, he thought, and bent down to strap on his leash.

Just then, two dripping wet surfers in their late 30's walked straight up to him. One of them said, "Hey buddy, do you know how big it is out there? The side shore winds and currents are out of control. You might just want to hang on the beach and take some pictures." Mitch smirked and walked right around them to the water.

Why does everyone think they're my buddy?

Finally, he reached the water's edge, barely noticing a calm but very solemn-looking surfer doing yoga stretches with the intensity of a warrior getting ready for battle. The only time Mitch had for stretching was to put on his rash guard. He walked out into the water and felt the surge of the massive swell pushing him back. He waded out, jumped over some whitewater, got to about waist deep, and jumped on his surfboard to start paddling.

After about five minutes, he looked over at the pier and realized he was no farther out than when he started. He tried duck diving and paddling as hard as he could through the breaking waves, but the surge of the whitewater and the currents pushed him back every time.

After about ten minutes, Mitch thought he might be making progress, but then a big wave hammered him. Rejected, frustrated and nearly exhausted, he let it carry him back to the sand. He sat on the shore for about five minutes, caught his breath, and decided to try again.

On the second attempt, the currents and the power of the ocean proved to be just too much. The waves were consistent, coming one after another, and Mitch grew more and more fatigued. After a ten-minute pummeling, a huge wall of whitewater plowed over him and ripped his board out of his clutching hands. He put his feet down to see how deep the water really was, and was surprised to learn it was only chest deep. He wasn't even twenty percent of the way out yet!

Back on the beach, the man with silver-streaked hair on the beach chair commented, "Well, he sure is determined."

Mitch rallied. Breathing like a runner, he got into a rhythm and did a couple of good strong duck dives. He did, in fact, get closer to the lineup. He was finally out far enough to get under the lip of the waves instead of duck-diving whitewash. Now we're getting somewhere, he thought.

Just then he saw another surfer riding a left, coming straight at him. He paddled even harder to get out of his way and over the top of the wave. Over his shoulder he saw the surfer pull out of the wave, grab his board, catch air, and then land in one motion, all with a huge smile on his face.

Mitch turned back to the horizon and saw a big fifteen-foot set wave about to crash down on his head. He knew that if the lip hit him, he would be in deep trouble, so he bailed his board, pushing it off to the side, and dove down to get out of the impact zone. As he held his breath under water, he felt the tug of his surfboard on his ankle, pulling him back toward shore. When he floated to the surface and looked for his board, it was "tombstoning". Still being dragged back to shore, the tension in the leash finally released and Mitch was able to pull his board to him.

The surfer who passed by Mitch just a moment before yelled out from behind him, "What are you doing, kook? Way to bail your board right in front of me!"

Then another surfer called out to Mitch, "Hey shithead! Beat it! You're gonna hurt somebody!"

Mitch didn't even realize what he had done, and he didn't care, either—he was so close to getting into the lineup. He wanted to flip the guy off and yell back, but he channeled all of that energy and adrenaline into paddling instead. He grabbed his board and started paddling like mad before the next wave hit.

Just as he got his momentum, another set wave loomed overhead. Mitch thought, I don't have enough breath for a long hold down so this time when I duck dive, I'm not letting go of the board.

He gulped a big breath of air, pushed the nose of his board deep to start the duck dive, but the whitewater hit him with all the force of a brick wall crashing down. He held onto the board with both hands. It spun, like an alligator, whirling in all directions so Mitch couldn't tell which way was up. They wrestled until finally the force of the water ripped the board from Mitch's hands. He and the board continued to tumble under the water and suddenly, Mitch felt a big thump on his head.

Almost out of air, Mitch finally floated to the surface. He looked toward the shore, reeled in his board, turned and saw another big wave coming. Realizing he was in over his head, he decided to go in. He turned to catch the whitewater, which spat him back on shore in a matter of seconds.

Dazed, exhausted, and feeling a pounding in his head, Mitch stumbled up the beach at dusk. The street lamps lit up on the boardwalk behind him. He looked down and saw dark drops falling to the sand and thought they were too dark to be water. He felt a trickle down his face and realized he was bleeding.

He reached up to feel the wound on his forehead, right above his left eye. What he felt was a gash so deep it might very well have pierced his skull. He swayed hazily as a series of images swirled around in his head: the Wall of Fame, Joe Weiss's bum knees, the giant $50,000 check, Gina's pouty lips, the black BMW rolling up at the valet, the zombie faces of his coworkers, the newspaper headlines, Reynolds Guilty!, Mr. Gordon's pointy nose, Agent Smith, the bills, the breakup, the bobblehead hula dancer, the whitewash...and then Mitch's eyes rolled to the back of his head and he collapsed, completely unconscious.

CHAPTER 3:

CRAWLING UP THE BEACH

We are called to be the architects
of the future, not its victims.

—R. Buckminster Fuller

When Mitch awoke, he found himself on a cot, lying on his back with a towel supporting his head. He blinked a few times until eventually he was able to focus on a single lamp hanging from the ceiling. The soft, yellow light created a peaceful ambience, and even though Mitch had no idea where he was, he could hear the sound of the waves outside, and somehow he felt safe.

Slowly, he turned his head to the right and saw a couple of simple wooden chairs and a desk with a first-aid kit on it. To his left there was only a hammock in front of some surf pictures on a wall. There was also a large wooden sign in the shape of a surfboard that read:

Jake's Surf School

Programs for beginner,
intermediate, advanced, and
professional surfers.

Mitch tried to sit up, but then recoiled in pain as he became aware of the wound on his forehead. He pressed his palm to it and groaned as he lay back down.

Footsteps approached, and Mitch forced himself to open his eyes once again. He saw the silhouette of the man with silver-streaked hair looming over him, looking for signs of life in his eyes.

"Welcome back," said the man.

"Unnnh," Mitch groaned, still not fully lucid, "the homeless guy."

The man smiled gently and turned to the desk behind him. He opened the first-aid kit and took out a few packets of alcohol-soaked wipes and gauze.

"Aloha. My name is Jake. This is my shop. You passed out. The lifeguards left over an hour ago, so one of my friends helped me carry you here."

Mitch groaned, "My head is pounding."

"I might be able to help with that," Jake said, and he held up the gauze and wipes for Mitch to see. "Is it okay if I clean this up a little bit and put a bandage on for you?"

Mitch closed his eyes and nodded slowly.

"On a scale of one to ten, how is your pain?" Jake asked as he tore open one of the packets.

"Eleven," Mitch said, really awake now and experiencing the full force of all his senses.

"A shaman friend once taught me how to move through pain. Would you like me to teach you?" Jake asked. He blotted the blood from around the gash and Mitch winced.

No, actually, I would not like to "move through" pain, he thought, I would like a seriously powerful painkiller to make it go away. But Mitch knew that it was unlikely the surf bum would have any pharmaceuticals on hand, so he just said, "Sure."

"Okay," Jake said, pulling up one of the wooden chairs next to

Mitch's cot. "We are going to integrate breathing with focus. First, close your eyes, take a deep breath, hold it, now release. Take slow, deep breaths. We are going to balance your chakras."

"Ha! I got a better idea," Mitch said. "How about a double shot of whiskey?" He looked at Jake expecting a laugh, but Jake's eyes were solemn and concerned, so Mitch said, "Just kidding," and began the deep breathing.

Jake closed his eyes and rubbed his hands together to warm them. He placed one on top of Mitch's head, the crown chakra, and the other on his heart, the fourth chakra. Jake said in an even, flowing voice, "Continue to breathe deeply, then exhale and relax fully. Every time you exhale, see if you can find the center of your pain. Can you feel the center?"

"Yes," Mitch said.

"Good. Now imagine diving into the center of it."

Mitch's head was pounding so it wasn't hard to feel the pain.

"Keep breathing. Now we are going to balance your third chakra," Jake said. Jake put his hand just above Mitch's belly button and Mitch continued to breathe deeply. "Now I want you to feel the outer edge of the pain. Can you feel the outer edge?"

"Yeah, I think so," Mitch said.

"Good," Jake said, "This time on the inhale try to feel the outer edge of the pain." For a full minute, the only sounds that could be heard were Mitch's breathing and the ocean waves outside.

"Let's go back and dive into the center of the pain," Jake said gently. He moved his hand up to Mitch's forehead, hovering but not touching. All of a sudden, Mitch felt a tingling in the center of his forehead. "That's your third eye, or sixth chakra."

Just then the pain began to melt away, and Mitch could even feel a warm and tickly sensation.

After a few final deep breaths, Mitch sat up slowly, eyes fully open, feeling good. "Thank you. Wow. I don't know what to say. The pain is completely gone. What are you, like some kind of witch doctor, or...?"

Jake held out his cell phone. "Do you have somebody we can call? You need a ride to the emergency room. You need stitches."

Mitch thought about it for a moment and decided to call his mom. She didn't live too far and there was certainly no way he'd be able to skateboard over to the ER. Jake gave Mitch the phone and then left to put away the first-aid kit. Mitch made the call and then took a seat on one of the wooden chairs to wait.

It was a nice surf shop, now that he had a moment to look around. Men's and women's bathing suits, t-shirts, flip-flops, backpacks, hats, all the usual items. The floor was clean and the place smelled like suntan lotion, which Mitch thought was the best smell in the world. He wondered why he'd never wandered inside before. Well, work comes first, right? He clearly remembered Joe Weiss saying that at the office.

"So what happened out there?" Jake asked, offering Mitch a bottle of water.

Mitch took the bottle and remembered his foray into the ocean. "Well, I'm a little out of shape. I haven't surfed in a long time. I tried to paddle out, but the waves and the current were so strong. I just couldn't get out to the lineup. And when I finally did, I had all these surfers dropping in. One of them almost hit me! Another one yelled at me because I had to ditch my board, and then I got so tired from getting hammered that finally a big wave just thrashed me and the board hit me in the head. That's when I knew I had to go in."

Jake stared at Mitch for a few silent moments, then said, "You are a thirsty pigeon."

Mitch looked puzzled.

"You ever heard of Aesop's Fables?" said Jake.

Mitch gulped some water. "Yeah, those are the nursery rhymes and stuff, right?"

Jake recited, "'The Thirsty Pigeon.' A pigeon, obsessed by excessive thirst, saw a bird bath full of water painted on a wall. Not realizing it was only a picture, he flew toward it with zeal, and unwittingly crashed into the wall and jarred himself terribly. Having broken his wings by the blow, he fell to the ground, and was caught and eaten by one of the villagers."

"Huh?"

"Zeal should not outrun discretion."

Mitch stared back and gulped down the rest of the water. Eventually, he asked, "Do you recycle?"

Jake pointed to a blue recycling bin next to the desk and Mitch tossed it in.

"Did you know the reason they were yelling at you is because there were dangerous conditions out there, and they know that only the best of the best are out on a night like this?" Jake asked.

"No, I just thought they were being assholes," Mitch said flippantly.

Jake closed his mouth and crossed over to his desk. He opened the top drawer, took out a piece of paper and handed it over.

"Here, this is for you," he said.

Mitch read the headline:


```
Surfer's Code of Honor:

Ten Rules to Live by!
```


"Thanks, I'll read it later, I promise." Mitch said as he folded it up and placed it on the cot.

"You mentioned that you aren't in shape. If you had been training for the last couple of months, do you think you would have made it out there?" Jake asked.

"Probably," Mitch admitted. He stood to look out the window, suddenly wanting his mother to come as soon as possible.

Jake pulled another piece of paper from his desk—a flyer with information about a class called Yoga for Surfers and placed it on the cot on top of the Surfer's Code of Honor.

"Here, this is also for you," he said. "I recommend yoga for all my students—especially the pros. It builds endurance, flexibility, strength, and calm under pressure so you can conserve breath. But can I tell you a secret?"

Mitch turned to look at him.

"You can be the strongest, most limber guy in the world, but if you don't know how to go with the flow, you'll get rejected every time."

"Rejected by who?" Mitch asked.

"The Force. Mother Nature."

Mitch tried to decide if Jake was crazy or not. He seemed sane—smart even—but the way Jake talked was so woo woo, all chakras and mother goddess whatever, and Mitch didn't really know what to do with it. Maybe too much sun fried this guy's brain.

Just then they heard the sound of tires on pavement and the honk of a car horn.

"That's probably my mom in the parking lot," Mitch said. He pointed to his own head and said, "Um, thanks man, I owe you one," grabbed his board and started to walk out.

Picking up the two flyers, Jake said, "Don't forget these."

Mitch tried to look thankful as he returned to take the flyers, but on the inside, he was thinking, Whatever. Jake nodded silently as Mitch showed himself out the door.

Fran Springer tilted her chin slightly upward in order to see over the steering wheel of her Ford Focus as she pulled out of the parking lot of the hospital. Mitch got patched up with stitches and was sent home with painkillers, which he wasn't sure he needed anymore, but still felt better to have them than not. He'd been telling his mom for years to get a car with adjustable seats so she could simply push a button and rise up the extra two inches she needed to look straight ahead, and every time she waved her hand. "Too many buttons."

Her blonde shoulder-length hair glowed blue in the moonlight as she reached over to pat his knee and send him a loving smile. As she drove, Mitch took some time to really look at her, and suddenly felt guilty for not calling more often and for opting to spend Thanksgiving last November with his girlfriend instead of his family. He wondered if she felt hurt.

He rested his elbow up against the door and leaned his gauze-wrapped head against his hand. He thought about the night—the whole week actually—his life collapsing like a house of cards and what he was going to do next. He couldn't afford to keep doing what he was doing, but he didn't know where to go. The thought of moving back in with his parents — even temporarily — felt so humiliating, and he didn't even know how to ask.

He looked out the window on the way home and saw a Starbucks and Quiznos side by side. He remembered when they used to be Mary's Café and a skateboard shop. One block down was a surf shop Mitch knew well. He smiled and tapped on the window and said, "Hey Mom, remember that's the shop where you and Dad took me to get my first boogie board."

"That's right."

They passed by the park bench where he kissed a girl for the first time, the restaurant where his whole family used to go together for brunch on Sundays, and the movie theater where his best friend worked as an usher in high school. He used to leave the back door cracked so they could sneak in and watch R-rated movies even though they were only fifteen. Mitch loved everything about his hometown, Huntington Beach—the surfer vibe, the rhythm of the waves, the boardwalk, the way the energy was busy but mellow. A BMW would be so out of place here, he thought.

Fran pulled the car into the driveway of the home she and Mitch's father, David, had bought back in 1972. It was the same house Mitch grew up in—a three-bedroom, two-bath single level. They bought it for $60,000, but now, because of its proximity to the beach, the value had appreciated to $1.2 million. Mitch's father called it their "cozy little retirement plan."

"Come on inside and I'll fix you something to eat," Fran said softly. "Your father wants to talk to you." Mitch took a deep breath and opened the car door, ready to face the music. It's not that his father was so terribly stern, but there was definitely a generation gap, a communication gap, an . . . an everything gap.

David Springer was a former Naval officer, and now nearing the end of his career as a purchasing agent for a large oil company that drilled off the coast of Long Beach. He stood among the chanters of "Drill baby drill!" at the last presidential election. Mitch was no expert in the subject of oil drilling, but he knew enough to be concerned about the rising oceans and the impact of fossil fuels on our environment.

"You gonna live?" asked Dad the instant Mitch stepped through the door.

"Uh," Mitch said, touching the bandage on his head, "yeah, I just got a few stitches. I'll be fine."

"Mom says you lost your job," he said abruptly.

Mitch pulled out one of the four chairs from around the plastic-cloth-covered kitchen table.

"David, be nice," said Fran, who had already pulled out plates, bread, peanut butter, jelly, and napkins.

David turned to Fran with his palms up, "What'd I say?"

"Yes, I lost my job," Mitch stated. "I still can't believe it. Just last week I was salesperson of the year and now the company is on the brink. They laid off half the office, including me."

"Did you see all the stuff in the newspapers about the FDA and the fines?"

"Yup," Mitch said with a tight-lipped grin. "Sure did."

"I noticed the stock took a nosedive. You owned a bunch of that stock, didn't you?" his father asked.

"Uh, yeah, thanks for reminding me," Mitch said, feeling the full weight of the week coming back down onto his shoulders.

"Hey, don't get salty with me, sailor. Just stating the facts."

Before anyone said another word, Fran placed a plate of peanut butter and jelly sandwiches on the table, with a bag of chips, a bottle of soda, and drinking glasses. Mitch poured some Coke and drank quickly, and finished two sandwich triangles before Fran even had a chance to sit down.

Mitch felt his father's stare burning a hole in the side of his head. He could already hear all the questions and accusations in his head, without him even saying a word. You'll be fine, Son, if you just keep working hard. That's the trouble with your generation, you don't know what hard work is. Success is simple: Work hard, get good grades, find a good company, make yourself indispensable to the company, and work your way up the ladder.

Mitch used to regard these as words to live by. He respected his father and heeded every piece of advice he ever got from him. But now, he was at an ugly place called rock bottom and if he was going to be intellectually honest, looking back at all his experiences, none of this "wisdom" seemed to be true.

Mitch remembered how he worked his way through college as a bartender. He paid attention in class, did his homework in the afternoon, then tended bar all night. He made decent tips, but never enough to start saving. Somehow the money he pulled in was always just enough to get him by.

Upon graduation, Mitch took an entry-level job in medical device sales. He picked a company with a strong reputation that had been around for thirty years—at his father's advice. "You want company stability," he said. "That way you can work there for life." But after working there for about a year, Mitch figured out that the company's reputation had been earned thirty years prior by its original founders. New leadership took over after a buyout and was nowhere near as good. They were bean counters with no vision, and they failed to innovate. Even though Mitch was a great salesperson (he worked his way up and came close to making six figures), he still couldn't overcome the fact that the competition's products were superior. It was like trying to sell a Commodore 64 in an iPad world.

Staying in the medical field, his next job was for a company that sold EMR, or electronic medical records. Once again, Mitch worked hard, excelled, and became a top producer, earning six figures by selling EMR systems. He was sure this company was the one that would stick, because it was the polar opposite of the previous—the leadership was all about innovation and staying on the cutting edge of technology.

A problem occurred, however, in development. The software wasn't beta tested thoroughly because the executives were in too much of a rush to launch in order to gain market share. The result was that it never delivered on its promise. It kept breaking down and customers were wasting time, paying high monthly fees for a system that didn't live up to its promises. Mitch came to the realization, and soon his customers did too, that he was selling vaporware. The company leadership spun a great yarn and tried to turn it around, but in the end, the company eventually folded. Mitch became a casualty of that implosion.

His next job after that was at Reynolds, where he thought he had finally found his path to wealth and the good life. This last wipeout stung as much as his head wound, and he wondered if he would ever be able to trust another company again.

"Dad," Mitch said sincerely, "I promise you, I'm a hard worker. I wasn't laid off for lack of working hard."

Something about Mitch's tone touched his father in the right place. He could sense Mitch's plea for understanding.

"I know you are, Son. I just think if you find another job and keep working hard, they're bound to notice, and you'll be rewarded. That's just how it works."

"I disagree," Mitch said—not in a combative way. "That's not how it works. Or at least, that's not how it has worked for me. I've worked hard and I've made all kinds of sacrifices for all the companies I've worked for, and where has it gotten me? Jobless and broke again, and now I'm just thinking there's got to be a better way."

"Oh yeah? What's that?"

"I...don't know."

David stood up abruptly. "Oh well, that's a great plan. Good luck with that." He started to leave the room when Fran stopped him.

"David, have a heart. The doctor said the boy is exhausted," she said. David stopped in the doorway between the kitchen and dining room. "Is there anything we can do to help you?" she asked Mitch. "What do you need?"

Mitch spoke softly, barely audible, "Can I stay here for a while until I figure things out?"

"Can't think in the penthouse, huh?"

"David!" Fran admonished.

David mouthed, "What?" and held his palms out at her once again.

"Go to my sewing room and get some sheets and a blanket?" Fran half-asked, half-ordered her husband. Then she turned to Mitch and said, "Yes you can stay here as long as you need to. Aunt Pat was going to use the granny flat over Christmas vacation but I'll just let her know there's been a change and she'll have to stay at Fairfield Suites."

David did an about-face and stepped out to fetch the blankets. Mitch sighed with relief and gratitude at his mother's words and stood to put the dirty dishes in the sink.

"Don't dear, I'll take care of it," said his mother. "Go lie down and get some rest."

Mitch walked through the living room to the patio door that opened to the backyard and walked toward the old converted garage. The horizontal wooden slats on the outside had been painted taupe, but it still looked very much like a garage. Mitch swung the door open, stepped in, and pulled the chain hanging from the single light bulb screwed into the ceiling. He coughed a bit as the faint smell of concrete dust touched his nose and looked at the futon set up against the wall. It was the same one he used in college—couch by day, bed by night. A shaggy, olive-green rug warmed the floor, and a dresser and set of dark brown wooden shelves defined the "bedroom."

A makeshift kitchenette had been set up on one wall with a sink, counter, microwave, hot plate, and mini fridge. Mitch walked to the far corner and saw that his parents had installed a small bathroom— simple but functional with gray tile, a small sink, toilet, and shower.

His father's footsteps plodded in behind him and crossed to the bed. He dropped off a set of white cotton sheets along with one of the patchwork quilts his mother made. "Stay warm," he said quietly to Mitch, as if calling a truce, and he shut the door behind him as he left. Mitch began to make the bed. Well, he thought humbly, at least it's affordable.

* * *

The first day, Mitch just rested. He asked his mother to drive him back to his apartment so he could gather some clothes and toiletries, and he settled into the small flat. When he was finally able to stand without feeling his head throb, and as he looked at the calendar and saw the end of August closing in, Mitch made the decision to hold a fire sale on Craigslist for all the items in his apartment that he couldn't afford to keep anymore, which was just about everything.

He couldn't believe how much stuff he owned. It didn't seem like that much when he was living there, but the number of knick-knacks and gadgets occupying the shelves and drawers in his apartment seemed endless as he took pictures, wrote descriptions, and posted them online for bargain hunters. As he held up a Bluetooth shower speaker and a leather cell phone case, and numerous items he never used, he thought, I spent money on this crap? Why? The only items he decided to keep were his clothes, laptop, skateboard, surf gear, and video camera.

It was painful to let go of his seventy-inch plasma TV, especially since it sold for only about thirty percent of what he paid for it. Many items brought disappointment upon sale: Watches, designer suits, electronics, stereo equipment. None of them held their value from the time he bought them. At the end of the sale, Mitch was left with a little more than $4,000. He took the money and almost half of the money in his checking account and bought a used 2008 Jeep

Wrangler. No leases or loans—he just bought it outright—and told his mother she was finally free from having to drive him back and forth. He felt a bit more independent.

In addition to the fire sale, Mitch sold his stock. Two months prior he could have cashed out for more than $100,000, but now it was worth only $25,000. He also took out a calculator and sat with the piles of bills he sorted the week before and found that he was carrying more than $100,000 of high interest credit card debt. He stared at the number and felt his stomach tighten as the realization hit. He owed all this money, was living in his parents' garage, had no real assets, had $30,000 in his account to live on, and no income. He thought his head might split open all over again.

He did, however, have supportive parents and a free place to stay. He decided to start every day by feeling grateful for that.

* * *

Alone one night while his parents went out to the movies, Mitch journeyed over to their kitchen. He put a bag of popcorn in the microwave and powered on his father's computer while he waited. He scanned help-wanted ads on various job sites to see what was available. He wasn't quite sure what he was looking for, but hoped he'd know it when he saw it.

His first instinct was to go where he was familiar: Healthcare, pharmaceuticals, medical sales. But then he thought, Once they realize that I was at Reynolds, no one's gonna hire me in this industry. As he started scanning other industries, he noticed an ad that caught his curiosity. "The Road to Wealth" read the headline, along with a picture of a kitten sitting inside a flower vase. What one had to do with the other, he had no idea, but he clicked anyway.

The ad directed him to a website for a success coaching company promising big wealth. A success coach, Mitch thought. Maybe that's what I need. He went back to Google and typed "success coach."

Hundreds of listings and ads filled his screen. "Get on track now! Click here for this FREE training session," and "How did this single mom make six figures in six weeks? Click here to find out!"

and "Secrets that only millionaires know!" called for his attention. The financial coaches eventually overlapped with life coaches and even weight-loss coaches, and there, all the headlines looked the same. "Do you want real results?" "Click here for real results." "Real results you never thought possible." "Top ten secrets to guarantee real results."

Mitch read them all and wondered, What's a fake result?

He noticed success coaches referring to themselves as success strategists, life strategists, and wealth strategists. Some of them got cute and called themselves business warriors, trouble-makers, and disruptors. Chief Fun Officer—that was his personal favorite. It made him laugh and cry at the same time.

He clicked on a few ads, purely for comedy's sake, and couldn't believe what he saw. There was an article titled, "Don't Fall for the Next Diet Scam!" The author was a hypnotist with a gorgeous head-shot next to her bio. Mitch clicked over to her website and read about her practice. He was impressed until he clicked over to her YouTube page and watched her latest video. "Wanda's Weekly Words of Wisdom" she called the videos, and in them she spouted advice for people struggling with their weight. In the most recent video, Wanda appeared to be at least ten years older than the photos on her website, and quite a few pounds heavier.

Not only that, but she didn't communicate one original thought in her minute and a half of wisdom. "Whatever the mind can conceive it can achieve" and "Whether you think you can or think you can't, either way you are right." Mitch had heard them all before and seen them a million times at previous sales trainings and on Facebook. What irked him the most was the fact that she didn't even give credit to the original speakers (in this case, Napoleon Hill and Henry Ford). She boldly looked at the camera, parodied Law of Attraction concepts, and spoke other people's words as if they were her own. What a hack, Mitch thought, and the microwave beeped.

"All right Mitch," he said out loud, popping a few pieces of popcorn in his mouth. "You have stitches in your head that make you look like Frankenstein, so you can't go on any job interviews yet, and even if you could, there aren't any job listings that look even remotely promising." Mitch stuffed a whole fistful of popcorn in his mouth and bit down hard for an aggressive chomp.

"Not only that" he said, spilling kernels to the floor, "you can't surf for at least two weeks. Cuz the doctor said the cut could get infected. So. Great. That's awesome."

He glanced over to the tan speckled granite kitchen counter to see if there were any other snacks he might add to his pity party, and noticed the two flyers Jake had given him the previous week. He slid them off and stepped over to the garbage can to toss them out, but something stopped him.

On the back of the Yoga for Surfers flyer was a picture of the instructor with a bio. She was stunning. It wasn't her beautiful hair, or long toned legs. It was...he didn't know what it was. The picture quality wasn't even that good—it was a photocopied flyer—but for whatever reason, this image had an energy to it that made him stop and stare. He read the bio:

```
Coco Sullivan is the founder of Trilogy
Yoga and a master yoga instructor from
Hawaii. She is trained in the disciplines
```

of Ashtanga, Sivananda, Iyengar, and Anusara, as well as sports medicine and rehabilitation techniques. She combines elements of these different styles into a dynamic class called "Yoga for Surfers" with a focus on balance, strengthening, and creating alignment.

"Okay, so, aside from the funky name, she seems legit," Mitch said to himself. He read further.

How Balanced Is Your Life?

At Trilogy Yoga we focus on total well-being. We believe optimal health comes from having balance in the three areas: Healthy body, healthy mind, and healthy spirit.

What's your Trilogy score? On a scale from one to ten, (ten being optimal) where are you now?

1) Healthy body:_____

2) Healthy mind:_____

3) Healthy spirit:_____

List one or two things you can do to improve each score:

1) Body:_____

2) Mind:_____

3) Spirit:_____

If you would like to learn more about creating balance in your life, come try our Yoga for Surfers classes.

A website appeared at the bottom of the page. Mitch put the pop-corn down, went back to the computer, typed it in, and clicked on class schedule. He put the time and location of the Yoga for Surfers classes in his calendar for the next few weeks. *I have nothing better to do*, he thought, *Might as well get in shape.*

The yoga studio was on the second floor of a strip mall a couple blocks from the ocean and Huntington Pier, between a hair salon and massage therapist. Mitch hurried to make the 8:00 a.m. class, trotting toward the door in his Nikes, t-shirt, and sweatpants. Once he stepped into the lobby, the whole world changed. All the sounds from the parking lot and busy streets faded away completely, and he heard only the tinkling of droplets from a Zen waterfall. The air smelled fresh, with a hint of Indian spices. Mitch suddenly felt that if he must speak, he should whisper. A painting on the wall featured Buddha sitting in the Lotus position, surrounded by all the colors of the rainbow, and to the left Mitch could see the classroom through a full-length glass door.

"Can I help you?" Mitch looked to the right where a young recep-tionist sat at a desk, smiling. He explained it was his first day. She asked him to fill out a registration form and sign the check-in sheet. She gave him a towel and a mat and told him his first class would be a free trial, and his instructor today would be Coco, the owner. If he liked it, he could come back at the end to learn about their packages and pricing. Mitch thanked her and walked into the class.

As he put his socks and sneakers in a cubby, he took a quick vi-sual survey of all the other people in the studio. What shocked him most was the sheer diversity. There were High School age girls and boys, hardcore locals with tattoos, a guy with dreadlocks meditating on a mat in the middle of the room, a few seniors with silver hair talking and laughing—people of all ages, races, genders, and sizes. Although, regarding size, Mitch found himself feeling shocked to re-alize he was fattest person there, and that didn't feel good at all. He set up his mat in the back.

The instructor, Coco, entered the room. Her face was the exact same face on the flyer—youthful, healthy, and serene. She wore black, form-fitting pants and a blue sports top, her long dark hair pulled back in a ponytail. Her eyes were a fierce blue, which Mitch thought looked exotic next to her smooth olive skin. She reminded him of his hula bobblehead, and he smiled like a lovesick high-schooler. Quickly, however, he shook his head and forced himself to look away. That was absolutely not the road he needed to go down right now.

Coco pressed play on the sound system, and the sound of native American flutes filled the air. She dimmed the lights and stood before the class, nodding, her hands in front of her heart in prayer position. Everyone, as if on cue, stood and went into posture with her.

"Good morning," she said with a soothing voice. "Let's start with some deep, grounding breaths. In through the nose, out through the mouth, making a 'ha' sound. Haaaaaa, and again, find your rhythm, long, slow, deep breaths in through the nose, long, slow, deep breaths out of the mouth. Haaaaaa. "

Mitch followed along. Easy.

"If you like, you can set an intention for this class," Coco continued, "knowing that when you quiet the mind, invigorate the body, and find your natural rhythm, you open up the channels of creativity and healing."

Oh geez, Mitch thought, Seriously? I'm in woo-woo central. I hope I'm actually gonna get a workout here. I hope it's not some séance where I'm gonna meditate all morning and never even break a sweat.

From the back of the room, Mitch watched everyone in front of him and copied their poses. Coco guided the class to adjust your posture and integrate with your breath, but he tuned most of that out. Boring! Also, every time she mentioned the "heart center" or instructed everyone to "find your breath," Mitch pursed his lips and fought the urge to roll his eyes.

Things started to heat up, however, about ten minutes into the class. They started holding poses for what seemed like an eternity. Coco led a series of Vinyasas, power poses, and deep stretches, constantly focusing on core and balance. Mitch's muscles started burning, and he could feel the lactic acid building up.

He looked at the senior citizens who were laughing and talking before and they were calm, holding their poses with poise and ease. Mitch tried to suck in his belly and stand up straighter, but he still couldn't hold the poses longer than a few seconds, if at all. He almost fell during the standing bow pose, and he shook like a scared Chihuahua during plank pose. Everyone in the room stood like graceful swans, while he tottered like an elephant in ballet shoes.

"Your circulatory system has a pump called the heart," Coco taught, "but our immune system doesn't have a pump. Fortunately, deep belly laughing, deep diaphragmatic breathing, and contracting and relaxing your muscles move the fluids of our immune system. Doing your yoga practice and quieting your mind can be very powerful in strengthening your body's natural healing."

Mitch dropped into his breath and began to get focused and intentional with his movement. He stopped rolling his eyes. He allowed the music to soothe his tired soul and he fell into a rhythm with the entire class. He felt his muscles come to life after being sedentary for so long. By the end, he was sweating buckets, his heart was pumping, and he felt lightheaded. Once he wiped away the sweat with a towel and drank water, he felt tremendous! Clear, calm, open.

Ohmygod, that was awesome, he thought, *I dig yoga!*

CHAPTER 4:

LEARNING TO FALL

Mistakes are great,
the more I make the smarter I get.

—R. Buckminster Fuller

Sweaty and tired, but also somehow feeling strong and vibrant, Mitch left the yoga studio and walked toward the parking lot. He looked out at the ocean and noticed the waves firing a couple feet overhead. In a trance, his legs started to carry him toward the pier. The ocean was a magnet.

Off to the north side, Mitch saw a man he instantly recognized as Jake out in the water. His silver-streaked hair glistened and stood out in the lineup of surfers. As Jake paddled for a set wave, Mitch noticed for the first time how strong he was. With his six-foot-two slender lean build, Jake looked like a lifeguard in peak condition. How old is this guy? Mitch wondered.

Jake took four strong strokes with his arms, the wave lifted him up, and in one fluid motion he elegantly slid up to his feet and dropped down the face, carving a slow bottom turn. Mitch's jaw dropped as he watched Jake shred. He turned his board straight up the face, smacked the lip and whipped his nose around back toward the shore, throwing a big spray out the back of the wave. Jake made a couple of pumps down the line, came up, did a floater, and then did a re-entry that flowed right into another bottom turn. He stalled just in time for the lip to cover him up for a few seconds, until he shot out of the inside section, kicked out and paddled back out.

Suddenly, Mitch got an idea and sprinted for his Jeep. He grabbed his video camera from the back seat and ran back to the pier, forgetting all about how tired he was from yoga and letting go of his self-consciousness about his jiggling thighs. Nothing else mattered to him now as he watched and videotaped Jake's effortless demonstration of mastery.

For the next two hours, Jake surfed and Mitch captured every one of his waves. There were several other good surfers out there, but Jake dominated, catching as many waves as he wanted. Mitch also noticed that every time Jake caught one, the other surfers in the lineup hooted and cheered for him. Not only did they really seem to like him, but the way they watched him, with such appreciation and admiration, you could tell they had a lot of respect for him, too.

When Jake left the water, Mitch strode briskly to his car and headed home, where he spent the next few hours on his laptop, working with the footage. He worked with such focus and diligence that he had the video done in a matter of hours. He hopped right back into his Jeep and drove to Jake's, stopping only to grab lunch at a drive-thru along the way.

* * *

As Mitch walked into Jake's Surf Hut, a woman and three young girls walked out. Mitch held the door as the little ones filed out in a line, each carrying new boogie boards. Their beaming faces and sun-bleached blonde hair made Mitch feel happy to be alive and grateful to be Californian. He smiled at their mother and walked into the shop.

The place seemed busy for a weekday afternoon. A group of teen-age boys stood together and talked about the surfboards on the wall, a father bought sunblock for his son. Mitch looked for Jake amid the shoppers, but didn't see him. He did see a friendly-looking young man behind the cashier counter, so he walked up and asked, "Hi, is Jake around?"

"Yeah" said the cashier, then called down the hallway behind him, "Jake! There's a dude here to see you!"

Jake rolled into the hallway, seated on an office chair with wheels, wearing a loose Hawaiian shirt, khakis, and flip-flops. He recognized Mitch and raised his hand. "Hey! Come on back," he called. Mitch walked around the counter to the back.

Mitch walked into the office, and before he even said a word, the artwork on the walls took his full attention. Custom-painted surf-boards with wild colors and striking shapes hung next to photos of perfect waves breaking on tropical beaches. Full-color, framed photographs of Jake riding giant waves, pictures of Jake standing alongside professional surfers like Kelly Slater, Mick Fanning, and local favorites like Rob Machado and Taylor Knox, covered the walls. Mitch stared, lost in a daze of admiration.

"This place is awesome!" he said. "Am I in heaven?"

"Some would say." Jake chuckled. "It looks like you're feeling better."

Mitch couldn't take his eyes off the walls. He took a few steps closer to see the writing on one piece that caught his eye. It was a simple eight-by-ten frame of a white sheet of paper with small, black writing in the middle:

```
To make the world work,
    for 100% of humanity
 in the shortest possible time,
through spontaneous cooperation,
  without ecological offense,
 or the disadvantage of anyone.
```

R. Buckminster Fuller

Mitch forced himself to peel his eyes off the walls and look at Jake, remembering why he was there in the first place. He reached into his backpack and pulled out a flash drive.

"I have something for you," he said, holding it out. "I took video of you tearing it up out there this morning. Wanna see?"

Jake looked at the flash drive, curious, and rolled his chair away from his desk making room. Mitch placed it in the slot, pulled up the file and hit "Play video." They both leaned in close to the screen.

Mitch had taken the best moments and compiled them into an energetic, inspiring surf montage. It featured Jake catching waves, having fun, so relaxed and at ease on the water. He added some cool Bob Marley music in the background, and at the end appeared the words, "To learn how to surf like this guy, check out Jake's Surf School at Huntington Pier!" Jake broke into a wide smile and turned to give Mitch an enthusiastic high five.

"Wow. You've got a real talent for video," Jake said.

"Thanks," Mitch said. "It's one of my hobbies. I was thinking you can post this on YouTube if you want and maybe get some new students out of it."

Jake nodded deeply, "I appreciate that. That's a very thoughtful gift."

"Um, well it's the least I can do," Mitch said, looking down and crossing his arms. "You basically saved my life."

Jake nodded with his eyes and turned back to the computer. He clicked "Play" again to re-watch Mitch's video.

"So, I gotta ask," Mitch said, marveling once again at Jake's surfing ability. "Not only did you catch pretty much every wave that came to you, but you were out there for more than two hours and you don't even look tired. I did a fifty-five minute yoga class this morning and was about to fall apart."

"You did yoga?" Jake asked, eyebrows up.

"Yeah, that one from the flyer you gave me," Mitch said.

Jake clicked "Mute" on the video and nodded approvingly. "To your question about how did I make it look easy, I've been surfing for almost fifty years, and here at this spot since I was a kid. I know this break like the back of my hand. I surf two to three hours a day, six days a week. On surf trips, I might surf five to six hours in a day, so I have a solid foundation. This video doesn't show the thousands of hours of training and practice—all you see here is the end result. But I assure you, I started out just like you, at level one, and had to work my way up to level five."

"Level five?"

"The Five Levels of Mastery," Jake explained, holding out his open palm. "Level one is unconscious incompetence. Level two is conscious incompetence. Level three is conscious competence. Level four is unconscious competence, and level five is conscious unconscious competence."

Mitch paused for processing. He remembered how cryptic Jake could be when he spoke, but no longer thought he was crazy. "Uh... wait, let me see if I can figure out what the heck you just said."

Jake held up one finger and said, "Level one. Unconscious incompetence."

Mitch glanced off to the side as the wheels turned in his mind. Finally, he said, "You suck, and you don't even know you suck."

Jake said evenly, "Yes. And your ego or lack of awareness prevents you from the possibility of improving. Level one is uncoachable." He took a slow deep breath and said, "Now level two: Conscious incompetence."

Mitch answered right away this time, "You suck, and you know you suck."

Jake nodded adding, "I prefer using the word competence because it implies there are skills that can be mastered to create competence."

"What's level three again?" Mitch asked eagerly.

"Conscious competence," Jake said, holding up three fingers.

"Okay so that's gotta be...you don't suck anymore, you're becoming competent, and you're aware you don't suck anymore."

Jake nodded. Then Jake held out four fingers, a faint smile forming on his lips as Mitch sailed through the definitions. "Unconscious competence," he said.

"Unconscious competence means you don't suck and you don't know it? Or...wait. I don't get this one."

Jake nodded encouragingly, "Good guess. At level three, conscious competence, you don't suck, you're competent, but like driving a car for the first couple of weeks, you've got to put all your attention on what you're doing or you'll crash. At level four, unconscious competence, you have developed a certain skill to the point where you can perform it well without even having to think about it. It's become natural for you and you make it look easy. So to continue the car metaphor, after years of repetition you can probably drive your car, shift gears with one hand, adjust the radio with the other, and not even blink an eye. In other words, you're so competent that you don't have to think about it and you make it look effortless."

"YES! While I was filming you, I kept thinking, 'Man the waves seem to come right to him.'" Mitch paused and imagined what it would feel like to be a level-four surfer.

"And the final step, level five, conscious unconscious competence, refers to masters," Jake finished. "These people have gone through the first four levels and understand the process so well that they're able to teach others how to become level-four performers."

"Like you. You're teaching pros how to surf and how to get better."

Jake nodded and turned back to the video and clicked "Unmute."

Mitch pondered the five levels of mastery and walked over to the tall corner bookshelf against the far wall in the office. He perused the titles, pulled a few off the shelves, and read the back covers. He found himself baffled, and perhaps a little amused, by the variety and diversity of genres and subjects. He found three-inch-thick books about sailing, ocean charts, books about quantum physics, business, philosophy, health, a Dr. Seuss book called The Lorax, a forty-five-year-old Batman comic book, and more.

"Hey, can you recommend a good book about surfing?" Mitch asked, realizing that he could probably find time for a little reading each day, now that he lost his job at Reynolds Pharmaceuticals. Jake glided over to the bookshelf on his swivel chair, grabbed a book called, Good to Great, by Jim Collins, held it up, then put it in Mitch's backpack.

"Thanks, man."

"Come back when you're finished so we can talk about it," Jake said.

"Okay, yeah, I will," Mitch said, taking the invitation seriously. He thanked Jake again as he showed himself out. Jake waved peacefully good-bye, then rolled back to his desk.

* * *

Back at the granny flat, Mitch made some instant coffee and sat on the futon. He pulled Good to Great out from his backpack, excited to discover surfing secrets from the masters. But within seconds of reading the subtitle and cover, however, he slapped it against the coffee table.

"What the...?" he said out loud. Mitch shook his head, then picked the book back up again, muttering, "That freakin' guy..."

Good to Great wasn't about surfing at all. It was a business book that described how companies transition from being average to being the best in their field. The subtitle was, Why Some Companies Make the Leap...and Others Don't. Mitch found the subject interesting enough, but he was so hyper-focused on surfing right then that he didn't want to switch gears. He fanned the pages with his thumb a few times while he considered his next move. Should he go back to Jake and ask for a different book? Should he go back to the computer and look at the day's job listings? Should he just take a nap?

Just then something caught his eye in the pages—another Venn diagram, three circles, all the same size, overlapping to create a sweet spot in the middle. This was the same diagram he saw on the flyer for the Yoga for Surfers class. He turned to that page to check it out.

The Hedgehog Concept, read the caption next to the diagram. The circles were labeled:

1) What are you deeply passionate about? 2) What can you be the best in the world at? 3) What drives your economic engine? Mitch scanned the text, looking for further explanation. He found he had to back up all the way to the beginning of the chapter in order to fully understand.

He learned there was a famous essay written by Isaiah Berlin called, "The Hedgehog and the Fox." Berlin divided the world into hedgehogs and foxes, based upon an ancient Greek parable: "The fox knows many things, but the hedgehog knows one big thing." A hedgehog has one single defense mechanism when encountered by predators—it rolls into a ball with its many sharp spikes pointing outward. Even though a fox is cunning, clever, and creative, it always retreats in response to the hedgehog's simple but effective defense.

The author of Good to Great applied this concept to business development, stating that many businesses behave as foxes, when they would do much better as hedgehogs. A fox is an opportunist, easily distracted, sniffing around trying to figure out where to find its next meal. Jim Collins noticed "Great" companies would find one single idea, or one basic principle to guide, organize, and unify all their decisions. By focusing on and mastering "one thing," often saying No to opportunities that were not on purpose, they'd be able to navigate the increasingly complex business world with far more success. Mitch found himself nodding in agreement, and drew a sketch comparing them, saying to himself, "Simplify, focus, master."

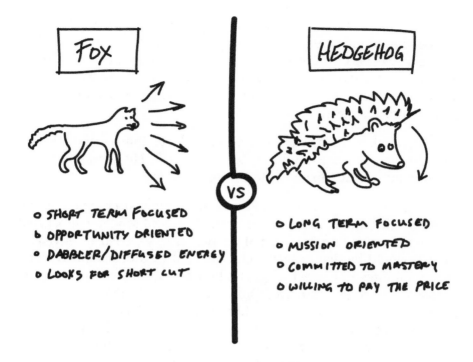

Fox
- SHORT TERM FOCUSED
- OPPORTUNITY ORIENTED
- DABBLER/DIFFUSED ENERGY
- LOOKS FOR SHORT CUT

VS

Hedgehog
- LONG TERM FOCUSED
- MISSION ORIENTED
- COMMITTED TO MASTERY
- WILLING TO PAY THE PRICE

The hedgehog principle could be employed by any individual or organization by applying these three principles. Number one, get crystal clear on what you are deeply passionate about. The impact you want to make, the causes that matter to you. If you made all the money you could ever need, would you still come to work? When you can say to yourself, "Yes! I was made for this job," you know you're in the right place. The goal is not to stimulate passion, but to discover and unleash your passions that are already there.

Number two, get clear on what you could be the best at. This went beyond mere competence and instead referred to natural gifts, talents, and abilities. The idea was that you could take one of your own natural gifts, and then improve upon it and develop it to the point where you could apply it and capitalize on it. There is something innate that drives us to get better in areas that matter to us.

Number three, identify the economic engine, or business model that fuels your ability to execute your mission.

The most important area of the diagram was in the middle, at the intersection of the three circles. Collins taught that organizations and people should constantly focus on staying in the sweet spot. This means you'd be doing something you're naturally good at, doing work you feel deeply passionate about, and get paid handsomely for it. In this spot, passion and joy drive your economic engine instead of need and desperation.

Mitch finished the chapter and grabbed a leather-bound journal he found in his father's office after the lay-off. He drew the Venn diagram and at the top he wrote Optimal Career.

In the first circle he wrote Passions, in the next circle he wrote Gifts/Talents, and in the third he wrote Busine$$ Model. Lying back on the futon, resting his journal on his chest he tried to envision what it would be like to live such a life. All he'd ever known were long commutes in heavy traffic, late hours, working weekends, gray cubicles, and numbers-driven, non-creative work. Even though he didn't like it, no one else did either, and so you just did it and you distracted yourself with addictive things like Facebook, keeping up with the Joneses, video games, gossip, alcohol, and in his case, food. He didn't see any way to change this, really, so for this Collins guy to come in and say, "Oh yeah, you can just do what you love tra-la-la," seemed a little naïve. Could it really be possible to feel so passionately positive about work?

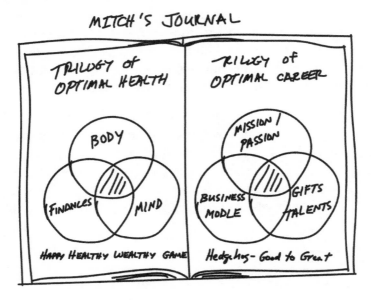

MITCH'S JOURNAL

Nevertheless, Mitch couldn't deny the diagram made sense, and his curiosity was piqued. He turned back to the beginning of chapter one, page one, and began to read. He finished in less than a week, taking copious notes in his journal. He asked himself some hard questions, like, "What do I care about? What am I deeply passionate about?" After years of devotion to Reynolds and pursuing a so-called "successful career," Mitch wasn't sure what he cared about anymore. After so many years of neglecting his passions in favor of climbing the corporate ladder, he found himself feeling kind of numb. He stared at the question on the lined page: What am I deeply passionate about?

After almost ten minutes of staring, he decided to leave it blank and move on to something else.

The things I don't know, I'll have to figure out. But there are some things I do know for sure right now:

1. Never again will I compromise my values in order to make a sale.

2. Never again will I become a sales rep for a company that sells products I know or suspect to be harmful.

3. My next job will have flexible hours so I can surf and have a balanced life.

That's what it was all about, in the end, for Mitch. He wanted to have a career that allowed him to follow his passion for surfing. He didn't want to be a homeless surf bum, wandering from beach to beach, contributing nothing, earning nothing, but he didn't want to be a workaholic anymore either. Balance = Success he wrote in large block letters at the bottom of the page, and then he closed the journal and turned out the light.

Hmm, he thought as he closed his eyes and settled down to sleep, this book is about surfing after all...

* * *

Mitch started going to Coco's yoga class almost daily. He improved significantly in a short time, in ways he thought were only noticeable to him. He even noticed changes in his attitude, starting to embrace the spiritual lessons Coco would offer at the beginning and end of every class. One lesson that resonated deeply within Mitch related to a Hawaiian practice of reconciliation and forgiveness called Ho'oponopono. "I love you. I'm sorry. Please forgive me. Thank you," Coco led, her voice soft yet powerful like ocean spray. Mitch found himself intoning the mantra every once in a while, when he was alone.

The scar on his forehead eventually healed and faded. He stayed in the back of the room, but he found himself able to hold the poses longer and longer without toppling over. Once in a while, Coco would venture back to his space and adjust his posture. He made it a point to look at the floor, or to choose some other focal point in the room when she did this. God she's hot, he thought, Okay, focus on the pose.

Twice he tried to say, "Thank you," and "Have a good day," to her after class, but it always came out in an awkward mumble. She usually nodded politely. One time she said, "Namasté," and Mitch stammered, "Uh, thanks. Same to you."

In an effort to get his mind off women, or at least this woman, Mitch threw himself into working on his hedgehog. He wrote in his journal every day, making lists of his likes and dislikes, trying to discover patterns. He figured out that he was passionate about nature, especially the ocean. And by extension, clean pristine beaches like those from his childhood memories. He realized his anger and sense of injustice upon hearing about all the oil spills, and polluted waters meant this is one of his passions. Corporations putting profit above any sense of responsibility and unconscious tourists leaving trash on the beach cut him to the core. Surfing, of course, was another passion. He acknowledged his talent for making videos, and his sales skills and ability to build rapport and strong relationships was another of his talents.

The one circle in the Hedgehog Principle that had him stumped was the one about the business model. What could he do to make money that also involved his passions, gifts, and talents? Try sales again? Maybe open a small surf shop like Jake? He came up with a few ideas that he liked, but none of them really lit a fire. The only thing that got him excited was the idea of becoming a level-four surfer. He decided to see Jake the next day to inquire about lessons.

* * *

Heavy rainstorms in September are rare in Southern California, but a big southern hemi started down near New Zealand, rolled across the Pacific, turned into a hurricane off the coast of Mexico, and worked its way up to Huntington Beach. Mitch woke up, saw the storm, and immediately worried for the Surf Hut. From what he could see, the structure appeared to be made of nothing more than bamboo, straw, and palm fronds, and this was a serious squall.

But later, as he pulled his Jeep into the parking lot, wind and rain beating against the windshield, he noticed the place stood solid. He ran from the Jeep to the outside of the hut, stood underneath the awnings and put his hands on the wall, examining it, wondering how it held up.

"The foundation is solid. Walls are made of concrete and steel," Jake explained, sticking his head out the front entrance. "The bamboo and palm are just for style." With a smile, he slipped back inside the hut. Mitch followed.

Jake led him through to the back of the hut, and out the sliding doors to the covered back patio. He invited Mitch to sit on a beach chair, sip hot tea, and watch the storm. If it had been anyone else, Mitch would have asked, "Watch the rain? What for? Wouldn't we be warmer and safer inside?" But since it was Jake, he kept his mouth shut and sat down.

Mitch rubbed his hands together, not knowing how to broach the subject of one-on-one surf coaching. Suddenly he remembered Good to Great inside his backpack. Perfect way to break the ice, he thought.

"I went through this whole book," Mitch explained, "and I really loved the Hedgehog concept, but I couldn't figure out my business model. I know what my passions, gifts, and talents are, but I don't know how to make money with them."

"That's common. Usually it begins to develop over time once

you get in the game and it often evolves. The good news is you've identified some of your gifts and talents, and you can start working on honing those," Jake said encouragingly. "Move in that direction."

"I'm definitely passionate about surfing," Mitch said, clutching his heart with one hand, "Even though I'm...consciously incompetent." He hoped Jake would laugh at that point, but Jake showed no change of facial expression. He simply nodded once.

"Hey could you..." Mitch hesitated, "take me on as one of your students? Man, if I could surf as good as you someday, that would be awesome!"

"Well let's talk about it," Jake replied. "Let's make sure this is a fit. Tell me what you are looking to do by working together?

Mitch felt invigorated by the drum of the rain and the whistle of the wind. He envisioned himself surfing big waves in Hawaii, the whole lineup cheering for him. He sat forward in his chair and asked, "I want to be good enough to surf the big waves like in Hawaii. How long do you think it would take for me to reach level four?"

Jake took a slow sip of tea and then set it down on a small bamboo table.

"Depends on how many mistakes you're willing to make," he said.

Mitch tilted his head and looked at Jake sideways.

Jake explained, "I've always learned more from my mistakes than my successes. If you're successful, you just confirm what you already know, which can lead to hubris and a comfort zone. On the other hand, mistakes keep you humble. Jake leaned forward and said, "The key is, you can't be afraid of making mistakes or else you'll hesitate, or worse yet, you won't take any action at all. If that happens, you'll get stuck in your own prison and never make progress. But if you're willing to make mistakes and learn from them, you'll accelerate learning and achieve success faster."

Mitch looked at the floor, unsure how to answer.

"Oh—there's one caveat," Jake added. "They've got to be nonfatal mistakes. Usually I don't have to say this, but I just remembered who I'm talking to."

Mitch looked back up at Jake with a good-natured grin.

"That wasn't a joke," Jake said directly, sitting forward in his chair. "You paddling out at Waimea Bay when it's fifteen-to-twenty-foot Hawaiian—that's a potentially fatal mistake. But you paddling out at Waikiki in two-foot and beginner waves, that's nonfatal. You get what I'm saying?"

Mitch said sheepishly, "Yes." Jake eased back into his chair, keeping his eyes on Mitch to make sure that grin didn't show up again.

"Now I can tell you that the journey from level one to level four is one that will stretch you to the end, challenge you, and I can guarantee that there'll be times you'll want to quit. But in my experience," he said, softening, "the journey is more valuable than the destination. You'll come out the other side a better person."

"Wow," Mitch said, his leg starting to bounce. "You make it sound like we're gonna climb Mt. Everest or something."

"We're not just talking about surf lessons here. If we decided to do this, my goal would be to help you become a waterman. It's not gonna be easy, and nothing is gonna happen overnight. It could be a couple of years before you knock on the door of level four. Do you get that? Years."

Mitch nodded seriously.

"Not only that, but if you want to be a big wave surfer, you're gonna take some on the head. It's not a matter of 'if' but 'how many' and 'how big.' You already learned that the hard way."

"What do you mean by 'waterman'?" Mitch asked.

Jake began to massage a knot out of the top of one of his tanned legs with one hand. "Watermen feel as comfortable in water as they do on land," he said. "When you become a waterman, you become one with Mother Nature, one with the ocean. She becomes your sanctuary and your playground."

Something about those words struck a chord inside Mitch. He had always felt the ocean calling him, like an Italian mother calling out the window to her kids that dinner is ready. Like a child, he wanted to come running and dive in.

"I have five rules that I give all my private students," Jake said, breaking the silence, working his thigh with both hands now. "I'm going to share them with you, and if you agree, we'll talk about coaching. Okay?"

"Shoot," Mitch said, focused.

"Number one: Take responsibility for your life. I cannot work with victims, whiners, people making excuses, or beating themselves up. There's no learning that way and you are wasting both of our time. Understood?"

"Yes."

"Number two: Be respectful and show respect to everyone and everything. That includes other surfers, the beach, the ocean, all of nature, and the whole planet," Jake said. He finished massaging his leg and stood up.

"What do you mean exactly, by 'show respect'?" Mitch asked.

"For now," Jake said, "let's start with the Surfer's Etiquette. Did you read that list I gave you?" Even as he said it, Jake walked over to a framed poster hanging up on the outside of the hut and knocked on it with his knuckles twice. The poster read:

```
        Surfer's Etiquette:
      10 Rules to Live By

1. Surfer farthest out and/or closest to
the peak has priority and right of way.

2. First on wave or first on feet has
priority and right of way.

3. First to call or communicate intent
```

(right or left) has priority and right of way.

4. Do not drop in on someone who has the right of way.

5. Do not snake (paddle around someone to try to get in position if they are outside).

6. Paddle out wide of the break. Do not paddle out through the lineup.

7. Do not kick out, bail out, or throw your board to endanger others or their boards in any way.

8. Beginner surfers please stay on the inside until you feel confident about your surfing abilities.

9. Respect the beach, the ocean, and others. Pick up your trash when you leave.

10. Give respect to gain respect.

Mitch walked over and read them again, one hand up against the wall, leaning in.

When he finished he pulled back and said, "Um, yeah so basically I broke just about every one of these." He chuckled nervously, but Jake didn't. Mitch re-read the entire list and continued, "I was running red lights and I didn't even know it."

Jake walked back over to the beach chairs and sat down, motioning for Mitch to do the same. Mitch felt as though he learned more about surfing in these twenty minutes than he had in the past twenty years. He felt inflated and humbled all at once.

"Rule number three: Fuel your body for excellence. I recommend eating something healthy every three hours, focusing mainly on lean protein and vegetables. Hydration is just as important, so a rule of thumb is drink 60% of your body weight in ounces of water daily," Jake instructed.

"Is that how you eat?" Mitch asked. Jake nodded.

"Rule number four: Show up 100%. We'll work out together plenty, but I'm also going to prescribe exercises you'll do on your own." Jake made direct eye contact with Mitch and said, "Unless you're injured, I expect those workouts to be completed one way or another, indoors or outdoors, rain or shine."

"Yes, sir."

Jake relaxed his gaze and eased back in his chair. "You've started yoga. How's that going?"

Mitch's whole face lit up. "I love it. I'm hooked. I'm going almost every day."

"Great, keep it up," Jake complimented. "Yoga, fitness training plus your nutrition plan are the perfect trilogy for surfing."

"Awesome, I will," Mitch agreed.

"Ready for the final rule? Follow me," Jake said and rose from his chair. Mitch followed him inside the hut and all the way to the bookshelves in the back office. Jake stood beside the corner shelf and said, "Rule #5. "Leaders are readers." Harry Truman said that. Many of these authors have spent twenty or thirty years mastering their specialty, and you can leverage that in a couple of days. I've read thousands of books and I only recommend a couple dozen to my students, so when I recommend a book for you to read, read it. We'll have conversations about the concepts to see what you take away."

Mitch was excited he'd finally get to read books about surfing. He appreciated Good to Great, but really wanted to study his sport.

"Awesome," he said. "Which one should I read first?"

"I'll let you know."

Mitch wanted so badly to whip out his credit card and say, "Sign me up!" He even touched his wallet in his back pocket, but then dropped his hand.

"Crap," he said, "I mean, yes, I'm up for the challenge, and I came here prepared to pay, but I thought it was just going to be a couple of sessions."

Jake raised his eyebrows.

"I realize how naïve that sounds now," Mitch said, looking down at the bamboo mat on the concrete floor. "I now know this may take years, and I have to confess, I don't even have a job. I can pay for like a month, maybe two months, and then when I get a job…"

Jake handed the clipboard and pen over to Mitch. "Perfect. We're on. Fill out this client profile, the liability waiver, and initials by the five rules. And…" Jake walked over to the bookshelf and pulled a small one from the top. "Here's your next book."

Mitch stood dumbfounded as Jake put the book in his hand: The Richest Man in Babylon, by George S. Clayson. "I don't want to be disrespectful, but I just said I don't have the money and I know you want a long-term, year or two commitment, right?"

Jake tilted his head sideways and said calmly, "You know what, the universe has a way of making things work out, especially when you take action and follow your heart. Let's start with a two-month agreement, and let the universe help out." With that, Jake left the room.

Mitch stood confused for a moment, looking at the clipboard and the book. Take action and follow your heart, he heard again in his mind, and filled out the registration form. The moment he signed on the bottom line, Jake reappeared, holding up a business card.

"This is a former student of mine. He built his company based on the concepts in Good to Great. I just had lunch with him last week and he said his business is exploding and he's hiring sales reps. I can't guarantee anything, but I'm pretty sure I can get you an interview. Interested?"

"Yes, yes, definitely," Mitch said, reaching for the card. "Ken Wilson," it read, along with, "Eco-Friendly Lighting: You can save money and save the planet." He put it in his wallet and made a mental note to research the company as soon as he got home.

Jake and Mitch scheduled their first few sessions for the following week. Mitch thanked him again for the lead and took his leave. As he walked to his Jeep in the parking lot, he noticed the rain had let up considerably, and the smell of fresh earth and minerals filled the air. He breathed it in and let it cleanse his system. "Here's to new beginnings," he said, and drove the slick, newly washed roads back to his flat.

CHAPTER 5

HOLDING YOUR BREATH

If I ran a school, I'd give the average grade to the ones who gave me all the right answers, for being good parrots. I'd give the top grades to those who made a lot of mistakes and told me about them, and then told me what they learned from them.

—R. Buckminster Fuller's Mission statement

When Mitch got the callback from Eco-Friendly Lighting to set up an interview, he was ready. He had researched the company, updated his resume, contacted all his references, and even secured a few written recommendations from old colleagues. Their headquarters was only a fifteen-minute drive from his parents' house, and the thought of saving all that commute time sounded great. He also really liked the work they did, selling energy-efficient lighting systems to residents and businesses—a stark contrast to how he felt selling pharmaceuticals with a mile-long list of harmful side effects.

As he drove up to the office building, he thought it looked like a large warehouse, made of concrete and surrounded by a well-maintained landscape of trees and grass. But when he walked in the front door to the lobby, he saw cascading waterfalls on both sides, and bamboo perfectly placed as a backdrop to the big Eco-Friendly logo above and behind the reception desk. There were a few chairs in the waiting area with what looked like an antique Japanese coffee and tea station, and Mitch felt a real sense of calm—a Zen-like vibe similar to Coco's yoga studio—even before he spoke to the receptionist. He wondered about Coco for a moment, what she was doing right then, where she was from, what she liked to do when not teaching yoga, but then reminded himself to focus.

"Hi," he said to the receptionist. "I'm here for an interview with Mr. Wilson."

To his surprise, she walked him right into the president's office! He thought he would be sent to HR or go on a round of interviews with a few lower-level managers first, but there he was in the corner office. Two glass walls looked out over a lagoon. Tall shelves lined another wall with photos, art, memorabilia, and a rich library. Another wall—the entire wall—was a whiteboard adorned with a few giant Post-it notes of drawings, notes, and diagrams related to various projects. The coolest feature was an L-shaped wooden desk that had an adjustable, stand-up desktop. Mr. Wilson stood behind it and looked up when he saw Mitch.

"You must be Mitch," he said, walking around from behind the desk to shake Mitch's hand. Ken stood about six foot two, with broad shoulders and wavy brown hair just past his collar. His skin looked tan against his pastel-blue, short-sleeved Quicksilver shirt, and Mitch guessed his age to be around forty, maybe forty-five. The striking thing, Mitch thought, was that Ken appeared to be so calm and grounded. Where was the stress, the urgency, and type-A impatience that was characteristic of so many business executives?

Ken led him over to a small brown leather sofa near the window next to a coffee table and invited him to take a seat.

"I...thanks," Mitch said. He had been expecting to be across the table, judge style. This felt more like meeting a new friend for coffee. Ken noticed Mitch's discomposure.

"Normally, HR does interviews, but you were referred by Jake so I thought I would meet you myself. It's not often Jake refers someone to me."

"Oh, thanks, that's good to know," Mitch said, relaxing a bit. "I hired Jake to be my surf coach. We start training next week."

"Really!" Ken said, impressed. "That's going to be a great experience. Jake was my coach too."

"He mentioned that," Mitch said, glad to discover right off the bat that they had something in common. "Jake told me you built your business based on the principles in Good to Great. I just read that book. I loved it."

"Yes, it had a major impact on me," Ken shared. "After reading it I decided to shut down all of our traditional operations and product lines and go exclusively eco-friendly. We did a total rebrand and decided to focus exclusively on clients that share our values."

"So you're focused like a hedgehog," Mitch said, smiling.

Ken nodded at the reference. "Very much. We're focused on what we're passionate about, which is saving our planet. All the employees here really care about the work we do. It's not just a job."

"Wow," Mitch said, shaking his head. "That's so much different than my last job. Their only focus was on earnings and driving the stock price up. Can you tell me what this position would entail?"

Ken leaned forward and explained the position. A lot of it was the same as other sales jobs Mitch had done: Outside sales, building relationships, setting quarterly and monthly goals with a sales manager, and reporting back. But one aspect was different, and that difference meant a whole new way of life for Mitch.

"Your manager will be your mentor," Ken explained. "And he'll teach you our system. We take a consultative approach to sales here. The hours are somewhat flexible based on how many appointments you have and where they are, but the previous sales rep for this territory usually worked from 10 a.m. to 5 p.m. Once in a while, you'll have an evening appointment, but our business clients close their doors at five, so you're usually done by then."

"Sounds great!" Mitch said enthusiastically. "My training time with Jake is 7 a.m. to 9 a.m. so these hours are perfect for me." Mitch was so stoked he could barely contain himself. To have a great job and be able to surf virtually every day meant he could have the balanced lifestyle he wanted so badly.

Ken stood to get Mitch's résumé from his desk. "I have your résumé here and I've looked it over," he said, coming back to sit down. "What would you like to tell me about your background and about yourself? And what is it you're looking for from this job?"

Mitch shifted his weight on the couch. "Well," he started. He had prepared for this interview at home and practiced talking about his achievements and how he won top producer at Reynolds. He was ready to paint a picture of himself as a major money-generator for any company that was smart enough to hire him, but for some reason he didn't go that route.

"To be honest," he said, speaking from the heart, "When I read about the hedgehog concept, I made my list of passions, gifts, and talents, but I got stuck on the business model. You figured it out, and I want to learn how you did it. Second, since my two biggest passions are surfing and the environment, the flexible hours mean I'll be able to surf almost every day, which, is so killer! Finally, I watched my dad, who worked in the oil industry his whole life. Every time I see those power plants and refineries spewing out fumes and tar washing up on the beach, it just makes me nauseous. The idea of working for a company that's trying to make a difference for our environment is very exciting. At the risk of sounding cocky...I feel like I'm the perfect fit!"

Ken laughed and sat back in his chair, casually crossing his legs.

"Yeah, I have people skills and I know how to build relationships. I've always made my numbers, and I'm sure I can make your company a lot of money. I can talk to you all about that if you want, but what really matters most to me is learning from you, helping the environment, and having time to surf. Does that sound selfish?"

Ken grinned and shook his head. "Not at all. We share a lot of similar values."

"Hey, can I just ask you one question?"

"Of course," Ken said.

"You're the owner of this company and I'm sure you work more hours than anyone else here. How often do you surf? Do you take surf vacations or just surf around here on weekends, or...?"

"That depends on if there's a swell or not," Ken laughed. "Sometimes once a week, sometimes every day. We're not based in Huntington Beach by accident. And I usually go on a ten-to-fourteen-day surf trip four times a year."

Mitch looked at Ken with all the wonderment and awe of a child who just met his favorite sports hero. "That's killer."

Ken gave Mitch's résumé one final review. "Well," he said, "one thing I've learned over the years is to trust Jake. I think you'd be a great addition to our team. I'm gonna give you a shot. How about we get you to over to HR so you can start on Monday? That's our training day and I'd like you to be there."

"Wow—thanks. You won't regret it!" Mitch said, standing to shake Ken's hand.

Ken escorted Mitch to HR, where he filled out forms, negotiated his salary, and scheduled his first day. As Mitch walked past the two waterfalls that flanked the front doors of the building, he closed his eyes and breathed in through his nose. Thank you, he thought, and smiled so wide he almost cried.

* * *

Monday morning, 7 a.m. The sun had been up for a just a few minutes so the air was still chilly, but the skies were clear so Mitch felt confident it would warm up soon. He wore his short-sleeved full wetsuit and carried his surfboard under his arm, eager to hit the waves—also eager to tell Jake how it went at Eco-Friendly. He knocked on the door at the surf hut and waited.

Jake suddenly emerged from the side alley next to the hut, holding a stopwatch and a clipboard. He walked purposefully toward the ocean, and neither stopped nor turned his head as he said, "Meet me down at the water." Mitch wheeled, startled, and by the time he turned around and spotted Jake again, he was already a quarter of the way down the beach.

Mitch followed, but even though Jake was only walking, Mitch found he had to break into a full run just to catch up with him. It was a clumsy run, because he was carrying the surfboard and some extra weight, but he made it eventually. By the time both men reached the water's edge, near the lifeguard tower, Mitch was out of breath.

"Dang, you walk fast!" Mitch panted.

"Lesson one: Go with the flow," Jake said, wasting no time.

"Wait," Mitch said, still catching his breath. "Wait, wait, I wanna tell you. I got the job. With Ken's company. I start next week."

Jake lifted his hand for a high five. Mitch slapped it. "Congratulations. All right. Now, put your board down. Interlock your fingers, put them behind your head, stick your chest out, and breathe slowly through your nose. It'll help you catch your breath faster."

Mitch did it and calmed down.

"Ken is a great person, a great student, and a great teacher. You're going to learn a lot from him."

Mitch stood tall and recomposed.

"Lesson one: Go with the flow," said Jake. Mitch stooped to pick up his board, but Jake stopped him. "You're not going to need your surfboard for this lesson. Here's what I want you to do. Starting here, swim straight out to the end of the pier. I'll be there with my stopwatch. Then swim back to the shore. Take your time as you swim back, because that's your recovery. We're only timing the swim out."

Jake led Mitch to the water's edge and clicked the stopwatch.

"Go," he said, and walked briskly to the pier.

Mitch waded into the water and started swimming, even though he really wanted to stop Jake and ask some questions first. Why don't I need my surfboard? Shouldn't I be paddling out on my board instead of just swimming? How come I don't just stay out there once I'm at the end of the pier to catch a few waves, and then come back to shore?

His muscles burned as he made his way out, each stroke harder than the last. This is probably my workout for the day, he thought. We'll surf after this. This is intense.

One minute and forty-eight seconds later, Mitch reached the end of the pier. He felt like he had just won a fight, or like Rocky when he ran up the steps. He looked up at Jake, who clicked the stopwatch and pointed him back to the shore. Mitch took it easy on the way back.

He met up with Jake back on shore, this time about fifteen feet from the pier. "Ready for your second lap?

"Starting from right here?" he asked.

"Yup, whenever you're ready," Jake said, holding out the stopwatch. Mitch took off.

This lap felt like a dream. The current carried him out like he was resting on a conveyor belt or one of those moving walkways at the airport. Each stroke carried him three times as far as his own power would normally take him. He made it to the pier in just fifty-eight seconds, almost half the time, and then swam back in.

Jake waited for him on the sand.

"So what was different about those two swims?" he asked.

"Well," Mitch said. "The first one was really tough, and the second one was a breeze."

"Right. Why?"

"I guess because on the first one, I was swimming through the lineup and against the current. On the second one, I swam with the current, and it pulled me out. Also, the waves are much smaller right next to the pier. I felt like I could just sit there, float, and ride the current all the way to the outside."

"You could," Jake said, looking Mitch directly in the eye. "That's the power of Mother Nature. So the lesson is, align with that power. From now on, you don't surf anywhere without first taking a look at the weather, the signs, nature, and the currents. Ride them. Don't fight them. That's why you ended up getting so beat up that night you got hurt. You were fighting the current the whole time and eventually the ocean threw you back to shore. But if you spot the current and get in front of it, Mother Nature will carry you right out to where you want to go. Go with the flow."

Mitch stood for a moment and let that sink in. Such a simple concept, such a small adjustment to make, but it gave him access to the ocean. Amazing.

Jake followed up by teaching the fundamentals of wave formation and wave dynamics. He showed Mitch how the underlying structure, sand bars, jetties, and changing tides create grooves in the ocean floor which create channels, which cause currents to speed up and go in a specific direction. He walked with Mitch in waist-deep water at various distances from the pier so Mitch could learn to feel the currents and the way they pushed and pulled. Mitch discovered that on both sides of the pier, the current pulled straight out to the peak. It was like Mother Nature was finally showing him the front door. It's a whole new world, Mitch marveled.

Back on the shore, Jake squatted to pick up a cigarette butt. Mitch looked at the ground and immediately spotted another one. He widened his gaze to include the entire beach and spotted fast-food wrappers, a few plastic bags, and some crushed soda cans scattered about.

"Can you believe how many people just leave their trash on the beach like this?" Mitch frowned.

"Let's pick some up." Jake said. He reached into his back pocket, pulled out a recyclable garbage bag, and handed it to Mitch, who bent over to grab a plastic six-pack ring. "Here, do it this way," Jake interrupted. He threw the cigarette butt onto the ground, then straddled it between his legs. He squatted down with his back straight, knees bent, and head up. Mitch then did the same with the plastic rings.

"Good. Make sure to keep your head up," Jake approved. "Head north up the beach and see if you can fill up this bag. I'll meet you back at the hut at eight o'clock, okay?" Without waiting for a response, Jake turned, grabbed his board and walked back to the hut.

Mitch spent the next thirty minutes picking up trash, using Jake's squat technique, and eventually filled his entire bag. He returned just before eight o'clock and saw seven soft-top beginner boards laid out on the sand in front of the surf hut, along with a small group of people standing around Jake, chatting and stretching. There were two adults and three giggling kids, probably around eight or ten years old, with sun-kissed hair and slathered in sunblock. Mitch could smell the coconut-scented lotion from yards away and it made him happy.

"Hey Mitch," Jake called out. "Throw that bag out in the back and jump in here. We're going to start the class in just a minute."

Mitch ran to the back of the hut, tossed the bag into the dumpster, and trotted back out to the front. Jake introduced him to everyone—a dad with his son and daughter, and a mom with her son. The kids appeared to be around the same age, eight to ten, and if they weren't friends already before, they were certainly becoming great friends now. Their lively chatter and wrestling in the sand reminded Mitch of his happy childhood. He wondered what Dusty, his best friend, was up to lately. Was he still in Mexico, and how did it go with those Canadian girls? Mitch made a mental note to shoot him an email when he got home.

"All right everybody, let's get started!" Jake said, clapping his hands together. The children and their parents gathered around. Mitch stood nearby, but slightly apart from the group. He wasn't sure where to go. Was Mitch supposed to be Jake's assistant and help teach the class, or go work on something else independently while Jake taught? He had no idea.

"Welcome to beginner's surfing! We're gonna learn a lot and have so much fun doing it. Are you ready?"

The kids shouted, "Yeah!" while the parents nodded nervously.

"Everybody take a spot next to one of the boards. We have six students and seven boards. One is for me, so there's enough for everybody," Jake instructed. Mitch stood by and watched them take their places, and realized there was one extra board.

"Oh!" he said out loud as it dawned on him that he was the sixth person. He walked over to the surfboard and stood next to it, finding himself feeling a little humiliated. Why does Jake have me in the kiddie class?

"Before we go over safety rules," Jake began, "by a show of hands, who here has ever done any snowboarding or skateboarding?" Four people raised their hands. Jake pointed to one of the adults with her hand up and said, "Okay, which foot is in front for you?"

"My right foot."

"Okay, you're goofy-footed," Jake said, to everyone's confusion. Then he pointed to one of the kids who had his hand up and asked, "How about you? Which foot goes in front?"

"My left foot."

"I'm left foot first, too," Jake said, giving the kid a fist bump. "That means you're regular footed. Mitch what are you?"

"Goofy."

"All right!" Jake said with a thumbs up. Then he turned to those who didn't have their hands up. They all looked befuddled as they put one foot in front of the other, then switched.

Jake walked over to the father of the two kids and spoke loudly so everyone could hear.

"Here's a simple and easy way to determine your natural stance on a surfboard." He said directly to the man, "Turn around and face the pier. Cross your hands over your chest." He did. Jake walked around behind him and shoved him forward, forcing him off balance so he had to take a step to keep from falling down.

"See how you put your left foot forward to break your momentum? That means you're left foot forward. You're regular." The man laughed as he recovered from the shock of Jake's little trick. The remaining students crossed their arms and smiled with anticipation as they waited for Jake to walk up behind them and push them forward. Soon everyone had been designated either goofy-footed or regular-footed.

Jake asked everyone to watch as he lay down on his surfboard on the sand, and demonstrated how to paddle, get up onto the board, and then balance.

"Balance is key," he instructed. "Mother Nature seeks balance. Surfers constantly seek a perfect dynamic balance with the ocean." Jake then asked everyone to lie down on their surfboards facing him, so he could demonstrate the technique. He shot Mitch a direct glance, extended his index finger and pointed down. Mitch dropped to his board.

"Okay, so you're lying on your board in the water and there's a wave coming your way. Here we go. Come on, let's paddle!" Jake called out to the class. The kids laughed as they paddled their arms as fast as they could.

"Great, now grab your board like this!" Jake continued. "Step one, up to your knees." He demonstrated and watched the class as they followed his prompts. "Step two, put your front foot forward. Step three, stand up! Stay crouched, stay balanced. Okay good! Let's do it again." Everyone returned to their bellies.

"Paddle, paddle, paddle. Step one, knees! Step two, front foot! Step three, crouch! Balance...balance...all right, good. Let's do it again."

Jake led the class through the routine a half dozen times until he was sure that everyone had it down, then he took them to the shoreline.

"Okay everyone, your leash attaches like this, on your back foot." The adults attached their leashes easily, but Mitch noticed the kids had some trouble. He immediately stepped over to help the ones nearest him.

Then Jake walked everyone into the water about knee-to-waist-deep and said, "Now here's the most important lesson of the day. You ready?"

"Yes!" shouted the kids, and the adults paid close attention.

"We're going to learn how to fall. Just flop backwards, like you're taking the Nestea plunge. Everyone all together, here we go!" and Jake fell back with a big splash.

Before they had a chance to think about it or even question it, all the kids fell backwards into the water along with Jake, as if they were flopping back onto a featherbed or soft pile of leaves in autumn. Then the adults followed suit. "Now, did that hurt?" Jake asked once everyone was up and recovered.

"No!" giggled the kids.

"Right. So now you know it's okay to fall." Jake pulled his board across the water in front of him and taught from it as though it were a podium in a university lecture hall. "That's the key to getting really great at surfing. You practice, you make a lot of mistakes, you fall, and then you get back up. To succeed, you make an adjustment, and try it again. Does everybody promise that even if they fall, they're gonna get back up and try it again?"

"Yes!" shouted the kids.

"Good! Now," Jake continued, "since you're going to fall a lot, I want to teach you how to fall safely. Don't dive straight down into the water, because we're starting in pretty shallow and you might bang your head. So when you know you're gonna fall, the best thing to do is just kind of flop over, like we just did. Just let it happen. Then, hold your breath underwater and put your hands over your head like this." Jake created a helmet with his arms.

"Then when you come back to the surface, you won't bump your head on your surfboard," Jake explained, motioning toward Mitch, "because that's really not good."

Mitch pointed to the scar on his head for all the kids to see. Upon seeing the wound, they all stood even taller at attention to Jake and clutched their heads even harder.

"So you'll come up out of the water with your hands over your head, and you'll find your surfboard. Then you climb back on and try again. Let's practice that a few times. All together now," Jake said. Everyone went under the water, and resurfaced, covering their heads—including Mitch. Once Jake was satisfied, he continued the lesson.

"Now let's try to do some paddling and popping up."

The kids caught on quickly and had a blast. The adults struggled a bit at first, but once they got the hang of it they were all smiles. Mitch managed the exercise well enough, though he started to feel tired at the end. What he couldn't believe was that his first private session with Jake was almost over and he hadn't actually done any surfing.

At the end of the class, everyone carried their boards back up to the hut, where Jake told them to leave them on the ground. He thanked everyone for coming and said he was looking forward to next week. The kids high fived him and walked off talking about their favorite waves, and the parents thanked him as they left for the parking lot. Mitch stood with his hands on his hips, head tilted toward the sand.

"Why did I just pick up garbage and then go through a beginner class?" Mitch asked. "I know how to catch waves already. I know I'm not a great surfer, but I'm definitely not a first-timer."

Jake checked his watch and with a pause and serious face said "Are you committed to being a learner, or a knower? UCLA Coach John Wooden, the most successful basketball coach of all time, started every season teaching his players how to put their socks on correctly and how to tie their shoes. If you're going to become a waterman, you need to have the strongest foundation possible, and your foundation starts at the beginning."

Mitch dropped his hands from his hips, nodded reluctantly, and turned to leave.

"Can I ask you another question?" Jake said softly.

Mitch paused.

"How much do you weigh?"

Mitch shrugged, "I'd guess 205. I was 175 in college, but I think I gained like thirty pounds when I went corporate."

"Wait here," Jake said, and ran inside the surf hut. He came back out with his clipboard and Mitch's paperwork, and a simple bathroom scale. He placed it on the patio and motioned for Mitch to come over and step on. Mitch couldn't believe what he saw.

"225?! What?!" he shouted incredulously. He stepped off and said, "That scale's broken, dude. No way!"

Jake calmly wrote "225" on Mitch's paperwork and said, "Listen. It's okay. It is what it is. This number is the result of all your past choices. Now you're going to make different choices, and soon you'll see different results. Starting now, commit to the eating plan I gave you and drink lots of water. Can you do that?"

Mitch nodded, clearly rattled.

"Good. Awesome choice. Now I have one last assignment for you today."

Mitch walked back, wondering how much they could really get done in only fifteen minutes.

"Take all these boards and carry them over to the shower. Not under your arm, but over your head and two at a time, like this," Jake demonstrated. "Rinse them off, then bring them back here and put them on the racks."

Mitch did it, and lumbered off the beach to the parking lot, his legs exhausted, his energy depleted, and his shoulders burning like hot iron in a forge. It was a good pain, though, he decided as he opened the door to his Jeep. He got in and looked at the clock: 9 a.m. In just one hour he'd report for his first day on the job at Eco-Friendly Lighting, and then the day would begin.

* * *

The conference room looked similar to the one at Reynolds, with its round table, whiteboard, projectors, and screens. Mitch walked in feeling confident, briefcase under one arm, ready to make the climb to number-one sales rep once again, as he had done at all his previous positions. He wondered what the sales record was for Eco-Friendly Lighting's current top producer. His goal for the first year would be to beat it. He nodded at the three other trainees seated at the table and took a seat.

At 10 a.m. precisely, Ken walked jovially into the room, accompanied by another man with thick brown wavy hair and green eyes.

They smiled warmly to the group, as if greeting new friends at a family barbecue. Mitch and the other trainees sat up, alert and ready to roll. It was the first time Mitch would notice this effect. He couldn't explain it, but sure enough there was something about Ken that multiplied the energy of everyone around him.

"Good morning! Welcome to Eco-Friendly Lighting. Have you all been introduced yet? Everyone in here is new, so there's no need to be shy." Mitch turned to the people on his left and his right and shook hands.

"I think I've met everyone," Ken continued, looking at each person directly. "But let me introduce you to our sales manager, Gustavo Sandoval. He's been with us for, what now, ten years, Gus?"

"That's right," said Gustavo, proudly, rocking back on his heels.

"We've got an exciting year ahead of us," Ken said. "We have some new products coming out, and some great government rebate programs that our clients are going to love. This training is going to occur in two parts. I'm going to lead the first part, covering the philosophy and foundation for the Eco-Friendly way, and then Gustavo will lead the second part, which will be exercises and practical applications to help you master the skills and habits. How many of you have attended sales trainings in the past?"

Everyone's hand went up.

"Great. Who can tell me the most important step in the sales process?"

Mitch's hand shot up like a schoolboy. Ken acknowledged him. "Closing," Mitch said assuredly. "The ABCs of selling. Always be closing, baby."

"Who else has been to a sales training where they were taught that closing was the most important step?" Ken asked. Again, everyone's hand went up.

Ken walked over to the whiteboard and drew a large pyramid on it. On the top of the pyramid he wrote the word "Rapport" and drew a line under it. As he spoke, he continued to write key words on each level of the pyramid.

"This is what traditional sales training techniques emphasize, and this is how I was taught when I first started. Step one was to build rapport. Step two was to qualify the client. Step three was to identify the problem. Step four was to handle objections, and the last step was to close—the most important step."

Mitch didn't bother taking notes on this part. Heck, he could have taught this part. This was the type of sales he'd been doing for years, and darn well. Sure it was aggressive, and he had to grow a thick skin, but there was something about the hunt and conquest that gave him a thrill.

"You know what I've found?" said Ken, putting the cap back on the dry erase marker, "Today's consumers, especially the higher-level executives we deal with, don't appreciate it. They're more sophisticated, more knowledgeable, and they know they have options."

True, Mitch thought, especially with the Internet.

"So here at Eco-Friendly Lighting, we use a completely different model," Ken shared. He drew another pyramid in blue ink, upside down, alongside the first one. Across the top he wrote, "Natural Sales Process." Mitch crinkled his forehead, the same way he did the first time Coco said she was going to introduce, "Ananda Balasana."

"If you spend most of your time building rapport, finding out who your clients are, identifying the problems they have, and figuring out if you can help solve their problems in any way, then closing becomes the shortest and easiest step of the process. As long as you've done your job up front, there should be no reason to use a hard close. So we're not going to teach you scripts, and we're not going to practices sales pitches. We're going to teach you simply how to build a relationship and connect with somebody."

Mitch wasn't sure he saw the logic in this. It seemed like an awful lot of time could be wasted in casual conversation, and time was money.

"So what we want to learn today is how to ask questions, how to really get to know clients and find out if what we offer is a fit for what they need. Then, and only then, if there is a fit, we're going to show you how to present our offering in an irresistible way, where they're going to be excited to write you a check."

Mitch almost let out an audible snort. Throughout his entire career, which was short but intense, he had rarely seen a customer happily write out a check or sign an invoice. Usually the only thing keeping them reordering was the calculator. As long as the numbers showed he was offering the greatest volume at the cheapest price, he kept his customers. And as long as he kept his customers, Mitch didn't worry about it.

"Our consultative approach is based on the premise that not everyone is a fit for what we offer. But, the only way to find out is to be interested and curious about them and ask a lot of questions, as opposed to the traditional method, which teaches you to go in, pretend to be interested then sell them what you got and make your commissions. Period! Who has ever heard the phrase, 'Everyone's a customer; they just don't know it yet'"?

Hands flew up. Ken nodded. "That doesn't work. Neither does, 'Always be closing.' As an energy consultant, your job is to help find energy partners who believe in our mission."

Mitch felt a bit exposed. Everything he knew about sales, he was just instructed not to do. Ken returned to the whiteboard and wrote, "Values-Based Presentation" off to the side of the pyramids—another phrase Mitch had never seen. He started to panic a bit, but then heard Jake's voice in his head, saying the words from this morning: Are you committed to being a learner or a knower? He pulled out his journal and began to take notes.

Ken turned to the trainees and said, "When you connect with someone's values and show them how partnering with us can help them reach their goals, you're using a values-based presentation. In our case, we show people how to lower their energy consumption and therefore their bills, while providing healthy lighting for their families, employees, and our planet. To make it irresistible, in just a few years the savings on their bills pays for the investment. Everybody wins."

Mitch stared for a moment at the two pyramids, marveling at this new system. It wasn't so complicated or difficult to understand—it was merely a shift in perspective—but what a difference it made to the overall buying and selling experience. Instead of focusing on making deals and earning commissions, he would shift his focus to the customers and helping them get what they want. Instead of asking himself, "How much product do I need them to order for me to make my numbers?" he would ask, "What's most important to them? What does this customer need? What can I do to help them get what they want?"

Ken concluded his talk by asking if anyone had any questions. He fielded a few and clarified some concepts. When everyone was satisfied, he said, "I'm going to leave you with Gus now, who's going to lead you through some exercises to show you how this works. First you'll get familiar with it here in-house, and then he'll take each of you out into the field, kind of like a copilot, and let you take this new way of selling around the block a few times until you've got it down. Thanks everyone, and welcome to the family!" With that, Ken took his leave.

Well, Mitch thought, closing his journal, this morning I thought I knew how to surf and how to sell. Now I know that I don't know crap. Hey, I've made it to level two: Conscious incompetence. I guess that's progress.

* * *

It took some adjusting, but Mitch eventually began to thrive in his new routine. He got into the rhythm of eating every three hours, he went to yoga three days a week, worked out with Jake three days a week, went to work, read a few chapters of Jake's book-of-the-week, then went to sleep and did it all over again. He felt tired the first week or so, but then his energy and sleep patterns shifted. Once his circadian rhythm started synchronizing with nature he was fine. Better than fine, actually—he started losing weight, his skin tone brightened, and he found himself feeling more alert, yet relaxed, all throughout the day.

One element of training that Mitch did not expect, but thoroughly appreciated, was the education. Jake introduced principles of biomechanics, functional training, isometrics, flexibility, strength, endurance, hypertrophy, speed, and agility. They started with basics, but once Jake saw how eagerly Mitch devoured the information, he added on and went deeper. They also studied nutrition from multiple angles—nutrition for weight management, performance nutrition, combat nutrition, nutrition for overall health, et al. Jake even gave Mitch oral and written tests every once in a while, so his brain got just as much of a workout as his body.

One morning when he walked into yoga class, he saw a first-time student come in, eyes darting about the floor, looking for a spot in the back. He remembered when he used to move with that same awkward, uncomfortable rhythm, darting and fidgeting, with an endless internal dialogue in his head. He gently approached the newcomer and offered a space for her mat in the back row, knowing she would feel more comfortable there. "Oh, thanks," she said, and placed her things on the floor. Mitch smiled encouragingly and moved up to a spot right in front of her.

After the class, he came back to see her again. She was seated on the floor, guzzling water. The other students grabbed their things and headed out the door to get to work, or chit-chatted lightly with one another and with Coco, but she lingered. Mitch recognized the feeling—when you're so exhausted you want to lie down and take a nap right there on the mat, and the thought of standing up just seems overwhelmingly hard.

"So how'd it go?" he asked. "Are you new to yoga?"

She slowly lowered the bottle from her lips and managed to utter, "Yes. That was tough."

"Yeah, well, you should have seen me when I first started. I sweat so much I was like a snowman melting."

"He's not kidding," came a woman's voice from behind. It was one of the other students, a woman in her thirties, about five foot four, Latina. "Your name is Mitch, right?" she said, joining the conversation. Mitch nodded and shook her hand. "I'm Lourdes. I know we've never really met but I see you here all the time so I feel like I know you."

"Yeah me too," said Mitch. "It's like I know everyone here, but I don't."

"Donna," said the woman on the floor, now rising up to shake hands with Mitch and Lourdes. "Nice to meet you." Mitch noticed she had perked up just a bit, and that made him feel good. For some reason, he really wanted to see her come back to class, and he wanted to see her succeed. He didn't know why. It was just one of those things.

"Um, so I hope you don't mind but I actually came over here to ask you a question," Lourdes said to Mitch.

"Me?" Mitch said curiously.

"Yes, I noticed you've lost some weight in the past month or so."

"Yes," Mitch said with his shoulders back proudly. "Eighteen pounds in four weeks to be exact."

"That's amazing. Can I ask what you're doing?

Donna listened attentively as well.

"I'd say it is a combination of things," Mitch shared. "First, I've hired a surf coach and we work out 3 times a week plus I take yoga 3 times a week. Second, my coach put me on this lean and green eating plan. Five or six small meals a day, mostly lean protein and non-starchy vegetables, and I've cut out all white sugar and flour. Third, I stopped drinking alcohol and started drinking eight to ten glasses of water a day instead. And...that's it."

"You make it sound so simple," Lourdes said. "I've got two kids in school, all the housework, I exercise five days a week on top of that, but I'm still not losing any weight. I try to eat healthy, but nothing seems to work."

Mitch hesitated. "I don't have kids, so I can't say I know what it's like, but don't give up. I'm sure your efforts will pay off eventually."

Just then he noticed Coco saying good-bye to two students at the front of the room. He waved to get her attention. When she joined the group, Mitch asked her, "What's your eating routine? Would you mind sharing it with us? You're in amazing shape." It was the first time he spoke to Coco without losing his mind. Nothing changed— she was still the most beautiful woman he'd ever seen—but right now he was focused on getting help for someone who needed it.

"Depending on my class schedule I eat five or six times a day to keep my blood sugar balanced and my energy up, and I drink a ton of water," she said. "In the morning I drink a protein shake and green tea. A few hours later, I have some eggs whites and vegetables. Lunch is usually a salad with chicken or tuna. In the afternoon I usually have a protein bar and a piece of fruit. I always have lean protein and vegetables for dinner, and then maybe a healthy snack before bed."

Mitch, Donna, and Janette exchanged a look. "She just basically said the same thing you did," Lourdes pointed out, amused. Mitch was surprised at the similarity. He wondered if Coco and Jake had read the same play book.

"I've been struggling with my weight my whole life," Donna shared with a sigh. "I think I just don't have any willpower."

"Well," Mitch said, "my surf coach told me 'when the Why is big enough, you'll figure out the How.' You'll just do it because it matters to you. I realized I would never be able to pursue my dream of becoming a big wave surfer unless I started to treat my body like an athlete. That was the shift for me. I don't really struggle with each individual food decision anymore. Surfing is too important to me. So what's your surfing? What's the most important thing to you that you want to be healthy for?"

Donna looked off to the side for a moment to consider the question, and then said thoughtfully, "It's my kids. It's about having energy and the ability to hang out and have fun with my kids."

"Great. So what's more important? Having your favorite fast-food dinner or being able to play with your kids? Do you need willpower to make that decision?"

After a few more minutes of conversation, Lourdes and Donna walked away with something to think about. They felt confident and motivated, and Donna said the words Mitch was hoping to hear, which were, "See you next time."

"I'm so glad she's gonna stick with it," he said to Coco once they were gone.

"Me too. That was so nice of you, giving them some encouragement," Coco said, looking at Mitch as if for the first time.

"Yeah, well, I don't feel qualified to give advice, but it does feel good that someone noticed I'm losing weight." Mitch combed his hair with his fingers and turned to get his shoes from the cubbies. Coco stayed with him.

"I've noticed your form has improved, and your endurance and strength as well."

"Thanks! I'm really enjoying this lifestyle. I think I'm hooked," Mitch said. As he bent down to put on his shoes he asked, "Hey, do you have any advanced classes? I want to step it up."

Coco took a step back. "How long have you been practicing yoga?" she asked.

"Two months."

"How long can you hold plank pose?"

"Um, I'm not sure."

"Do you know all the basic poses and proper form?"

Mitch stared blankly back at her.

"It seems you are in the right class for now," Coco advised. "You're a great student though. Let's revisit this conversation in a few more months."

"Yes, definitely," Mitch admitted, and he walked over and grabbed his gym bag.

Mitch said goodbye with a smile, sliding the bag over his shoulder. Coco nodded cordially and returned to her clean-up duties at the front of the room.

Mitch headed to work. Patience was not his strong suit, but the idea that Coco would be keeping an eye on him from then on sent a surge of energy through his whole body. Because try as he might, he couldn't keep his eyes off her.

CHAPTER 6:

DUCK DIVE

Don't fight forces. Use them.

— R. Buckminster Fuller

As Mitch continued to work with Jake, he learned more about the ocean than he ever learned about any other subject in his entire life. Every workout session and every exercise included a lesson about swell direction, swell period, wind direction, tides, bathymetry, and more. He read articles on Surfline.com and book excerpts recommended by Jake, and in just four months found himself becoming somewhat of an amateur meteorologist.

Mitch's learning carried over into his work life too, as he started to make connections between marine ecosystems and mainland economic systems. For example, he learned that replacing just one light bulb in every American home with an Energy-Star-rated light bulb would reduce greenhouse gas emissions by nine billion pounds, or about the amount from 800,000 cars. One Energy Star light bulb replaces about six incandescent light bulbs, which saves waste and pollution from the manufacturing, transportation, energy production, and disposal of incandescent light bulbs. With every new sale and every new client acquired for Eco-Friendly Lighting, Mitch thought about what a significant, positive difference he was making for the health of the planet and the ocean.

However, while Mitch certainly appreciated Jake's extensive

knowledge of the subject, he also found himself feeling frustrated, and with increasing frequency. He'd been working with Jake for four months now, and still never got to surf out at the main peak. That was where the biggest and best waves came in, and where all the best surfers hung out. Mitch watched them catching and shredding the best waves, day after day, and wanted to be part of that action.

Instead, Mitch spent his sessions with Jake picking up trash, Sumo style, along the beach, carrying surfboards over his head after classes, rinsing and putting them away, and even going spearfishing. Usually once a week Jake sent Mitch out to "catch us some dinner." Mitch enjoyed the experience; while he was down below the surface, he could see the bathymetry, the sandbars, and the schools of fish. He could feel the currents gently carrying him across the floor and watched the seaweed plants sway back and forth. With each dive, he fell deeper in love with the ocean. But at the end of the day, truth be told, he just hadn't done much surfing.

It didn't bother him at first, because conditions hadn't been ideal, and he also knew there was a pecking order in the lineup. Beginner and intermediate surfers were expected to stay out of the way of advanced surfers for both respect and safety reasons—Rule #7 of the Surfer's Etiquette. But one crisp, clear morning, as Mitch walked down the beach with Jake, he noticed there was no wind, and the water was glassy. The waves were slightly overhead, and with good form. After months of training and conditioning, he decided he was ready. Jake, however, shut him down.

"Remember the Thirsty Pigeon," Jake said simply and kept walking.

Mitch stopped abruptly in the sand, clearly riled.

"What?! Really?"

"Really," Jake answered, unaffected by the caustic tone.

"I can handle it. It's not that big," Mitch pleaded, trotting to catch up to Jake.

"I have your lesson planned out for today. Would you like to hear it or would you like to argue?"

"Are you kidding me?" Mitch said, throwing his arms up in exasperation. "I've been training my ass off. Picking up garbage, carrying your beginner class boards, spearfishing for your dinner. I've done everything you ever said. I've been busting my butt. I want to do some real surfing already!"

Mitch started to walk away and kicked the sand in frustration. Jake observed Mitch the way a mother might contemplate a pouty toddler. Eventually, Mitch circled back and put his hands on his hips, looking at the ground. For a few moments, which to Mitch seemed like hours, Jake just stared at him. Finally, he spoke.

"There are four levels of capacity. Each one builds on the previous. One of the biggest mistakes I see people make is putting themselves in situations where they don't have the capacity to deal with the challenge at hand. When I met you, you were overweight, out of shape, had just been beaten up by Mother Nature, and had almost zero capacity for paddling out, let alone popping up. You were in the first level, which is called, 'Repair and Recovery.'"

Mitch wouldn't look Jake in the eye, but it was clear he was listening. Jake continued.

"Now your head is healed, you're losing weight, getting healthy, building some endurance and strength, and you're building your foundation, which is level two. Yes, you're able to catch waves without putting yourself or others at risk, but you're also only one mistake away from being back in repair and recovery. You've got just enough capacity to practice and train well."

He remembered Coco giving him a similar "talk" and said, "Okay, so when will I be ready for bigger waves?"

"When you reach the next level, which is called, 'Reserves.' That's when you have more than enough capacity. Soon you'll have the ability to paddle for hours at a time. You'll be able to hold your breath for sixty seconds or longer. Your mental and physical capacity to deal with adversity and challenging conditions will be to the point where even if you have one tough wipeout, it's not gonna break you or send you back to level one. You'll be able to handle yourself with or without my supervision."

"Is that the goal?" Mitch mumbled, hands on his hips.

"No, not for you," said Jake. "The goal is level four. Mastery. This is when your capacity is abundant—so great that you've got enough to share. You'll be a waterman, completely comfortable in the water in virtually any conditions. You'll be able to paddle for four to five hours, hold your breath for at least two minutes, which will give you a ton of confidence and the ability to stay calm when those big waves are crashing on your head. At this level, you'll not only be able to take care of yourself, but also have enough excess capacity that you might be able to help somebody else who might be in need."

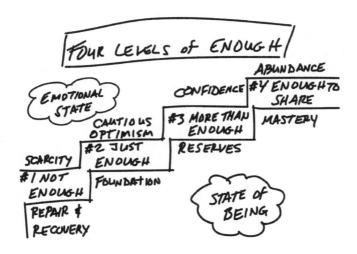

Mitch shuffled his feet. "And how is this different from the 5 levels of mastery and competence?"

"A world class surfer like Kelly Slater could be at level four, unconsciously competent, but if he breaks his foot, he won't be able to surf because of the injury. He'll be in repair and recovery, or level one of capacity. Mastery and capacity are two different things. They go hand in hand, though. There are mental, emotional, and physical components to each. You'll learn."

Mitch took a deep breath, looked up at the sky, stretched his arms behind his back and tilted his head left and right. "Okay...so...I'm in foundation. How do I get to reserves?"

Jake turned toward the ocean. "Over time, with discipline, and deliberate practice. Sumo squats to pick up garbage strengthens your legs for popping up. Carrying the soft boards over your head strengthens your shoulders for paddling out. Spearfishing is designed to help you learn to hold your breath for longer and longer periods under water. The middle peak is a good place to practice. That's where you're going to surf today."

Mitch froze. In his mind he started reviewing every exercise he'd done over the past few months, reprocessing them, seeing how they all fit into the grand plan. He realized how smart and well-thought-out each of his sessions were, and how they all led him to this point. Finally, he turned to Jake, looked him in the eye and said, "Ohhhh."

They continued to walk toward the water.

"I'll be surfing the main peak and I want you to surf between the second and third peak," said Jake. "Work on your duck dive so we can make sure you've mastered the ability to get under big waves and out of the impact zone so you can get out to the good ones. Also work on your pop up. Try to see how fast you can get up to your feet and plant yourself. I'll see you back on the beach in about an hour and a half."

Mitch nodded, flashed him a shaka sign, grabbed his board, and started jogging down to the water.

Being in great shape, he caught plenty of waves and even got a few hoots, as he made several big carving turns and put out some nice sprays.

On his last wave, he jumped down on his belly to ride it all the way to shore. He went through the beginner zone where all the first timers and soft-foam boarders were practicing. The water was only knee-to-waist deep, but for a beginner, that was enough of a challenge. From the corner of his eye, Mitch saw a boy, maybe twelve or thirteen years old, struggling just to stay on his board. Mitch observed him for a while. He had blonde hair, a strong build even for his young age, determined eyes, and feisty temper. He got angry at himself after a few failed attempts, and even started splashing and hitting the water.

"Hey," Mitch said, approaching the boy. "Learning how to surf?

When did you start?"

"Aw man I suck, I've been doing this for a couple of weeks," he said, holding his board with one hand. He pointed out to the main peak with the other hand and said, "My big brother is out there with all the good guys and he won't even teach me."

Mitch glanced out to the main peak and watched the advanced surfers for a moment. He saw the desire in the boy's face and related immediately.

"Hmm, that's frustrating. Have you ever taken a lesson?" Mitch asked.

"No, I just watch him and try to copy him," said the boy, watching one of the advanced surfers catch a wave and pop up. Then he looked down at his own board and frowned. He could totally empathize. He also knew that at this beginner level, he could probably do something to help.

"Hey, I can teach you one thing in five minutes that will make a big difference in your ability to catch these waves and get up. You want some help?" he said with an encouraging smile.

The boy lifted his head and said, "Yeah!"

"Okay," Mitch began. "You know how you keep paddling the wave and it keeps hitting you and then knocking you off? Or you try to catch the wave but it passes right by you and keeps going? I want to teach you how to catch almost every wave so you can get really good at getting up to your feet. So. One, catch the wave. Two, stand up. Those are the first two things you've got to do."

The boy nodded obediently, and Mitch walked with him over to water that was about waist deep.

"By the way, I'm Mitch. What's your name?"

"Isaac."

"Cool. All right, Isaac, the first thing I want you to do is learn how to time the waves. This next wave, paddle when I say and just ride it on your stomach. Feel what it's like for the wave to take you and grab you." Mitch held the board steady while Isaac laid down on it, and as the wave approached he let go.

"All right here it comes," Mitch said. "Paddle, paddle, paddle..." The wave picked up Isaac and Mitch called out instructions. "Hold on...go straight...all right, good job! Come on back out here!"

Isaac grabbed his board and carried it back out to Mitch.

"Did you see how when the wave comes, if you have enough speed, it'll catch you, but if you don't have enough speed, it'll just knock you over?" Isaac nodded. "So the key is to wait for the wave to get about two to three board lengths from you, then to paddle really hard and build momentum before the wave gets to you. Got it?"

"Got it," said Isaac, pushing his wet hair back from his forehead. Mitch walked over to the sand, Isaac close behind. Without even thinking about it, he went through Jake's beginner class, which he'd seen a dozens times, teaching it almost verbatim to how Jake taught it. He taught the three-step pop up and explained each step. Then he drilled it, using just a few key words.

"Paddle, paddle, paddle. Step one, knees! Step two, front foot! Step three, crouch! Okay balance! All right, good. Let's do it again."

They did the drill four or five times, and then Mitch took Isaac back into the water. To his surprise and delight, Isaac caught the very first wave and rode it all the way to the sand! He turned to Mitch, raised his fists over his head in victory, and shouted "Woohoo!" Mitch raised his arms as well. Isaac ran back in the water, happy and eager to do it again.

"All right, well, you got that. Practice that. And then next week if I see you around, I'll give you the next tip," Mitch said, holding out his hand for a fist bump.

Isaac made a fist and bumped Mitch's hand. He got on his board, began to paddle as hard as he could, shouting, "Thanks dude!" as he paddled away.

Later that evening in his journal, Mitch wrote, "I can't believe how good it felt to watch that little grommet ride his first wave and really get the three-step process." He added to his list of passions, gifts, and talents, "Coaching & Teaching."

* * *

Another three months passed in the blink of an eye. Mitch stayed focused, worked steadily, and practiced patience. He showed up for Jake's sessions three days a week without fail. He built up his capacity to the point where he could hold his breath under water for more than a minute. He also reached his ideal weight of 175 pounds.

His yoga practice had become so strong that he was now one of the people in the front of the room that everyone else modeled. Coco used him regularly as the example for the class. "Notice how Mitch's back leg and arms form a perfect 'T'...this is Warrior III Virabhadrasana," she'd say. New students often asked if he was an instructor or Coco's assistant teacher.

It became common for people to approach him after class and ask him how he stayed in such great shape. It seemed like everybody wanted to tell him how hard they tried and how hard it was to keep their weight under control. Mitch started to call these stories, "Woe is me's." He used it like a noun. Everyone had one. Linda just got back from a cruise, and gained weight, so she'd tell Mitch her woe-is-me to explain why it wasn't her fault. David went out with some friends and they all stopped and ate at a fast food joint, he also had to eat the fast food, and so woe-was-him. Rebecca's desk was right near the break room at her office, and people kept bringing in cakes, donuts, and other pastries, clearly with the intention of destroying her life, so woe-was-her. Mitch listened, showed compassion, never judged, but he often wondered how they would react if they could hear themselves talk.

At work, Mitch found himself feeling a strong sense of personal and professional fulfillment. He loved meeting people, helping them save money, and also knowing he was doing something to move the needle on climate change. He was one of the best sales reps at Eco-Friendly Lighting, but that wasn't his main focus anymore. He was committed to the entire team and the mission. One morning, one of the other sales reps got stuck in traffic on I-5. He called the office to ask for help, because his first meeting of the day was supposed to take place in an hour, and he knew he would be thirty minutes late.

"This meeting is with the president of one of the biggest factories in Long Beach," he panicked. "I've been working for months to get this appointment. This is my only shot!"

"I got you covered," Mitch assured him. "I'll keep them busy until you get there."

He immediately loaded up his Jeep and went to the factory in his coworker's place. He told everyone at the meeting there would be a two-part presentation. He would deliver the first part, and his colleague, "the specialist" would come in later for the second part. Mitch began by asking lots of questions, warmed up the room with his sense of humor, and when his coworker showed up, he recapped the client's needs better than the client could have done themselves, edified his coworker, and then transitioned the meeting seamlessly over to him. In essence, Mitch let his co-worker be the hero.

This wasn't entirely selfless. The pay structure at Eco-Friendly was designed in such a way that part of his pay came from a percentage of his own sales, and another part of his pay came from a pool of the whole team's sales, so the better the team did, the more each individual benefited. This was one reason they had a win-win culture. "Cooperation not competition." The culture at Reynolds Pharmaceuticals was the opposite: Win-lose. "Beat and compete."

At the Monday morning meeting, Mitch's coworker sang his praises to everyone, including Ken. He told them all about how Mitch saved the day and helped him land the account. The recognition made Mitch feel great, but he was most excited about Ken's approval. He looked up to Ken as a hero and role model for the kind of business and life he wanted to create for himself. To create a lifestyle where he could surf whenever and wherever he wanted, and there was Ken, living the dream. A thumbs-up from Ken made Mitch feel like he was making progress, or at least on the right path.

Mitch continued to read all of Jake's book recommendations, which by now included, Good to Great, The Richest Man in Babylon, Dr. A's Habits of Health, The Power of Full Engagement, Rich Dad, Poor Dad. Cashflow Quadrants and The Go-Giver—none of which were about surfing. He did, however, notice overall improvements in his performance at work and in life in general. In addition to his health, the most significant positive change had to do with his finances. For the first time in his life, he was able to pay down a large portion of his debt, start an automatic savings account, establish a spending plan, and pay his bills on time.

By the beginning of June, Mitch was able to move out of his parents' garage and into his own condo. His mother made him promise to come over for dinner at least once a week. His father shook his hand and simply said, "Work hard!" His father didn't disapprove of Eco-Friendly Lighting. He knew it was respectable work; he just didn't jibe with "the whole granola cruncher, save-the-planet thing," as he called it. As Mitch pulled his Jeep out of the driveway and headed over to his new place, he reminded himself that now he was living his own life—not his father's, not keeping up with the Joneses—and this path was the right one for him.

* * *

Far from a penthouse, but certainly an upgrade from the converted garage, Mitch's condo consisted of a small living room, a bedroom, a den that he decided to use as an office, a simple kitchenette and bathroom, two parking spots, and a storage room in the garage. What it lacked in sophistication, it made up for in location. Just one mile from the beach, Mitch was able to jog or skateboard to and from his sessions with Jake. He also started taking walks along the beach on weekends to relax.

One Sunday afternoon, while Mitch sat reading on the couch, he heard a knock at the door. He put his book aside and got up, wondering if it might be his mother with some sandwiches, or maybe the landlord. Mitch swung the door open and was blown away to see who it was.

"Dude!" called out the wavy-haired surfer. He stood in the hallway in a hoodie and board shorts, with one hand raised for a bro-style handshake.

"Dusty!" shouted Mitch. He clutched Dusty's hand as if they were going to arm-wrestle and patted him on the back with the other.

"Yo, bro! I'm back to SoCal!" Dusty said as they hugged. "You missed some epic surf down in Mex!"

Mitch stepped back and took a look at his best friend from childhood. Happy, slightly dazed, slightly wet, as if he'd just stepped out of the water, Dusty looked exactly the way Mitch always remembered him.

"I know, man, I wish I could have gone," said Mitch as he led Dusty inside.

"Check out these new digs, man!" Dusty said, looking mostly at the brown tapestry and leather couch, which was about the only eye-catching thing in the room. Mitch found it on eBay for less than a hundred dollars. But then Dusty turned around and realized there wasn't much else to see.

"What happened to your penthouse?" he said.

"I, uh...well," Mitch began, and put one hand on his hip and rubbed his neck. Dusty looked at him and understood.

"Hey, these are cool digs, man," he said. "How many rooms you got here?" Dusty took a step forward and stretched his neck to see through the doorway to the bedroom, he saw the bedroom and bathroom, and took a step backward. "Wow. All right!"

"I couldn't afford the penthouse anymore. I got laid off," Mitch was able to say finally.

"What?" Dusty said, wheeling. "So you're not workin' for the man anymore? Who was it, Harolds? The big corporate guys..."

"Reynolds, yeah. Pharmaceutical company."

"Really. I thought you were killin' it there."

"Yeah, so did I," Mitch explained. "They ended up marketing this weight loss drug that was causing all kinds of problems for people and, at first, I didn't know about it, but then I did know about it, and I just...Anyway, now I'm working for this really cool company that sells environmentally friendly lighting. And the owner is a surfer, so I'm super stoked."

"Aw, that's cool, man," Dusty said with his signature laid-back nod and perpetual smile.

"What about you, Dusty?" Mitch asked, motioning for Dusty to take a seat on the couch. Mitch rolled his home office chair over to the couch and took a seat.

"Well, you know, doing odd jobs, making ends meet," Dusty said, touching the fabric on the couch. His voice trailed off as the texture of the fabric against his fingers stole his attention. Suddenly he snapped back up in an alert smile and said, "Check out my new board!" He stood and opened the door to the hallway, where his surfboard leaned up against the wall. He brought it inside and said, "I just got this. Snagged it on Craigslist, man. This thing is rad!"

"Aw, that's awesome," Mitch agreed. "How much was it?"

"Three fifty. Barely used. This thing will catch any wave but can also handle overhead waves easily. It's super responsive. I can turn on a dime with this baby."

"Cool," Mitch said, examining the shortboard.

"So, yeah," Dusty continued, "I'm trying to find some work, you know. I got a couple of leads. I was wondering if maybe I could crash on your couch for a couple of days."

"For sure, man, stay as long as you want," Mitch said casually, quite lost in the shape of Dusty's board.

That was the day Dusty moved in.

A couple of days turned into a couple of weeks, and before long it was understood that Dusty was there to stay. Mitch found him easy to live with because he spent most of his time at the beach, sometimes even overnight. Dusty had no possessions except his clothes and his surfboard, so there was no new clutter in the tiny apartment, and all he ever ate was peanut butter and jelly, so Mitch was still able to stay within his food budget. Once in a while, Dusty would work a construction job or other temporary gig, and he always gave most of the money to Mitch. They had no formal rental agreement, but Dusty was honest.

Sometimes Dusty forgot to close his bathrobe when he walked into the hallway and downstairs to the laundry room, which gave Mitch's neighbors quite the surprise, but nothing ever came of it. In fact, the people in the complex found him amusing, even endearing, as they discovered Dusty lived in a state of continual happiness and cluelessness. He always had time for a friendly conversation, would help little old ladies carry their grocery bags up the stairs, and never—never—missed a party. Before long he knew everyone in the building, and even found a girlfriend on the third floor where he often crashed as well.

Mitch thoroughly enjoyed surfing with Dusty on the weekends. It was a whole different feel from his sessions with Jake. With Jake, Mitch strove for mastery. With Dusty, Mitch just let his hair down and had some fun. At the end of their long surf sessions on Saturday mornings, Mitch and Dusty would hang out on the sand as children splashed, women in bikinis walked by, seagulls called, and waves rolled in. More than once, as Mitch took a bite of one of Dusty's special pb&j's, he thought, "Man, this is the life." Surfing on its own was a joy, but surfing with a friend, was joy multiplied.

* * *

Mitch brought Dusty along to Coco's yoga class a couple times, which Dusty enjoyed, but not enough to stick with it long-term.

"I don't get up that early unless the waves are firing. And it costs mucho dinero," Dusty said one Thursday night as he left the condo to go to a party. "Teacher's a babe, though," he said, closing the door behind him. Mitch knew not to insist, the same way Dusty knew not to insist when Mitch said he didn't go out on weeknights anymore. They gave each other their space.

The following morning, Mitch went to yoga as usual, felt tremendous at the end as usual, but found himself unable to leave as usual. People kept coming up and asking him questions about health and fitness. At one point he spoke to a group of eight students all at once, each one peppering him with questions about what he ate, how often he worked out, what type of workout he did each day, how much weight he'd lost, how long it'd taken him to lose it, and more.

Glancing at his watch, Mitch realized that if he didn't cut the conversation short, he'd be late for work, so he thought of an idea.

"Hey, you know what?" he said to the group. "Part of the reason

I've been able to stay focused on my goal is that I have a mentor who taught me the fundamentals, and for accountability. I bet if we ask him to come do a little workshop on healthy eating for athletes, he'd be happy to arrange it. Would you guys be interested in something like that? Maybe if we each pitch in twenty bucks, we can get him to come do a group training session."

Everyone in the group thought it was a terrific idea and said twenty bucks was no problem. Even Coco offered her support by volunteering the yoga studio as the venue for the workshop.

So Mitch went to see Jake.

"I have a better idea," Jake suggested, after listening to Mitch's request. Seated at his desk, Jake rolled his chair back and forth a couple of times, taking a moment to review his thoughts before he spoke. "Why don't you lead the workshop? I'll help you, but you run it."

"How do you mean? We team-teach it?" Mitch asked.

"I mean I think this might be a good challenge for you. You recently discovered you have a passion for teaching and coaching. I'll help you organize the five to ten bullet points, and then you run the workshop. Maybe this can be the beginning of something."

"But I'm not qualified to teach. I mean, I know the material, but I don't have credentials or certifications or anything."

"Actually," Jake said, rising to open the drawer of a tall file cabinet. He pulled out Mitch's file and opened it on the desk, revealing copies of all the written tests Mitch had taken for Jake since they started working together. Score sheets ranged from 85% to 100% on all, and one final sheet that Jake picked up and placed directly under Mitch's nose said, Trilogy Fitness Institute Certification Checklist. All boxes were checked except for Health Screening and Evaluation, and Special Populations.

"I can teach you those two last modules and then you can take the final exam, and then you'll have your certification from Trilogy Fitness," Jake explained. "There are two other certifications it would be a good idea to pursue, and those are First Aid, CPR and automated external defibrillator."

"Yeah I can get those," Mitch said, knowing the certification courses and training were offered by the Red Cross at various locations nearby. "So..." he continued, trying to figure out how this happened. "You've been teaching me from this Trilogy certification curriculum this whole time? Why didn't you tell me?"

"You never asked," Jake answered, and gathered up all the paperwork inside Mitch's file. He put it away, cleared his desk, and invited Mitch to pull out a notebook. "Now let's plan this workshop. I'll adjust our training schedule to include finishing up this curriculum right away, so you can feel better about teaching. It really should be you and not me."

Obediently, Mitch pulled out a notebook, and the two got to work.

"Who is your audience? What are their expectations?" Jake asked.

"A broad mix of athletes from yoga class. They expect to learn how I lost weight and got in shape so fast."

"Alright and how much time do you have? What are the top three to four things that you want your students to learn?" Jake asked.

"We have at least one hour, plus some time for Q&A. I definitely want to do a section on letting go of excuses, and how it's just impossible to make progress with the 'woe is me' mindset," Mitch said, writing fervently in his notebook. "Can I talk about the 'woe-is-me' stories? Or would that offend people?" Mitch wondered.

"Not if you do it right. Be sure to talk about your personal experiences," Jake advised. "Tell stories about how you let go of excuses and how applying these principles changed your life. Also spend some time on the importance of drinking water," Jake instructed. "More than you think is necessary. In my experience, people nod and say they get it, but they don't really get it."

"Oh and basic nutrition," Mitch remembered. "When I started I had no idea how to eat to stay lean and fuel for my activity level."

Hours went by and they barely noticed. By midnight, the workshop outline was complete: Talking points, exercises, questions for discussion, handouts, and a shopping list with a few simple recipes to help everyone get started. Mitch woke up the next morning with a work hangover—a combination of exhaustion and exhilaration. His body screamed for sleep, but his spirits were high.

Twenty dollars per person, maybe I can get those eight people to come, plus a few more if they bring a friend. He did the calculations in his mind as he got dressed and brushed his teeth. Can I really make a couple hundred bucks in an hour and a half?

He packed his gym bag, gathered his clothes for work, grabbed the flyers to hand out for the workshop, and paused. He stared at the flyers and found himself suddenly gripped by anxiety and uncertainty. He called Jake.

"Hi. Um...what if nobody wants to come to the workshop anymore once they find out I'm teaching it instead of you? What if they do come and they hate it and say it's stupid and demand their money back? What if I forget everything while I'm teaching? What if I'm a hack because I'm just repeating the things that you taught me?"

Jake listened to Mitch's long string of what-ifs, which grew increasingly ridiculous the longer he went on.

"What if someone asks a question and I don't know the answer? What if someone starts texting while I'm talking? I don't know if I can do this."

When Mitch finally ran out of steam, Jake said simply, "Do you know what Greg Noll said about his first time surfing Waimea Bay, Hawaii, on a big day?"

"What?"

"He said, 'I took off on a wave, went down the side, popped out the other end, and said, 'Shit, I'm still alive!'"

Mitch laughed and massaged his forehead with his fingers.

"You'll be fine, kid," Jake said with a laugh. "Let me know how it goes." He hung up the phone.

Mitch's fears turned out to be unfounded. In fact, everyone seemed even more eager to participate in the workshop because Mitch was teaching it.

"I don't know this Jake," said Marisa, a middle-aged, weathered woman who came to yoga twice a week with her husband, Raoul. "But I know you, and I like you. I'm glad you're going to teach."

Mitch passed out the flyers, which had the basic information—a brief description of the workshop, date, time, and location. Coco watched Mitch hand out flyers and speak with students while she put away the blocks and mats. When the last students left, Mitch remained.

"Do you have to run off to work now?" she asked, putting away her iPod.

"Yes and no," Mitch answered. "My first appointment isn't until eleven o'clock today so I'm not in a big rush."

"Ah," she said. "Good thing. You're becoming such a celebrity around here."

Mitch smiled. He crossed the room to pick up his gym bag and paused as he approached the door.

"Hey, I'm gonna go grab a smoothie. Do you want to join me?"

Coco looked up and smiled, "Sure! I'm hungry. Where to?" She looped her bag over her shoulder and slipped into a pair of pretty white sandals. Mitch opened the door and held it.

"How about we go to the place down by the pier? We missed sunrise already, but it's still really peaceful and serene this early in the morning." Coco looked at him with just the slightest sense of surprise, as if she didn't expect him to be the type of guy who would notice such things. She slipped past him through the doorway.

Even though he knew the answer already from the back of the brochure, while they walked to the boardwalk Mitch asked, "So where are you from originally? Sometimes when you talk, I think I can detect just the slightest accent, but it's so slight that I'm not sure if I'm really hearing it or not."

"I grew up on the North Shore of Oahu," Coco answered.

"Wow. How long have you been here in Huntington Beach?" Mitch asked. He had been curious about her for so long.

Coco told him the story of how she came to the mainland. Her mother was Polynesian, her father was a haole.

"That's what they call a white man, or a mainlander. He was in the Navy when he met my mother. They had a whirlwind romance. He married her, but then left Hawaii on his ship soon after I was born. I basically grew up without him. He was never around, and when he was, he was never really a good dad."

"I'm sorry. I understand about the military dad thing. Mine was in the Navy too. But he and my mom are still married so it's kind of not the same. What happened next?"

"Well," Coco continued as they approached the smoothie shop, "do you really want to know? It's not a happy story. "

"Yes, please," Mitch said. The morning air, the seagulls, the shops on the street held no interest for him—he was completely attuned to Coco's voice and stopped to face her in front of the shop, listening only to her.

"My father started getting into trouble a lot. He'd get arrested for drunkenness or fighting. He even got demoted and lost a rank in the Navy. Eventually, my mother divorced him. I remember thinking that would be a good thing for us, to finally be able to disconnect from him and his destructive ways. But instead, she just kept finding more destructive men to date. One of her boyfriends got her to experiment with drugs, and soon she became addicted. That's when I left."

Mitch stood with his mouth gaping, completely surprised. He never expected to hear a story like this coming from Coco. Not knowing anything about her, he used to try to guess or imagine a background for her that made sense. Like maybe she moved to L.A. to try to make it as an actress, and she was teaching yoga to pay the bills. And one day her big break would come along and she'd leave the studio for Hollywood. But a runaway from an abusive home in Hawaii? Never crossed his mind. She carried herself with such dignity and poise.

She finished the story while they got their smoothies and returned to the pier.

"So I was still very young, just a teenager, but fortunately I had Ohana. Do you know what that means?" Mitch shook his head. "Ohana means family. My grandmother and my mother's aunties and uncles took me under their wing. Your surfing coach, Jake, is one of my uncles."

Mitch stopped in his tracks. "Jake's your uncle? No way!"

Coco laughed. "Well, he's not really my uncle—not my blood relative. We just call anyone who is an elder, who is caring and supportive, auntie or uncle. Because in Hawaii, ohana doesn't just mean someone in your blood family. It means your community. If not for Jake, I might never have made it. I might have just followed in my mother's footsteps."

"How did Jake do that?" Mitch asked.

"He started me thinking about making my own choices, following my heart, what I wanted to do with my life. That's why I got into yoga and opened my own studio. He told me to read the book The Richest Man in Babylon so I could learn how to manage my money."

"He made me read that book too!" Mitch interjected. "He recommended that book to me when I hired him as my surf coach."

"And then as I started building my yoga business," Coco continued, "he kept recommending books to me like, Good to Great."

"No way—me too."

"Really?" Coco said, "Did he recommend The New Wellness Revolution to you as well? That one helped me integrate my lifestyle, my passion for yoga, and a business in an industry that was exploding. That one was key."

"No, not yet," Mitch said as he pulled his cell phone from his pocket. He texted the name of the book to himself as a reminder to pick it up later.

"By Paul Zane Pilzer," Coco added. "You don't have to buy it. I'll lend you my copy."

What was supposed to have been a quick morning snack turned into a two-and-a-half-hour first date. Mitch and Coco discovered so many connections and commonalities between them, it was like reconnecting with an old friend. Mitch never stumbled for words, never tried to impress her the way he used to try to impress his old girlfriends, with his car or his designer clothes. He was just himself. The conversation flowed back and forth, natural and connected.

Mitch wished he could have stayed longer but at ten thirty it was time to head out and clean up for his appointment. He turned to her to say good-bye and realized he saw her in a whole new light. She was still beautiful as ever, but now he saw someone with courage and strength, thoroughly grounded and able to live life on her own terms. He admired that she made it on her own. He was impressed and inspired by it.

"Can we do this again?" he asked.

She didn't say a word—just looked up at him and smiled huge. For a brief moment, Mitch got the notion she was too giddy to speak, like a high school girl looking up at her football-player crush. She turned to walk back down the pier, and after about twenty paces, turned back to see if Mitch was still watching her. He was. Mitch went to work feeling like the king of the world.

CHAPTER 7

NAILING THE TAKE-OFF

Whenever I draw a circle,
I immediately want to step out of it.

—R. Buckminster Fuller

On Saturday morning in the surf hut parking lot, Mitch shivered in the predawn darkness and wondered why Jake requested such an early start time. He alternated between checking his watch (four a.m.) and gazing out at the ocean while he waited. The lights on the pier shined like bright orange stars over a sea of black ink. Soon the sky would start to glow pink, then gold, and then there would come that skin-tingling moment when the ocean came to life. Mitch wanted to be out there for the morning glass.

Mitch looked beyond the pier and entertained the idea that perhaps today was the day. Maybe today Jake would finally let him paddle out to the main peak, now that he had the capacity and endurance to make a long paddle in big waves, and the strength to fight against a nonstop, brutal current. He knew how to read the ocean and get quickly to his feet. He checked an app on his phone and saw that the forecast was perfect. He could think of no reason to put this off any longer. With fists pressed into his jacket pockets, Mitch bounced on the balls of his feet and even did some squats to try to get warm.

Jake emerged from the front door of the surf hut carrying a large cooler with a few bags and boxes precariously balanced on top. He set them carefully on the ground, pulled a set of keys from the front pocket of his windbreaker, and locked the door. Mitch approached.

"I really think I'm ready today," he blurted, without even looking at the items by Jake's feet.

"Good morning," said Jake.

"I've done everything you've told me to do. I've practiced, I've done the drills, I've read the books. I'm conditioned, I'm ready, and I want to go out to the main peak."

"Noted. I asked you to come earlier than usual today because I need to ship a package to Hawaii and I have to get it to the drop-off site before the first pickup. Will you drive me? After we drop off the package, we'll grab a surf."

We'll grab a surf was all Mitch needed to hear. He sprang to help Jake load the cooler and other bags into the back of his Jeep for what he assumed would be a quick errand run, and fastened Jake's surfboard to the roof. Jake climbed into the passenger side of the Jeep and buckled his seat belt.

"Where to?" Mitch asked, both hands on the steering wheel.

"Turn right out of the parking lot," directed Jake, calmly settling back into his seat.

Jake never actually told Mitch their destination. He gave each direction as it occurred. Turn left here, turn right at the light. Eventually, Mitch found himself driving up the ramp to I-405 North. He started to wonder how far this drop-off location really was, and if they were almost there. He asked Jake twice. The first time, Jake said, "Soon." The second time, he said, "Ever notice how peaceful the sky is at dawn?" Mitch stopped asking.

But when several exits went by without a word from Jake, Mitch became unsettled. He looked at the clock more than once and tried to calculate their return time. Jake appeared to be peaceful and re-laxed, and Jake had never lied to him before about anything, so he decided to trust his teacher. Mitch continued up the freeway, and tried to look at the clock less often even when he hit traffic jams.

Two hours later...

Mitch and Jake arrived at a Postal Annex just off the 101 in Santa Barbara. Mitch pulled into the parking lot, completely downcast, and found a spot. He slowly put the car in park and pulled the key out of the ignition, then glanced over at Jake, who speedily unbuckled his seat belt and reached into the back seat to grab a small, padded envelope.

"Be right back!" Jake said and hopped out of the vehicle. He trotted up to the entrance and walked right in. Mitch raised his elbow to rest on the car door and rubbed his forehead with his hand. Postal Annex. He couldn't believe it. There was one on every street corner back home. Why they had to come to this one, two hours away, he couldn't fathom.

It was already six thirty. Mitch knew that by the time they drove back through weekend traffic, the entire morning surf session would be over. The main peak would be super-crowded, teeming with locals, tourists, and maybe even some kooks who shouldn't be there.

Mitch turned to the back seat and lifted the lid of the cooler with his finger. He saw sandwiches in plastic bags, bottles of water, and fresh fruit.

"You want a sandwich? Help yourself," Jake said affably as he climbed back in. Mitch let go of the lid and it slammed shut. WHAP!

"You knew we were gonna be gone this long, didn't you?" he accused. "That's why you packed food." Jake answered in a single nod.

"You could have told me. I never would have agreed to this," Mitch said with daggers in his eyes. Jake nodded again.

Mitch sighed and looked away. Then Jake buckled his seat belt, and said with alacrity, "Let's go!"

"Go where?"

"Surfing!"

Thoroughly vexed, Mitch snapped, "You know we'll never make

it back in time to surf the main peak."

Jake stared at Mitch for a few moments in silence until Mitch looked up and Jake was sure he was listening.

"A reed got into an argument with an oak tree. The oak tree marveled at her own strength, boasting that she could stand her own in a battle against the winds. Meanwhile, she condemned the reed for being weak, since he was naturally inclined to yield to every breeze. The wind then began to blow very fiercely. The oak tree was torn up by her roots and toppled over, while the reed was left bent but unharmed."

Mitch closed his eyes and didn't know whether to laugh or cry. "Go with the flow?" he groaned. "Seriously? Are you seriously telling me to go with the flow?"

Jake sat back in his seat, looked forward, and waited.

Muttering something unintelligible, Mitch put the key in the ignition and drove.

Again, Jake gave directions. Left at the sign, right at the light, just follow this road. On one street in a residential community where all the houses looked alike, Jake had him make a U-turn, prompting Mitch to laugh and shake his head. Eventually, they arrived at the dead end of a cul-de-sac, and Mitch parked.

Jake hopped out of the Jeep and grabbed his bags from the back seat. Mitch slinked out of the car and stretched his arms and neck. Jake tapped the surfboards that were fastened to the roof, indicating to Mitch that he needed to take them down. Mitch yawned as he lifted them off, and lumbered after Jake, who carried his bags vigorously up the sidewalk. He stopped and waited for Mitch when he reached a point where the concrete sidewalk ended and a dirt path extended down a cliff.

"It's about a five-minute walk from here," Jake said, inspiring Mitch's curiosity. "You need help carrying the surfboards?"

"No, I got it," Mitch said, and set out upon the dirt path. He stepped carefully, avoiding the many roots and thorny bushes along the way. The slope was just steep enough to require his full attention and focus on maintaining balance with the surfboards over his head. He couldn't see a thing up ahead—all he could see was each next step.

When Mitch finally reached the bottom and lowered the surfboards, he looked up, and almost stumbled backward in the sand from shock. He saw Jake standing before a vast ocean expanse on what appeared to be a private beach. The small cove had grayish-white sand, an outcropping of rocks, and a point to the right where the waves wrapped around into the cove. Farther down the beach were cobblestones and a somewhat rugged terrain with lots of trees and shrubs. From this little secret hideaway, Mitch couldn't see any houses or signs of life. It was completely surrounded by nature. Not only that, but majestic blue waves rolled in from the water, head-and-a-half to double-overhead. Mitch saw just a few surfers hanging out at the peak with a few more paddling out, so it wasn't crowded at all. He rubbed his eyes, as if he'd seen a mirage in the desert and needed to make sure it was real.

Jake beckoned with two fingers for Mitch to come over. "What time is it?" he asked. Mitch checked his waterproof watch.

"Seven o'clock."

"Perfect," Jake said as he unzipped one of his bags. Inside, Mitch saw a medical kit, sunscreen, a wetsuit and booties, an extra board leash, and wax. Excitement began to well up in him and the color returned to his cheeks. Jake took out the bottle of sunscreen and gave it to Mitch.

"So let's talk about this," said Jake.

As Mitch squeezed the lotion onto his hand, and looked out at the waves, he felt a mixture of elation and fear. This surf spot was even better than the main peak back home, but the waves were so much bigger than what he was used to or what he expected for his first venture out this far. He relished the challenge, but also knew he needed to focus. While Jake spoke, Mitch put on his two-millimeter, short-sleeve full wetsuit and paid close attention.

"We've got a couple of hollow barrel sections," Jake continued. "The lines are very consistent. Watch. How many waves are in this set?"

Mitch watched and counted. "Six wave sets."

"What's the period?" Jake said.

"Every eighteen seconds, another wave comes."

"Good. What's the swell direction here?" asked Jake.

"Well, let's see," Mitch said, pointing out across the water. "That's west. The swells are coming in from there, so it's a northwest swell."

"And which way is the beach facing?"

"West southwest," said Mitch.

"With this swell angle, what do you think is the predominant direction of the current?" Jake asked, not as a test, but clearly driving to a point.

"Well, if it's a northwest swell, then the current is going to go south," Mitch answered, wondering how he was going to handle the two opposing forces.

"This means that if we want to stay on the peak, we're going to have to be paddling nonstop. Do you understand that? The key to this spot is constant paddling against the current to stay in the same place, while still respecting the other guys in the lineup and without getting in their way. Have you ever heard of the Deming principle?"

"No, what's that?" Mitch asked.

"Edward Deming was a management consultant for government, business, and industry starting in the 1950s. One of the many principles he taught was that every process has a beginning and an end. And when you focus on the first fifteen percent of any given process, and get it right, the remaining eighty-five percent practically takes care of itself. In other words, if you can get into position to nail the take-off out there, then riding the wave will flow effortlessly."

Mitch listened while watching the few surfers already out in the lineup. One of them timed a wave poorly and got crushed by the lip. Mitch winced, breathing in through his teeth, as he watched the guy recover, coughing and clutching his surfboard.

A wave of fear came over him as he realized how difficult this surf spot really was, but when he turned and saw Jake's face, he regained his confidence. Jake was so relaxed and cheerful about the whole situation, as if he was already one hundred percent certain that Mitch would handle it like a pro. The teacher's belief in his student translated to the student's belief in himself. Mitch walked forward to the water, stepped in, and paddled out.

But just as he approached to within visual range of the few guys in the lineup, he saw something that made him freeze and almost fall off his board: it was the surfer who threatened to kill him the night he got his head injury! Even though their run-in was a year ago, Mitch would never forget his bright red hair, tattoos, and massive frame. The guy was the Hulk on a surfboard, and Mitch felt all the air escape from his lungs. He kept his head low and slowed his paddle.

"Hey, kook! Get off my wave!" he heard a voice call out. To Mitch's relief, the call wasn't directed at him. It was to one of the other guys in the lineup, who cowered in response. The Hulk then got set to catch the next wave.

One of the other guys pointed and said, "That guy's in position." The Hulk turned his head to look at the lineup, shrugged his shoulders and said, "He's a kook." Then he dropped in and rode all the way back to shore.

Mitch considered turning tail and catching one in. He didn't need this kind of intimidation or bullying on his first day big day.

He looked back at the beach and saw Jake jump in and begin his paddle out. Thoughts of quitting were immediately vanquished.

Finally, he decided, You know what? I'm just gonna be really respectful, surf the shoulder and wait for the lineup to thin.

So Mitch paddled out to the lineup and stayed on the shoulder.

He started catching waves, popping up, making drops, and in fact did really well on the inside. The Hulk, who Mitch now knew was named Joe, didn't bother him—ignored him completely as a matter of fact—much to Mitch's relief.

But at one point, Joe rode a wave and it closed out on him. Mitch watched as Joe's leash snapped and his board started to float in. Because Mitch was on the inside, he paddled over quickly and grabbed it. Then he dragged his board by the leash as he paddled Joe's out to him. When Mitch got to Joe, he was tired. He did a double-take upon seeing Mitch, as if saying to himself, I recognize this guy but I don't know from where... Joe just looked Mitch up and down and said, "Thanks."

Mitch bowed his head in relief that Joe still didn't recognize him and breathed a little easier.

"You going in since you broke your leash?" Mitch asked.

"Hell no," Joe replied, climbing back on his board. "So good today. I ain't missin' this."

They turned back toward the lineup just in time to see Jake drop in on a big double overhead set wave. Mitch hollered, "Yeah Jake, go!"

Joe turned to Mitch and said, "You're here with Jake?"

"Oh yeah, he's my surf coach," Mitch said proudly. "He's my mentor."

"He's a friggin' surf god!" Joe said, with much respect. "You're good if you're with Jake. Come out to the peak."

Mitch followed Joe to the outside, and once again Joe returned to shredding. One by one, everyone in the lineup went, until Mitch remained, all by himself.

His heart started pounding as a wave approached. It was a serious double-overhead wave, and he had to paddle out even farther because he could tell this one was going to break on the outside of the reef. Mitch paddled as hard as he could and got into position.

He got himself lined up and turned his board around as the wave hit the reef behind him. Moving forward, slowly building, with Mitch paddling as hard as he could. Just as it was about to break, he popped up to his feet, slid down the face, and made his bottom turn. Just as he did it, the whole lip threw over his head and he found himself inside the barrel.

All of a sudden, time stopped. There was no sound except the soft, constant whisper of the ocean, like being inside of a seashell. The experience for Mitch was complete flow. He wasn't thinking. It was all instinct and reaction.

He shot out of the barrel and did a backside cutback. He rose up and snapped the lip. He slid back down, hit the inside section, made a couple of nice turns, and then pulled out, perfectly poised on his surfboard. He looked over at Jake, who clapped his hands and called out, "Go, Mitch! Go hydra!"

Huh? Mitch wondered. What's hydra? Is that like hydraulics? At any rate, he knew it was a compliment when Jake gave him the shaka sign, so Mitch let out his victory cry, "Wooooo-hooooo!!!!"

In that moment, Mitch thought he could die and it would all have been worth it. The countless hours of drills, practice sessions, classes, the thousands of burpees and squats, the long dives under water spearfishing, carrying the boards over his head day after day, the cutbacks, the drop-ins, the pop-ups—it was all worth it. The soreness, the bruising, the cuts on his feet, the struggle to get better faster, waking up at dawn, exhausting himself and then going in for a full day of work—they were such small sacrifices to make for such an incredibly giant payoff.

That was amazing, he thought, I want to do it again!

The drive home was long, but Mitch didn't mind a bit. He recapped every turn on several of his best waves. He was jubilant, like a grommet that just learned how to stand up. The rest of the way home Mitch felt pure joy as he kept replaying surf scenes over and over in his mind.

When they finally arrived back at Jake's Surf Hut, Mitch felt exhausted, but it was the best kind of exhaustion—well-earned, satisfied, and proud. He put the car in park and even though his legs felt as thick and heavy as lead, he asked Jake if he needed any help bringing his gear inside. Jake nodded, and the two got out and began to unload Jake's bags, cooler, and surfboard.

"Hey, are we ever gonna do this again?" Mitch asked as he lifted Jake's board from the Jeep. "I know it's a long drive, but that secret spot was so awesome."

"Sure," Jake said. "We can go any time you want. I'm up there a couple times a month."

"Really?" Mitch asked, tucking the board under his arm. "Well then how come we didn't go sooner? I don't mean to sound disrespectful, but I probably could have surfed that spot a long time ago."

"The Monk and the Butterfly," said Jake in the tone of voice Mitch had come to recognize well. He braced himself for story time.

"A young monk walked along a creek and spotted a butterfly breaking out of his cocoon." Jake began. "Amazed by the beauty he sat to watch it emerge and take its first flight. The butterfly struggled for hours. Wanting to help, the young monk carefully used two twigs to open the cocoon to let the butterfly free. But when it tried to fly, the butterfly fell to the ground and died."

Mitch stopped in his tracks. He looked at Jake, who motioned for him to lift one end of the cooler while he lifted the other end.

"He hurried back to the monastery and went straight to his elder to explain what happened. Saddened and frustrated he said, 'I sat for hours marveling and watching God's creation coming to life. It struggled very hard so I gently helped it, yet only moments later it dies. How can this be right?' The elder said gravely, 'You didn't understand that the struggle was part of God's design. The only way a butterfly can strengthen its wings is by breaking free of the comfort and safety of the cocoon. By trying to help, even though you had good intentions, you prevented it from being able to develop the muscles it would need to survive.'"

Mitch and Jake lowered the cooler to the ground, and Jake reached into his pocket for his keys. He unlocked the front door of the surf hut, looked at his watch, then turned to Mitch and said, "Often, hardship and adversity are there to help us prepare for the journey ahead. Mentors, teachers, and parents really have just one job: To help us strengthen our wings."

With that, Jake slipped through the door of the surf hut and disappeared inside. Mitch lingered outside, looking at the door. He wanted to remember everything about that day—the way the sky looked at dawn, the feel of the ocean under his belly as he paddled out, the heat of the sun on his wet hair, the rush of wind as they drove along the freeway, the scent of salt, sand and asphalt, lessons from Jake and even the sound of silence right now after Jake said good-bye. Mitch breathed gratitude.

***

The workshop wasn't supposed to start until 7 p.m., but Mitch already stood by the front entrance of the yoga studio at 6:30, eager and excited to welcome his class. He checked the room one more time to make sure he didn't forget anything. Coco had helped him clean up, set up folding chairs, and connect a laptop to a large projection screen. As a surprise gift, she bought some colorful flowers and large potted plants and placed them in the corners of the room.

"Oh wow," Mitch said. "You didn't have to do that. You've done so much to help me already."

In addition to giving him use of the venue free of charge, she had also set up a nice display case in the reception area for his worksheets and handouts. She let him hook up his iPod to the stereo system so he could play background music while waiting for his students to arrive.

"Next time you have a night off," he said, "I'm taking you out to dinner. Really, I can't thank you enough for all this. The studio looks amazing."

Coco's cheeks turned the same shade of pink as the lily in her hair. She smiled and said, "You're welcome. Are you even nervous? You look completely relaxed."

"Yes, a little," Mitch admitted. "But in a good way. I guess I feel like if I could surf those double-overhead waves up in Santa Barbara last week, heck, I can do anything."

Coco smiled as she touched "Play" on the iPod, and the room quickly filled with sound.

Mitch's playlist included, I Got a Feeling, by the Black-Eyed Peas, Hall of Fame, by Will.I.Am, the classic We Will Rock You, by Queen, and other high energy songs to get the group fired up and excited about transforming their bodies, their health, and their energy.

Coco danced as she set up a table with a water pitcher and glasses in the back of the room, while Mitch waited by the front door for people to arrive. If I can just leave one person feeling inspired to make a breakthrough, he thought, even just one person, then this night will have been a success.

The first person to arrive was Mitch's coworker from Eco-Friendly Lighting—the one he had helped when he was stuck in traffic and couldn't get to his meeting on time. Mitch was thoroughly surprised to see him, very pleased, and even more pleased to see he brought along his wife. Mitch had posted one of his flyers about the workshop up on the corkboard in the break room, but he wasn't sure if anyone had seen it or was planning to come.

"I told a few people about your workshop, actually," said his coworker, putting his arm around his wife's waist, "including Claire. She wanted to come, so here we are. I'm just here for moral support, of course, because I'm already in tip-top shape." He patted his beer belly for emphasis and exchanged a joking look with his wife. They walked in to take their seats.

Mitch turned back to the door just in time to see Marisa from Monday yoga class enter with her husband, Raoul. He welcomed them with a friendly hug and invited them to get a glass of water and to mingle with others.

"You're going to teach us to be skinny tonight, right? We're excited!" said Marisa, warmly. Raoul smiled and nodded.

Mitch was happy to see Donna and Janette from the Wednesday yoga class come in next, each with a guest.

"We got a babysitter," said Donna, her arm linked in her husband's. Mitch noticed how different everyone looked in their regular clothes as opposed to their yoga pants and sweats. He saw them in a more three-dimensional way—as real people with jobs, obligations, and families. He felt humbled and grateful that they all took time out from their busy lives to come learn with him.

A couple more people Mitch knew from the yoga studio showed up just as the clock struck seven, so Mitch greeted them and walked to the front of the room to start. He looked at his audience and counted ten guests, which was a nice group. He expected eight, he hoped for twelve, so ten was all right. He picked up the remote control for the slideshow, gave Coco the signal to turn off the music, but just as he was about to begin, the front door swung open once more.

"Dude!" called Dusty as he appeared at the studio entrance with his arms outstretched and a smile on his face. Behind him stood three people Mitch had never seen before.

"Dusty!" Mitch said brightly.

"Check it out. This is Tiffany, Emily, and Mo. They're our neighbors, dude, and I told them your workshop was gonna be killer!"

The three new people stepped forward, and Mitch walked over to shake hands. Tiffany introduced herself and then Emily, her daughter, a college student still living at home. Mo was a very tall African-American gentleman Mitch had seen before in his apartment complex. Mitch remembered Mo because he always walked up the stairs slowly, as if he had knee problems or perhaps back pain. Mitch never asked, though, because he didn't want to seem rude.

"Hi, I'm Mitch. Thank you for coming," he said, extending his hand.

Mo shook his hand. "Mo. I've heard a lot about you."

"Oh yeah? From Dusty?" Mitch said playfully. "Don't believe a word of it. I deny everything."

Mo chuckled, signed in, paid his $20 and lumbered over to the last available seat in the front row. Dusty linked arms with both ladies and led them to three empty seats directly behind him. Mitch returned to his position at the front of the room, bolstered by the sudden increase in the size of his audience. He looked up at Dusty's smiling face and made a mental note to buy Dusty a new leash for his board.

"Okay, let's get started!" Mitch said, grabbing the remote control. The first slide showed a tanned, muscular surfer riding a perfect blue wave with a big smile on his face. "This is why I decided to quit making excuses about how busy I was and decided to make my health a priority. Surfing is my passion. Just being in the ocean fills my spirit, and there's nothing I would rather do on earth than what you see in this picture right here."

From the second row came Dusty's voice, along with a shaka sign thrown up in the air, "Surfing rules!"

"So what I'd like to do to start," Mitch grinned, "is to ask all of you, why are you here? What made you decide to attend a workshop on health, nutrition, and weight loss this evening? And what is it you want to walk away with tonight?" Mitch scanned the room and saw Donna with her hand up. He nodded for her to speak.

"Well, I've tried ten diets and none of them worked, so I want to figure out why that is, and what I'm doing wrong."

"That must be frustrating," Mitch said. "Anyone else confused on what to do and frustrated with the results they're getting?" Several nodded and raised their hands.

"Why are you here, David?"

"It's surfing for me too. That's why I go to Coco's Yoga for Surfers class. I'm thinking now I want to add a workout routine also, but I want it to be like, specifically for surfing."

"Awesome," said Mitch.

One by one, everyone shared their most pressing issues, except for Dusty, who sat in the back, bobbing his head in time with some steel drum reggae music in his head. When asked why he was there, he said, still bobbing his head, "Just scopin' out the babes and helpin' my bro."

Mitch covered all the fundamentals of health and weight loss. He talked about eating small, frequent meals; balancing carbs and protein; balancing cardio, strength, and flexibility in a fitness routine; stretching beyond your comfort zone; and even the importance of rest and recovery time in the form of meditation. He spent extra time on the importance of drinking water, as Jake advised, and how to dig deep to find your "why."

There was a short break in the middle of the workshop when everyone could get up and chat. During the second half, Mitch led them through some exercises and did a Q & A session. At the end of the two-hour workshop, Mitch told everyone, "All right, so go out and get healthy! Did everyone learn something about how to balance fitness, nutrition, and achieving a healthy weight?"

He looked out at the group and saw mild, friendly smiles and nods. Somehow Mitch was hoping for more enthusiasm. He saw Tiffany with her arms crossed and head cocked to the side in her seat, as if still processing some of the information.

"Did you have a question?" Mitch asked, powering down his laptop and stepping out in front of the table.

"No it's just that...look at you. You're like, a real athlete and staying in shape is so easy for you. It's different for the rest of us. I've been struggling with my weight for ten years. I've had three kids. You don't know what it's like."

Suddenly Dusty curled forward, as if someone were tickling his stomach. "What?" he laughed. "No way! Mitch used to be a lard ass!" Everyone's eyes bulged and nervously looked over at Mitch, who was too shocked to say anything.

"Dude," Dusty continued, "show 'em that picture of me and you from your birthday. Wait I have it..." He fished into his Baja hoodie, pulled out his cell phone, swiped it and clicked, and then held up a photo for the class to see. Mitch and Dusty stood on a beach next to their surfboards, flashing shaka signs, and smiling wide for the camera. Dusty looked tan, wet, and happy—his usual self. Mitch, however, looked pale and pudgy. His pasty belly hung over his board shorts, and his legs stuck out like two stuffed sausages at the bottom.

From the front of the room, Mitch stared, horrified, at the photo. First of all, he couldn't believe he used to look like that. Second, he couldn't believe Dusty was showing it to everyone. He felt the urge to slip out of sight and hide away forever.

But just then came the turnaround. "Wow! What a transformation!" Donna said, thoroughly impressed.

"That's you??" asked Tiffany, squinting at the photo. Then she looked back at the real Mitch. She continued to look back and forth from the photo to Mitch.

Emily leaned over to see, and then said, "That's amazing."

Mo took one look at the photo, and one look back at Mitch at the front of the room and said, "Do you do personal training?"

Three other people raised their hands immediately after and said they were interested in hiring Mitch for personal training as well. Mitch was caught off guard and didn't know what to say. He got the certification through Jake, but didn't expect to actually use it—he just wanted some sort of validation as a teacher, and proof for his audience to know that his information was solid. He told them it might be hard because of his day job, but he'd certainly consider it. The idea appealed to him, but he was already so busy.

Thinking on his feet, Mitch simply bought himself some time. He passed around a pad of paper and asked everyone to write their names, cell phone and best time to reach them, so he could call them later to discuss possibilities.

The paper went around the room, along with the photo of Mitch. Each person looked down at Photo Mitch and then up to Real Mitch, as if trying to verify that it was really him. They shook their heads in wonder, wrote their names on the paper, and then turned to each other saying, "Can you believe it?" and "When I met him in October, he was even bigger than in the picture" and "Well, that's it then. I'm following his plan." The lively chatter continued as the gathering came to an end and people thanked Mitch one by one for his time and for sharing his story.

"Hey Dusty," Mitch called as the last group left Coco's studio. Dusty turned around, thumbs looped in his front pockets.

"That picture of us on my birthday," Mitch continued, "is truly awful. I completely and totally hate how I look in that photo."

"Aw, no!" Dusty said, slapping his forehead. "I'm sorry, man. You want me to erase..."

Mitch interrupted, "No, but do me a favor and send it to me. I'm gonna have it enlarged and put on a poster so I can bring it to every workshop I ever do. Thanks for breaking it out."

It took a few seconds for Dusty to process Mitch's reaction. Finally he smiled, forwarded the image to Mitch, and jogged out the door to catch up with Emily.

Mitch turned to see only Coco remaining in the studio. She looked at him expectantly, studying his face as if to say, Well...? How do you feel?

Mitch let out a howl of relief and celebration as he just about crumbled to his knees. "I did it!"

Coco gave him a hug, knowing exactly how he felt. She experienced the post-public-speaking high many times in her early years as a yoga instructor. Every class felt like a Broadway show and she looked forward to the glowing reviews. If a student ever came up to her after class and thanked her, or said they felt fantastic and energized for the rest of the day, she'd just about melt with relief and joy. Over time, her classes started to fill up and stay full, but the feeling of being on stage, with the anxiousness before and exhilaration after, never got old.

"It went great! You were amazing!" she said. "I'm so impressed."

"Aw, man," Mitch said, pulling back and pressing his palms to his eyes. "Thank you. Thank you. I really can't thank you enough for all your help."

"Of course, you're so welcome," she said. "Let me know if you ever want to do another one. I thought this was terrific." Coco crossed to the stereo, unplugged Mitch's iPod, and started to clean up.

"Okay, yes, definitely," Mitch said, looking about the room. He picked up a couple of folding chairs and stacked them.

They worked together to get the room back in order for the yoga class tomorrow morning. The last thing they moved out of the studio was the front table, which still had Mitch's laptop and pad of paper on it with the workshop students' names and contact information. Mitch didn't take his eyes off of it while he and Coco lifted the table and carried it back in the reception room.

Coco noticed. "What are you thinking about?"

"These people," Mitch answered. "They said they might want to hire me to be their personal trainer. I've never done that before, but I think I can do it. I'm sure I can do it. I just don't know how to set it up."

Coco set her end of the table down and stood up tall with her hands on her hips.

"Can't you just model what Jake does with you?" she asked.

"Oh, for sure, yeah. And I'm certified now, so that's not what I'm worried about," Mitch said as he gathered up his notebook and laptop. "What I mean is, do I need to write up formal contracts for this? How much should I charge them? And how do I accommodate people's schedules when I have so little wiggle room in my own schedule? Really, the only time I can train anyone is evenings and weekends. Early in the morning I'm with Jake, and I have my full-time day job Monday through Friday, so...I guess, I don't know, I don't want things to get too complicated. Maybe I shouldn't do it."

Coco listened and then grabbed a pen from her front desk. She gave it to him and said, "Let me ask you some questions. If any of those people would be willing to train with you on evenings and weekends, would you do it?"

"Absolutely. That'd be perfect," Mitch replied.

"Do you feel like personal training is aligned with your passions, gifts, and talents, like in Good to Great?"

"Yes," Mitch said, starting to see where Coco was going. He opened his notebook to the most recent page. "Maybe even more so than my current job."

"Well, maybe it's time to start thinking about running your own business. Does the idea of entrepreneurship turn you on, or do you like the security of your day job?"

Mitch wobbled his head back and forth. "I...well, it's a little of both. I definitely want to try being my own boss, being an entrepreneur. Ever since reading Unlimited Wealth and seeing how my boss Ken built his company, I've been thinking that would be my path to wealth and freedom. Working for someone else and having a salary is nice, but it's limited and it's fixed. I like the idea of making my own schedule and being able to earn as much as I want."

Coco nodded, "Right. When you run your own business, it's all up to you. That can be a good thing or a bad thing. I have a feeling that for you it's a good thing. You're so disciplined and so driven."

"Thanks," Mitch said, as the wheels continued to turn in his mind. He scribbled notes while he spoke. "You know what else? I think all the time about how if I ran my own business, I could organize my time however I want. If I want to take a two-hour lunchtime surf break and then work until six or seven, great. If I don't want to work Wednesdays and prefer Sunday instead, great. I can't imagine how cool that would be."

"Yup. Time freedom is huge," Coco agreed. "Notice how I teach a lot of classes very early in the morning and very late at night? It's because that's exactly the way I like it. Then the whole day in the middle is mine."

"That's awesome," Mitch said. "And I have to say, I'm also really inspired by you. You're another reason I want to start my own business."

Coco paused while pulling her coconut-colored cardigan out of the closet.

Mitch continued, "You live life on your terms. Your way. You set up this studio and the whole place just vibrates with...I don't know how to describe it...Coco-ness."

"Aw, thank you. And that's really cool that you noticed," she said, grabbing her gym bag and purse. "I feel that finding that vibe, my own authentic self-expression, is one of the keys to my success."

Mitch closed his notebook and grabbed his bags as well, seeing that she was about ready to leave. As Coco pulled out her keys she said, "I hope you think seriously about training them. Don't worry about all the numbers or contracts or business stuff yet. Just think about the difference you can make."

Mitch liked that advice. No pressure, just take some time and think about it. They walked out of the studio, and Mitch waited while she locked the front door. He walked her to her car and thanked her again for "all your help, and for the inspiration." As Coco drove off, Mitch heard Jake's voice in his head repeat: Maybe this can be the beginning of something.

CHAPTER 8:

GETTING INTO POSITION

*Pollution is nothing but the resources we are
not harvesting. We allow them to disperse because
we've been ignorant of their value.*

—R. Buckminster Fuller

Mitch couldn't believe he made it up out of bed and to the beach in time for his 7 a.m. surf lesson the following morning. He barely slept all night because he kept reviewing the workshop like a movie over and over in his mind, examining and analyzing it, thinking of all the things he could have done differently or better. He started to give Jake a play-by-play of the workshop, but he interrupted Mitch and asked only three simple questions:

"What went well?"

"What did you learn?"

"What's your next step?"

"I don't need all the details." Jake explained. "I guarantee you nobody even noticed half the things you're obsessed about. So don't dwell on mistakes, celebrate them. That's how we learn. So tell me: What went well?"

"Well," Mitch said, planting his six-six go-to shortboard upright in the sand, "Dusty showed an old picture of me when I was really overweight. It was brutal. But everyone loved it."

"Great! You had a 'before-and-after' that showed them what's possible, and that your program works. Nice! What else went well?"

"I was prepared, I had a good turnout and great feedback." Mitch listed.

"Ok, Next question, what did you learn?" asked Jake

"I learned..." Mitch paused as he looked down at the sand. "This may sound strange but I learned that I can do this. I was terrified to run the workshop by myself, but I did it. And everyone liked it, so...I learned I can do it. It's like, if I can surf that heavy wave in Santa Barbara, and I can lead my own workshop despite my fears, then, I don't know, I feel like I can do anything."

"Great," Jake said, giving him a strong high-five. "What's your next step?"

Mitch drummed his fingertips on the white surfboard behind him while he thought about it. Eventually he shrugged and said, "I don't know. A few people asked me if I do personal training, so I guess I've got to think about that."

Jake said simply, "Don't think. Visualize."

And just like that, all conversation and thoughts about the workshop ended. Mitch and Jake did their surf lesson as usual, Mitch went to work, and back to his weekly routine. He did start visualizing, however, whenever he could steal a moment during the day, and certainly before bed at night. Images and conversations swirled through his mind as he imagined what it would be like to coach someone to good health, just as Jake had done for him.

He imagined Mo getting stronger and his limp slowly disappearing as they spent week after week together, building muscle and correcting posture. He imagined Donna looking and feeling like the vibrant, energetic woman she wanted to be, enjoying her children, and letting go of stress and exhaustion.

Sometimes, during particularly slow afternoons at the office, the visualization took on a life of its own, and Mitch found himself standing inside a huge fitness facility in his mind, right near the beach and next door to a surf shop. He stood in the center of a large, clean floor and listened to the sound of waves in the distance. Large windows and high ceilings with skylights allowed loads of natural light to pour in. He envisioned a classroom off to the side of the gym floor, designated for workshops and group support as new members started their journey to good health. He envisioned a logo, colors, and himself as the CEO...and that's usually when he snapped out of it and returned to reality—purchase orders and phone calls.

He kept the list of names from the workshop, and called them all a week later, just to ask how they were doing. He asked if they had started making any changes in their diets or workout routines. He asked if there was any particular aspect of the workshop that resonated strongly with them and listened with interest to their responses. Almost everyone said they had started to make healthier choices and expressed appreciation for his follow-up.

Although two people asked if he was going to do another workshop, Mitch never brought up personal training. He still wasn't prepared to talk about it, and he didn't want them to think he was calling just to try to sell them. Because the truth was, he cared about Mo's ailing back, David's desire to become an elite surfer, Donna's wish to be healthy for her children, and everyone else's goals and desires. Every once in a while, one of them would appear in his mind as he visualized that new fitness facility, but then he'd pull in the reins. It was too big, too much, and overwhelming.

Finally, over the course of the last week in July, visualization translated into action. It was the week of the US Open of Surfing at Huntington Pier, and the week Mitch officially took the leap and became an entrepreneur.

***

Mitch had wanted to go to the US Open of Surfing for the past few years, but never quite made it due the workload he carried at his corporate job. Eventually, he let the competition fall off his radar, because looking forward to events he knew he'd never be able to attend felt like torture. But this year, on an otherwise ordinary morning in mid-July, he overheard someone joking as he walked past the breakroom at work. "...a buddy of mine is surfing in the trials this weekend. You think if I tell Ken I'm going for networking purposes, I can get my expenses comped?"

Instantly, Mitch whipped out his smartphone to Google the dates. The men's and women's final rounds would take place on a Sunday, just thirteen days away. He put it on his calendar.

When that Sunday came, Mitch sprang out of bed, slipped into his board shorts and favorite Billabong T-shirt, and dashed to the beach. It was a good thing he went on foot, because parking was brutal. He had read online that bleachers would be set up for forty thousand people, but a far greater number of people would likely be in attendance—probably more like fifty thousand.

Throngs of tourists and surf fans swarmed around the main entrance. Once Mitch made it past the bleachers, the crowd became less dense and he was able to see the pier on the right, lined with dozens of bright sponsor banners and logos. White vendor tents dotted the beach in addition to the usual souvenir and trinket shops already there on a typical weekend. Teenagers danced to music that blared over the loudspeakers by the skate park, tourists studied their maps, and the smell of chili dogs and cheese fries wafted through the air as the food court opened.

Mitch appreciated the energy of the event, but also found himself feeling a little put off. Tourists always left such a mess behind, and he could just imagine how bad the beach was going to look the next day. As a resident of Huntington Beach, with all his happiest childhood memories connected to the place, it kind of made him sick.

Mitch looked up at the Jumbotron, but because it was such a hot, sweaty day, he soon realized he wasn't really in the mood for watching a movie. Every once in a while, the music would quiet down and announcers shouted out the current scores, but Mitch could barely make out what they were saying because of the echo.

A horn sounded at the beginning and end of every heat, and people would cheer. Mitch didn't. He couldn't see any of the surf action, because of the mob of people between him and the water, and eventually he grew frustrated. He sent a text to Jake.

Hey, Where are you?

Jake: VIP section. Right in front of the announcer's booth.

Mitch dropped a shoulder and bulldozed through the crowd to the VIP section, where he found himself barred by a red velvet rope divider. A tall, beefy Samoan-looking bouncer dressed in black stepped directly in front of Mitch, crossed his arms, and asked, "Do you have a pass?"

Mitch cowered, but then caught a glimpse of Jake just behind him, and spoke fast.

"No, but my surf coach is right there. Hey Jake!" Mitch said, pointing. Jake turned and saw Mitch, walked over and gave the bouncer a nod, who then stepped aside, allowing the two to talk to each other across the divider.

"Is this crazy or what?" Mitch said. "How are your students doing?"

"So far they're doing great," Jake replied. "The surf is pretty mediocre today, so it requires a lot of athleticism and creativity on these small waves to earn points. They're putting on a show."

"I have to say," Mitch said, squinting, "I'm kinda over this. I can't see, I can't hear, it's hot and muggy..." He raised his hand to shield his eyes from the sun, but it didn't help.

Jake shrugged and said, "You can always watch the highlights later."

Mitch stopped for a moment to consider what to do, but just then he felt a slight breeze on the back of his neck. He looked toward the water and said, "I want to check period and swell direction on Surfline." Noticing the surf was shoulder to head high, south swell, with a slight texture from the northeast side-shore wind, which meant the water was a little bit choppy at the pier.

"Hey," Mitch said, thinking out loud. "With 14-16 second intervals, and this wind direction wouldn't the Point be good right now? This northeast wind should be offshore over there, and the swell direction and the incoming tide..."

"Ah, yeah," Jake said, smiling to see his junior waterman learning the ropes. "It's probably all time right now! It should be a little bigger because it's south facing, and the crowd might be light because of the contest."

"I think I'm going to bail this mess and see if I can get lucky," Mitch said.

"Go for it," Jake nodded. "I'd go too if I wasn't coaching."

Mitch took off, agreeing to check back in later. He jogged home, hopped in his Jeep, and drove down the road to the Point.

He caught it near-perfect. The swell hit straight on and although there were a few people in the lineup, it wasn't crowded at all. Mitch caught over 20 waves in two hours and paddled in feeling refreshed, stoked, and hungry. He stopped on the way back to his apartment to grab a salad with grilled chicken, and at about two o'clock in the afternoon headed back to the pier.

As he walked up Main Street, he noticed a small crowd gathered around the statue of Duke Kahanamoku in front of the Huntington Surf and Sport shop. He also saw a cameraman with a small video camera set up on a tripod among the spectators, who stood far enough away to give him room to shoot. Mitch stood up high on his toes, trying to see over everyone's heads. Then he crouched down low, peeking through elbows and hips, to try to catch a glimpse of who might be at the center of the shot.

What he saw gave him a huge personal thrill. Standing right there in front of "The Duke" was twelve-time World Championship Tour winner, two-time Surfer Hall of Fame inductee, Waterman of the

Year, and one of the most consistently top-seeded competitors in the Association of Surfing Professionals, Rob Machado. Mitch thought to himself, *Nooooo waaaaay...*

Standing next to Rob was Pete Mel, easily one of the best television announcers in the world of competitive, big-wave surfing. Pete held a microphone in front of his chest, looking composed and dignified, waiting for his cameraman to give the signal.

"Good afternoon, ladies and gentlemen," Pete said once the camera was rolling. "I'm standing here with Rob Machado, the Southern California surfing legend, professional surfer, and environmental activist. Hey, Rob, you made it to the semifinals this morning. How do you feel about your performance?"

"Well," Rob replied, smiling and gesturing toward all the admiring faces around him, "the crowd's amazing, I have all my bros out here with me, it's a beautiful, sunny SoCal day, so really I have to say it's all good. I have no complaints."

"Well, the fans certainly love you in these parts, no question," Pete agreed, and everyone applauded and whooped. "I understand you've got a fundraiser coming up for the Rob Machado Foundation—a surf contest down at your home break at Seaside. Tell us about it?"

"We're raising money to save our planet, bro, and get more people to go green! All the money in the Rob Machado Foundation goes to environmental projects for young people, like beach clean-ups and habitat restoration. We also support school greening initiatives, like reducing lunchroom waste, providing environmental education, water conservation, supplying recycling bins, walk-to-school programs—you name it. All kinds of really cool stuff."

Rob's sea-blue eyes lit up as he spoke about the foundation, and his wild, Rasta, sand-colored hair swished over his shoulders.

"So what would you say," asked Pete while the cameraman drew in close, "to those individuals who don't think their actions make a difference? How do you motivate people to go green and do their part no matter how small?"

Rob rubbed the back of his neck while he considered his answer, and turned to look at the statue of Duke Kahanamoku.

He turned back to the microphone and said, "First of all, I'd let them know they already are making a difference—it's just a question of whether it's a positive difference or a negative difference. Every day, each of us either contributes to problems in the environment, or we contribute to a solution. The solutions are in the products we buy, the food we eat, what we do with our trash, and how we take care of our beaches. It all starts with each of us taking responsibility for our footprint. I'm stoked to see how many businesses are going green. When all these different groups of like-minded people join forces and work collectively, that's when bigger structural changes can happen."

"So tell us, for those of us who want to contribute to the solution and come out to the surf contest at Seaside, where can we go to get more information?"

"Check out our website," Rob said directly into the camera. "Rob-machadofoundation.org. We're also on Facebook, Twitter, YouTube, and Instagram—there are plenty of ways to connect."

"Thanks so much," said Pete. "Good luck with the rest of the surf contest and thanks for stopping by and talking with us." Rob flashed the shaka sign and Pete gave the signal to cut. Fans immediately closed in on Rob, requesting autographs and photo ops. Pete helped the cameraman wrap up the equipment and signed a few autographs as well.

Mitch stood in awe, frozen in place while everyone pushed past him to get to Rob. What an incredible guy, he thought, and how cool would it be if I could get involved with Rob's fundraiser.

When the crowd finally thinned, Mitch stepped up to Rob and tried to maintain every element of cool as he introduced himself. It took a conscious effort, because his heart was beating in his throat and he felt a massive urge to spout out his entire life story, including everything surfing ever meant to him throughout childhood, his passion for it now as an adult, what it was like to watch Rob in 2006 when he won the US Open of Surfing, the Monster Energy Pro at

Pipeline, and the Summer X Games in Mexico, and of course how much they had in common which meant they should become very best friends.

Just before he opened his mouth to speak, Mitch noticed a half-empty paper plate of French fries spilled on the ground near the base of the statue of the Duke. Red ketchup smeared all over the plate and part of the gray pedestal like a mini fast-food homicide. Habitually Mitch stooped and carefully cleared the crime scene, tossing the plate into the nearest trash can. Someone followed up by wiping the ketchup off the pedestal with a towel. When Mitch stood up he saw that it was Rob Machado himself.

"Hey, thanks for cleaning that up," said Rob, folding up the towel to put back in his backpack.

Mitch looked left and right to see if Rob was talking to some-one else, but there was no one. He stepped up and held himself together well enough to be able to say, "Sure. Um, hey, that was a great interview. My name is Mitch and I was wondering..." Mitch patted his board short pockets to see if he had any business cards on him, but didn't, so he just kept talking. "I work for a company called Eco-Friendly Lighting, and my boss is a big-time surfer and environmentalist. Do you think we could get a booth at your event? Who would I talk to about that?"

Rob pulled out a business card from the front of his backpack and gave it to Mitch. "Here," he said jovially, "call and ask for Tricia. She's in charge of the sponsorships and can get you all the informa-tion."

Mitch took the card and held it in both hands, as if it were something holy and he was afraid to drop it. He managed to utter, "Thanks, man," and started to back away.

"Sure thing," answered Rob. "Hey, what was your name again?"

"Mitch. Mitch Springer."

"Hope to see you there, Mitch. Nice meeting you."

Rob turned and walked away, and Mitch continued his afternoon stroll back toward the beach. He was still stoked from his surf session out at the Point, and now he just met a living legend. He didn't know if it was possible to fly any higher.

He kept walking, looking down at the business card, turning it over in his hands, until he came upon a row of white tents. He looked up and realized he'd arrived at the Sponsor Village. One tent in particular caught Mitch's eye because of the large, bright green banner stretching across the top that read, "GreenLight Products: Save Money on your Electric Bill." Mitch placed Rob Machado's business card safely inside his wallet and walked over to check it out.

His chest tightened as he pretended to be a casual passerby, inspecting the samples on the display shelves, looking over brochures and product information. GreenLight appeared to be another version of Eco-Friendly Lighting. They sold almost all the same types of products and even served the same parts of California, but their prices were lower. Mitch gathered one of each of the brochures on the main table.

A neatly dressed Asian man in a collared shirt and slacks stood quietly behind a table with his hands politely folded behind his back while Mitch collected the materials. He didn't speak or attempt to engage with Mitch in any way, but he did appear to be attentive, so Mitch asked, "Hi...so...if I were to replace all the lighting in my office, how would I go about that? Where do I start?"

The man nodded and slid a thick product guide across the table to show to Mitch. He opened it to a page showing several types of office light bulbs. He slid his finger down the list to show him the product names and then across the page to the corresponding prices. Then he turned to a page at the back of the guide, "How to Order," and invited Mitch to read the simple instructions.

"I just find the product I want, call this number, and order it? Just like that?" Mitch asked.

The man smiled and bowed slightly. He also handed Mitch a flyer that read across the top in all caps,

GREENLIGHT'S PRICE GUARANTEE: IF YOU

SHOW US ANY OF THESE PRODUCTS FOR A LOWER PRICE ELSEWHERE, WE'LL CUT OUR PRICE TO EARN YOUR BUSINESS!

"Okay, thank you," Mitch said and quickly turned to walk away. Visions of cancelled accounts entered his mind. Customers apologizing, explaining they couldn't say no to the savings, saying that it wasn't personal...Once his customers found out they could get Eco-Friendly products for so much less, they'd for sure switch their allegiance. He felt a churning sensation in his stomach for the rest of the day.

Mitch forced himself to stop and take three deep breaths. He went to the beach to try some yoga poses to clear his head and calm down, but he couldn't focus. The US Open was dying down, but there were still so many people scattered about, and even more trash.

Furthermore, all Mitch could think about was how the first company he ever worked for went under when the competition put out better products. The second company went under when its product failed to live up to its promise. The third company, Reynolds, was in the process of going under because its products were determined to be harmful. Would Eco-Friendly go under now because a competitor offered the same products at lower prices? Mitch didn't think he could handle another layoff or financial crisis. And he had grown very fond of Ken and didn't want to see his company fail.

As the sun began to sink into the horizon, Mitch felt like sinking too. He went home after dark and lay awake all night.

***

"What's on your mind?" Ken asked Monday morning. Mitch dropped into one of the plush chairs in front of Ken's desk. With heavy hands, he pulled out the brochures he collected from Green-Light's booth the day before and handed them over.

"This new company just opened up in Long Beach. Their prices beat us across the board, on every product. The guy at the booth showed me their price guarantee and they'll even under-bid any other company. All the customer has to do is show them a product or package for a lower price, and they'll beat it. I'm really worried about this," Mitch explained. "How are we going to keep our customers once they find out about GreenLight?"

Ken read carefully through the materials, placing each page face down on his desk as he finished and moved on to the next one. At first, he seemed concerned, but as he read through the pages and listened to Mitch, his expression softened. In the end, he said, "Well, you can stop worrying. They're not our competition, and that business model is unsustainable. I've seen lots of companies like this come and go, believe it or not. They don't understand DyVal, and they're always stuck in the price trap."

"They don't understand what? DyVal?" Mitch asked.

Ken pulled his chair back from the desk, opened a drawer, and pulled out a dry erase marker. He made a motion for Mitch to follow him as he crossed the room to the whiteboard. In large letters at the top of the whiteboard he wrote, "DyVal."

Dy-VAL = DYNAMIC VALUE

DIFFERENTIATION		
↑	TRANSFORMATION	PRICELESS
	EXPERIENCE	$3.00
	PRICE BARRIOR	
	SERVICE	$1.00
	PRODUCT	50¢
	COMMODITY	10¢

"DyVal means 'dynamic value.' Everything I'm about to explain was taught to me by Marshall Thurber. Have you ever heard of him?"

Mitch shook his head. "Marshall is a positive deviant, a business-man, attorney, real estate developer, educator, scholar, inventor, public speaker, he's one of my most trusted friends and advisors," Ken explained. "You should look him up on YouTube."

Mitch pulled his journal and a pen from his portfolio and wrote down the name.

Ken then wrote "Commodity" at the bottom of the board. "If you're offering a commodity, the only thing your client cares about is price. Let's say you're an entrepreneur and you start up some sort of company around surfing. If you're offering a commodity, you'll be selling the fiberglass, the foam blanks, fins and the components that make up a surfboard. All the client cares about is to get those components at the cheapest possible prices."

Then he turned back to the board and wrote "Product" right above commodity. "The next level up on the value chain is a product. Now, if you buy all that fiberglass and foam and put it all together to make a surfboard on your own, then good for you—you just created a product. The actual cost of your product in terms of parts and labor might be only a couple hundred bucks, but if you put a brand name on it, like Rusty, or Channel Islands, that same product might sell for six hundred fifty or seven hundred fifty dollars. Once you create a brand, you create the opportunity for customer loyalty and you differentiate yourself."

Mitch nodded. Above product Ken wrote "Service" and said, "The next level of differentiation is providing a service, such as, I don't know, surf lessons or a custom board made to the buyer's specs. For this, customers will pay even more. Some companies bundle their product with a service, like your cell phone, for example. You buy the phone and the monthly service, and we call that an offering."

Ken wrote the word "Offering" next to Product and Service. Mitch took copious notes. Ken walked over to take a sip of water from the bottle on his desk to give Mitch a chance to get everything down, then came back and continued.

"At this point you are still stuck in the price trap, you can easily be duplicated. You might have a great product or a great service and still your competition can come in and knock you off. What cannot be duplicated is the next level of DyVal, which is creating an experience."

Ken drew a line on the board above "Service" and wrote "Experience."

"So if we go back to our surfing example, we can offer our customers a surfing safari—an experience. We can take a group of people to some destination, plan out the entire itinerary for them, provide an expert surf guide, make the trip all-inclusive with food, drinks, accommodations, and... you get the idea, right? Give them an awesome life memory. It's all organized by an expert and they get to live the dream."

"Totally," Mitch nodded. "Taking a killer surf trip like that is one of my goals!"

"And keep in mind now," Ken continued, "that in the business sense, 'Experience' doesn't have to refer to an exotic vacation. It can be at your local coffee shop, too. Customers often drive past four or five different coffee shops while they're on their way to their favorite one. Why do they do that? Can't they get good coffee at any of the other places? Sure, but they want more than just good coffee. They want the experience they've come to know and love from their favorite coffee shop. They walk in and immediately the aroma pleases them. They like the décor and the atmosphere of the shop itself. Maybe the barista knows them and calls them by name. Everyone is friendly, the coffee is always good, always just the right temperature, they can sit in a comfortable chair and work on their laptop at a table—whatever they want. And it's the consistency that keeps the customers coming back day after day, even paying higher prices for the cup of coffee, because they just can't get this experience anywhere else. Make sense?"

"Hmm," Mitch said, thinking about all the places he liked to shop. He realized that if he had 1 or 2 bad experiences somewhere, he rarely went back. "So," he said, thinking aloud, "we should be trying to create an experience not just get a client?"

"Yes. At the level of experience, you're no longer in the price trap," Ken answered. "But believe it or not, there is another higher level." Ken turned to write one final word on the whiteboard.

"Transformation" appeared at the top of the list. Ken circled it.

"The highest level of DyVal is 'Transformation.' With our surf business example, transformation would be where our customers change their view of the world through surfing. Maybe they become watermen. Their point of view about the ocean, the world, their relationship with nature, would all change to align with the point of view of surf culture. Maybe it's a giving adventure where you go to a village and build a hospital or a well for fresh water? At this level, as a businessperson, you create such a positive experience for your client that they not only continue to be loyal in giving you their business, but they become raving fans and brag about you to everyone they know. And when you have that, no price-cutting and no amount of slick advertising would be able to compete."

Mitch thought about Jake, and how he had become way more than his surf coach and the transformation he'd undergone as Jake's student. The thought of taking a surf lesson from anyone else or buying a surfboard from any other shop seemed absurd, even if the prices were significantly lower.

"I totally get it," Mitch said, mind blown.

"So what we always need to be working on here at Eco-Friendly," Ken concluded, "is to constantly increase our value so that we're creating that world-class experience for our clients, and optimally a transformative experience. When we do that, we don't need to worry about competitors or price cutting. We won't even have any competition because what we offer is so unique."

Mitch reviewed his notes, putting it all together.

"So what I'm hearing is, I shouldn't go down to the level of fighting GreenLight on price. Because even if I did, and I won business based on the lower price, it won't serve us in the long run. I'd basically just have to keep discounting and discounting and discounting in order to stay the cheapest, and even then, it wouldn't matter because at the higher levels of DyVal, price is irrelevant."

"That's right," Ken said, tossing the dry erase marker back over to his desk. "You don't create wealth by chasing the bottom."

"So...how do I create an experience?" Mitch asked. "I'm selling lightbulbs."

"Creating an experience happens with every interaction—every touch point between you and our clients and our company. Do you remember how we taught you consultative selling and empathetic coaching? By using that model and asking questions, finding out what our clients need and want, you've already differentiated yourself from ninety percent of the transactional, product-oriented companies and commission-focused sales reps out there. And that's just at the experience level. What we really offer is a transformation, because as we educate our clients, they start to think of themselves as environmentalists. For many, our lighting systems are just the first step in journey to becoming more eco-friendly. It starts off with saving money on lighting and electricity, but then develops into something much bigger. They become advocates of our mission to save the planet. Next thing you know they're marching with us on Earth Day."

Suddenly Mitch remembered the other reason he wanted to talk to Ken first thing in the morning. "Speaking of saving the planet," he said, perking up, "you'll never guess who I met yesterday at the US Open."

"I don't know. Who saves the planet? Superman?"

"Close. Rob Machado."

Ken's face lit up like a light bulb. "Cool! How did you meet Rob?"

"He was doing an interview at the US Open with Pete Mel right in front of the statue of "The Duke," Mitch said. "And he's got this fundraising event coming up—a surf contest—to benefit the Rob Machado Foundation. They offer all kinds of programs to teach kids about protecting the environment. I really want to go if we can. It'd be a great way for me to get some leads and meet homeowners and businesses that we might have synergy with. It's only five hundred dollars to sponsor a booth and I got the event person's contact info."

"I love it," Ken said. "And I like that you're thinking synergy. Co-operation with other businesses is much better than competition. Get me all the details and I'll let you know by tomorrow. You have to introduce me to Rob, though, or else I'm calling it off."

As Mitch walked down the hall to his desk, he felt yesterday's worries fall away. Ken just offered him a whole new way of seeing, and he felt renewed.

***

By the end of the workday, Mitch should have been exhausted, but wasn't. He spent the evening thinking about DyVal, and tried to come up with new ways to add value to his client relationships. He also remembered the people who attended his workshop and asked for personal training. He brainstormed how he could provide a completely transformative experience for them—how to get from where they were now to their vision of optimal health. He envisioned Mo, Donna, and David transforming into the best possible versions of themselves, and exactly what his role would be in that process.

Mitch feverishly wrote out all his ideas. His journal became filled with notes about his new venture. He started mapping out his business model and how he could launch by working just part time in the evenings.

He drove to Coco's studio and caught her just before she was about to close for the night. Rushing through the door, still in his work clothes, he held out his notebook and said, "What do you think of this? I think I've turned a corner here and I'm finally figuring it out."

Surprised and delighted at his sudden entrance, Coco held out her smooth bronze hands to take the notebook. She let her bags slide off her arm onto the reception desk and sat to review Mitch's notes. Mitch stood close, rereading his own notes upside down and backward across from her.

"Oh, it's the business model for your hedgehog!" she smiled. Mitch loved that she knew exactly what she was looking at. It made communication so easy.

"I'm thinking," he said, "what if I do one group class one night a week, and then I work one-on-one with each client one time per week? That way they get two exercise sessions per week, but everyone's second hour is combined so they get a sense of community like your yoga crew?"

"Smart," Coco agreed.

"And the group class would be divided into two parts," Mitch said, and walked over to take a seat on the bench near the window. "The first part would be like a health seminar, kind of like a mini-version of the workshop I did here. I'd introduce a particular issue or challenge in health and fitness and discuss solutions and plans for success. It would be very interactive with Q & A at the end, and it would be a good opportunity for everyone to just check in, learn something, and even gain support from the rest of the group. The second part would be a group workout with two or three options for each exercise based on their fitness level. That way everyone leaves sweaty and feeling good."

"That's an awesome way to structure it," Coco said, still studying the notebook.

"What if I charge a hundred dollars a week for all that?" Mitch continued.

"Sounds like a great value for the clients," she said, looking at the section where he calculated his potential earnings.

"Okay, so a hundred a week," Mitch continued. "If four of those twelve people who were at the workshop agree to hire me to be their coach, I can potentially make four hundred dollars per week, or sixteen hundred per month."

"Ish," Coco said. "Sixteen hundred-ish. Some months it'll be more, because of five weeks in the month."

"Right. So that's a nice income for a part-time job, six hours per week, that I'm creating for myself and setting my own hours, right?" He rubbed the belly of the Laughing Buddha statue on the windowsill. He made the same jolly face and looked up at Coco, who laughed.

She grabbed a pen from a cup on the desk and held it up, indicating that she'd like to write in Mitch's notebook. "May I?" she asked.

"Sure."

Coco wrote, "Ten clients" underneath Mitch's numbers and filled in the weekly and monthly amounts. She also added another column to show the amount per year. "Once you get ten clients, you'll make about four thousand dollars per month and forty eight thousand a year, working about eleven or twelve hours per week."

"Not bad" Mitch said scratching his head. "That's almost my full-time base salary at Eco-Friendly...and that's working forty hours per week. Wait...really? Is that really possible?"

Coco lowered the notebook, looked Mitch directly in the eyes with a little smile, and said, "If you set your mind to it, anything is possible."

It was a moment of instant connection. Mitch found himself bubbling over with positive energy and new ideas. He went on to talk with Coco about how he'd been visualizing himself as a personal trainer and coach, how he would organize his time, what his logo might look like, and how he wanted to save money for an exotic surf vacation one day. He shared all his dreams, and she openly and compassionately received.

While Coco listened, she felt inspired with a few new ideas to add to her yoga studio, and she ran them by Mitch. The entrepreneurial spirit seemed to bless the room as they shared back and forth, talking about all the possibilities for the future. Later that night, after they left the studio and both went home, Coco and Mitch lay awake in their beds, dreaming of their lives as they could be, as they could create them.

CHAPTER 9

GO WITH THE FLOW

Love is metaphysical gravity.

—R. Buckminster Fuller

The first two candidates signed up right away. Mo, the tall, lumbering neighbor who came to the workshop with Dusty, said he knew he wanted to work with Mitch from the moment they met. He felt a good rapport, learned a lot from Mitch's talk, considered Mitch to be a role model for how he wanted to look and feel, and the evening hours worked perfectly for him. Mitch had created simple, one-page documents—an overview, liability release, and a coaching agreement—by using Jake's as templates and modifying them to suit his own business. He emailed them to Mo, who had them electronically signed before they even hung up the phone.

Mitch also made sure to advise Mo to check with his physician before beginning a nutrition or exercise program, because if there was one thing Mitch had learned in the pharmaceutical industry, it was that liability was no joke.

David, too, signed up in an instant. He and Mitch shared a passion for surfing, and it was hard to find trainers who really understood the sport. David didn't want surf lessons—he wanted targeted exercise sessions to better his surfing ability. Mitch shared David's excitement as they envisioned his transformation from novice surfer to, as David put it, "Dominating the main peak!" Laughing together, they scheduled David's first few sessions.

This is easy, Mitch thought, feeling good as he called the third candidate, but then he heard, "No," "No," and "No" again—"No" three times in a row.

Raoul, Marisa's husband, was interested, but really needed a trainer who could speak Spanish. He and Mitch barely made it through their phone conversation, as Marisa had to step in and translate multiple times. Emily and Tiffany couldn't meet in the evenings, because that's when Tiffany went to work at Growlie's—the local restaurant and bar where she met Dusty. Emily went to community college at night. "Besides," Emily added, "I think I would just feel more comfortable with a woman trainer."

Mitch felt disappointed, but he understood. Personal training is personal. People had the right to try to find the trainer who would be the best fit for them, just as much as Mitch had the right to try to find clients who would be the best fit for him. He wasn't going to waste one moment lamenting the fact that he didn't speak Spanish, or thinking about all the things he wasn't. All his years working in sales had taught him not to take it personally and move on.

When he picked up the phone and called Donna, he felt certain he would get a "Yes." They'd been taking yoga together for quite a few months, and they often engaged in great conversations after class. He thought it would be fun to work with her.

"Gosh, I would love to," she said, "but I'm way too busy. I don't know when I would ever be able to get together. It's already hard enough to go to Coco's yoga classes. I'm lucky if I make it there once a week. Between my two kids, my work, and taking care of the house, by eight o'clock, I just want to crash into bed!"

"I hear you," Mitch said, relating one-hundred percent with her situation. "I know what it feels like to be so busy that you almost never have time for yourself. But that's how I blew up to 225 pounds. Can I just point out one thing? If you're too busy to take care of yourself, that's actually one of the best reasons to hire a trainer."

"But it's just going to add another thing to my to-do list," she objected.

"I'm not talking about adding another thing. I'm talking about making the best use of the time you have. How many hours a week do you currently exercise?"

"About three to four hours per week," Donna said. Yoga class, some time on my treadmill, and walking the dog on the beach."

"How long have you been doing this routine?"

"Almost 2 years now."

"If you only have a few hours a week to exercise, you've really got to make those hours count. Coco's classes are great, but then if the other few hours you spend yawning while walking on a treadmill or taking a stroll to decompress, you're really not getting much benefit from those hours. The health goals we talked about—the ones that involved transforming you into the happiest, healthiest version of yourself so you can be there for your kids—those aren't going to happen without some focus and discipline. Time is too precious. Why waste it?"

Mitch heard nothing for a few moments, and then Donna admitted in a low voice, "You're right. I'm spinning my wheels here. Nothing ever changes."

"So let's do this," Mitch proposed. "Commit right now to working out four hours a week—just like you already do. Do two of those hours with me, and the other two you can do at Coco's or on your own. The program includes a weekly seminar, just like the workshop we did at Coco's studio. Then, at the end of the month, let's see how it's going."

"Hmm," she considered. "I like it. Sounds like a good plan." Already her voice sounded calmer.

Mitch made another call to Janette, and though she seemed interested, she had one major objection: "I can't afford it." The reason she couldn't afford it, she said, was because of the high cost of her diabetes medications and doctor visits.

Mitch, remembering what he'd learned about consultative sell-ing, asked a couple questions about her finances with relation to medicine, doctor visits, groceries, and eating out. Together they added up those expenses, and Janette realized they were costing her almost $1,000 a month. Mitch also asked if her doctor had ever told her that if she lost some weight, she could possibly reduce or eliminate some of her medications. She said, "Yes, he says it a lot, actually. And every time I ask him what to do to lose weight, he says to exercise more and eat less. Well, I've been trying that for three years and failing."

"Ever hear the quote from Hippocrates?" Mitch asked. "'Let food be thy medicine and medicine be thy food.'"

Once Janette saw the bigger picture, living life more simply, with fewer medications in her blood and more money in her pocket, the $100 a week really didn't seem like such a high price to pay. She and Mitch scheduled her first session.

After these first few calls and conversations, Mitch realized for the first time how meaningful this work could be and how important it was to his clients. He finished calling his list, created files for each of his four new clients, and spent the rest of the afternoon planning the weekly seminars.

At the end of the day, Mitch put his journal in a backpack and went to see Coco at her studio, and he was so glad he did. She imme-diately came up with the idea of creating a Plan B-type of offer for candidates who were either on the fence, weren't ready to make the commitment, or genuinely couldn't afford the $100 a week.

"Maybe you can develop a sort of do-it-yourself workout plan, designed for overall general conditioning that anyone could follow, and then also let them come to the weekly group workout. You can charge much less," she said as she wiped down a yoga mat with disinfectant spray and a cloth. "Then later, if they decide they want more, they can easily switch to the full personal-training program."

Mitch thought that was brilliant. He stepped outside, whipped out his cell phone, and called back two people that had each ex-pressed interest in working with him, but said they weren't ready.

So Mitch offered them the B package for only $25 a week, and told them they could upgrade whenever they felt ready. Both candidates signed up.

When Mitch came back inside, before he could even say a word, Coco piped up, "Hey, I've got another idea."

While stacking up the last of the clean yoga mats, she explained to Mitch how the referral program worked at her studio. "If a member brings a guest, the guest gets a twenty percent discount when they buy their first package of sessions. Also, the referring member gets a free bonus session added to their account. So it's a win for the guest, a win for the member, and a win for me. If you come up with some sort of referral program for your business, it could make finding new clients much easier."

Mitch sat on the bamboo floor with his back against the wall and started jotting notes in his journal. "I love how simple it is," he commented while scribbling with his pen, "and so smart."

Coco grinned at the compliment. "So now you're off and running, and you've got a marketing plan to grow from four clients to ten. How does that feel?"

Mitch looked up. "I'm stoked! I feel awesome. There's a little fear, but it's the good kind—exciting." He put away the journal. Coco held out her hand and pulled Mitch up from the floor. She led him out of the main studio and into the front lobby, shutting off the lights behind her.

"I wish there was something I could do for you," Mitch said as he stood near the window with the Laughing Buddha. "I really appreciate all this help, but saying 'thank you' just doesn't seem adequate."

"'Thank you' is adequate," Coco said as she picked up her sweater, purse, and gym bag. She pulled out her keys from her purse and locked the closet and cabinets.

"Did you eat dinner yet?" Mitch asked.

Coco suddenly froze as if remembering something cosmically important. "Is today Tuesday?" Mitch thought about it and then froze as well as he made the startling realization.

They looked at each other and said at the same time, "Taco Tuesday at Sandy's!"

"We're going," she said, breezing right past Mitch to the front door. He helped her lock up, and they made a beeline for the beachfront restaurant on Huntington pier.

***

Coco groaned and her eyes rolled up to heaven as she took a bite of the hand-pulled chicken taco with Sandy's "Nacho-Average Salsa," onions, cilantro, and sliced radish on top.

"Mmm, I've been waiting for this all week," she said. "For two dollars and fifty cents, you can buy nothing better on this earth." A tiny drop of salsa slid down her chin and she caught it with her napkin.

Mitch took a bite of his own taco and had to agree—it was perfection on a plate. The salty sea air mixed with the aromas of California cuisine swirled around them at their small table on the open-air patio with an ocean view. The flavors, the lively reggae music in the background and seeing her smile like that made Mitch feel like a million bucks. When he looked at Coco, he noticed the vast sky glowing behind her in dazzling shades of red and orange, and he experienced a whole new kind of happiness—the chicken-tacos-at-sunset-on-my-favorite-beach-with-the-most-beautiful-woman-in-the-world   kind of happiness.

"Are you going to eat that?" she asked, pointing to his coleslaw.

He nudged the cup in her direction and said, "It's all you." Then he relaxed back in his chair, head slightly tilted to the side, and loosely clasped his fingers around a glass beer bottle.

As the sun disappeared, the evening lights turned on around the patio, and all the lamps along the pier began to glow. They finished their meals, and Coco sat forward to talk in earnest.

"I thought of how you can help me," she said. "I need help figuring out how to create leverage."

Mitch leaned in, as if he hadn't heard her correctly. "Leverage?" he asked. "What do you mean?"

"Oh I thought you knew, because you designed your hedgehog with leverage built in," Coco said, but Mitch just stared. She picked at a few stray veggies on her plate and teased, "Okay, so maybe you just made that genius choice by accident. The rest of us have to actually try..."

Mitch wanted to feel flattered, but he still had no idea what she was talking about. He went over his business model in his mind, trying to figure out what part might have something to do with leverage. Coco took a sip of ice water, folded her napkin and placed it on the table, and explained.

"Leverage is a universal natural principle that with the right conditions you can do massive amounts of work with little effort. Like moving a big boulder with a fulcrum and lever. Let me back up a bit and I can put this in the right framework so it makes sense. A few months ago, I attended a weekend seminar called, 'Business and You' taught by Marshall Thurber. There were three critical elements to make your business successful and sustainable."

"Marshall Thurber?" Mitch interrupted. "No way—I just heard about him the other day. My boss Ken taught me about DyVal and said he learned it from Marshall Thurber."

"Right! DyVal was the first main lesson at the seminar. The second lesson was about system, and the third was about network science."

"Ah, okay," Mitch said. "Tell me more."

"Your system, Coco explained, "has to do with the processes and methods you put in place to deliver on your promises to your client. And just like DyVal, you have to constantly think of ways to make them better. You measure, analyze, and tinker with your systems until you can predictably give your clients what they want and need.

What happens when eight out of ten customers are stoked?"

"You get repeat business and referrals," Jake said.

"That's right. When your system is predictable, duplicable, and successful, you're ready for the next step. But if you have only two satisfied customers out of ten, obviously your system isn't ready."

"Makes sense," Mitch said, following. "What's the next step?"

"Network science. And leverage is a big part of that. Leverage means impacting more people, and reaching more people, without necessarily expending more dollars, hours, or energy. So, for example, you're offering one-on-one personal training to your clients, and you're also offering a group class, right? In the class, you still work for only one hour, you still deliver your service, but instead of reaching just one person in an hour, you're reaching many people in an hour. You go from one-to-one, to one-to-many. You're creating leverage," Coco explained.

Just then the waitress came over to their table with the check. Mitch took out his credit card and paid, and suggested they continue talking while going for a walk on the pier.

"Marshall said it's really important to do each of these three steps in order. First DyVal, then System, then Network Science. Otherwise, you could lose all credibility."

"Why?" Mitch asked as they approached the pier entrance.

"Well, you can have the greatest marketing and advertising campaign in the world, but if people get into your product or service and have a bad experience, or if the product isn't fully developed or doesn't work, you're gonna have a serious problem. Or another scenario would be this: Your system has the capacity to deliver top-notch service, but to one only customer at a time. So when more customers come, you can't meet the demand and your service gets sloppy. A satisfied customer will tell two or three people how great your company is, but a dissatisfied customer will tell eight or ten people. The bad press goes viral so fast that you'll never be able to catch up."

GO WITH THE FLOW

"That's so true," Mitch said. "Let me ask you a question then. You're an entrepreneur, and you teach classes at your yoga studio, and classes are a form of leverage. So why are you saying now that you need help to create leverage? Haven't you already created it?"

Coco nodded and shook her head at the same time, dipping it back and forth like a horizontal figure eight. "Sort of. Not nearly enough." She took a few moments to think as they passed by the first street lamp. "Let me give you the example Marshall Thurber gave us. Think about the best teacher you had when you were a kid, and how much value he or she added to your life. Next, think about a superstar athlete, and how much value he or she added to your life. Which one added more value?"

"Teacher. No question."

"All right, so now answer this," Coco challenged. "Between the teacher and the athlete, which one made more money?"

With a scathing laugh, Mitch answered, "The athlete, about a thousand times over. They make millions. Teachers are lucky to make $50,000 a year, and then people complain they're overpaid."

"Why is that?" Coco asked.

Mitch looked down at the concrete and made fists inside the pockets of his windbreaker. "I don't know," he said. "Doesn't seem fair."

"It's because of the amount of leverage they're each using. The teacher had great DyVal. She offered high, lasting value. But she delivered her value to around thirty people a year, or however many kids were in the class. The football player had a lower impact upon your life, but his value was delivered to millions of people per week. The leverage through the stadiums, radio, television, commercials, and the NFL—all these networks made it possible for his value to be delivered to more people, without him having to work any harder or for a longer period of time."

"Right..." Mitch said, looking out at the dark water while processing her argument.

"So the success formula is actually really simple: value times reach equals financial success. The higher your value, and the greater distance you're able to reach, the greater impact you'll make. Your teacher had high value with very low reach, which, unfortunately, produces low financial reward. It may not seem fair, but it is the way the principle of leverage works. And we don't get a vote. It's a universal law."

"Yeah, I see what you're saying," Mitch nodded. "So if we go back to you and your yoga studio, what we want to do is figure out a way to take your products and services out to more people. You are cutting back on private lessons and already teach classes, so you definitely want to fill those up to maximize the leverage you've created there, and then you also want to expand your reach even beyond the classes somehow. Become the NFL of yoga, right?"

"Yes!" Coco said.

"Okay, let me think."

For a few minutes, neither of them spoke. The sound of their footsteps mingled with the whoosh of the waves and faint voices of other passersby. Finally, Mitch scratched his head and said, "Well, you know what hooked me was the yoga-for-surfers workshop you taught. What if you turned that into a video product?"

Coco looked slightly off to the side as if trying to see the video in midair. "That would definitely create massive leverage. The only problem is I don't know how to make a video. I don't know how to sell it online, either. I never studied online marketing; everything I've ever done has been in person—handing out flyers, networking, meeting people at health and fitness events, referral programs. How much would it cost to make a professional video like that?"

"Heck, we can do it for almost free," Mitch said, running his hand along the metal railing at the side of the pier. "I've got a mac-daddy video camera and killer editing software. I use them all the time to make surf videos. I made one for Jake once—I'll show it to you. And...I know a beautiful yogini who could be our model and I'm pretty sure she knows all the poses..."

Coco blushed. Mitch continued to think out loud as they approached Ruby's Surf City Diner on the pier. They walked past the hexagonal-shaped building, past the fishermen to the end guardrail, where there was nothing in front of them except endless ocean.

"Probably the most expensive part would be packaging and running our first batch," Mitch mused. "But these days, you can publish DVDs on-demand, and we can also test it digitally as a download before spending a lot of money on our first run."

"You make it sound so simple," Coco said, grasping the rail.

"It is simple," Mitch smiled. "I do it all the time. I love it."

Coco let go of the rail and turned to Mitch, not knowing what to say. She just threw her arms around his neck, leaned in close, and kissed him. "It's perfect," she said. "Thank you."

Mitch's whole world disappeared in that moment. Even when she pulled back, he couldn't open his eyes.

"Let's make the video together," she said happily. "We'll be partners. I'll cut you in on the revenue."

Mitch managed to nod in his glazed stupor, which caused her to chuckle and kiss him again. This time he managed to pull her in close and responded with strength. Finally, they parted, she took an extra breath and they walked back down the pier holding hands, their bodies silhouetted in the silver moonlight.

***

Mitch's first month of training his new clients went well. Everyone paid on time, showed up for their appointments, and even the two clients who agreed to "just give it a try" ended up registering for a second month. Mitch arrived prepared and energetic for each session. He worried he might be spreading himself too thin by surfing with Jake in the morning, then going to his job at Eco-Friendly Lighting, and then training clients in the evening, but so far, with just four clients, he was holding up quite well. He had less time for leisure, but given what he was trying to accomplish, it didn't seem like much of a sacrifice. Besides, there were plenty of weekend surf sessions with either Jake or Dusty to keep him happy.

Mitch arrived at the beach one Sunday expecting peaceful, easy feelings. It was one of those mild California days with clear skies, calm winds, glassy water, waves a foot or two over-head with five or six wave sets. Mitch would have cried if he still worked at Reynolds and had to miss out on these near-perfect conditions. He agreed to meet up with Jake at the Surf Hut early in the morning—not for a lesson, but for a "free surf." When he arrived at the back patio, he was pleasantly surprised to find Ken waiting there, too.

"I didn't think you'd mind if I invited him along," Jake said amiably as he slid open the screen door and stepped out to greet them.

"Ha! You kiddin' me?" Mitch said, tucking his board under his arm. "I feel like the geeky freshman who gets to hang out with the cool kids. Let's catch some waves!"

Ken, Jake, and Mitch talked and joked as they strode down to the water, and as they paddled out, Mitch felt nothing but good vibes... until they got close enough to see who was out at the main peak.

Mitch recognized a few of the locals who had vibed him the night he injured his head. They were easy to spot, with their tattoos, loud voices and the uber-confident way they sat on their boards and kept watch over the lineup. "Locals only, get out of here kook," they'd call out like police officers, turning foreign surfers away. Even though Mitch was, technically, a local, he had established himself as a kook. On that big day, he showed no respect for anyone's safety, no respect for the ocean, and no respect for the more advanced surfers. By ignoring the locals' warnings, he did the opposite of what gains and shows respect, and that was enough to get him banned from his own home break.

Ken and Jake were seasoned vets and all the locals knew them and respected them, so they paddled right out. Mitch also saw Joe— the same Joe whose board he rescued up in Santa Barbara—but apart from a what's-up nod, Joe didn't pay him any mind. In fact, he paddled right past him to get out to the main peak without saying a word.

So Mitch decided to stay on the shoulder, by himself, and out of the way. If they see me and recognize me, he thought, they'll jump all over me. If they see me and don't recognize me, then I'm a foreigner and they'll still jump all over me. Either way I'm screwed.

He caught his first wave, turned right, and went backside. He got a couple of nice turns in, and then a big slap off the lip with a floater re-entry. It was a great ride, but problematic because he ended up right at the pier. To get back into position for another wave, he had only two options: Either he could try to paddle against the current back to the shoulder, or he could ride out with the current along the pier. If he rode the current, though, it would drop him off right at the main peak.

Mitch remembered his lesson about "Go with the Flow" and what a losing battle it was to try to paddle against the current to get into position. He thought maybe he could ride the current out to the main peak and then quickly paddle over to the shoulder and out of the way before anyone even noticed he was there. He decided to give it a try. He lay down on his board, put his head down, and started to float out with the current.

But the instant he got close to the main peak, one of the locals picked up on him.

"Hey!" the local shouted with a nasal voice, which of course drew the attention of almost everyone nearby. Quickly, Mitch scanned the lineup, looking for Jake or Ken—somebody who could vouch for him—but they weren't there. They must have just caught a wave.

"Hey!" the guy shouted again and paddled over to get a better look at Mitch's face. "Aren't you that coach guy who's always at that yoga studio?" Mitch knew it was useless to try to lie. He took a deep breath and faced the music.

"Um yeah."

"What's your name, bro?" said the surfer, using one hand to sweep his blonde hair to the side.

"Mitch" he said sheepishly. By now there were about ten other surfers watching and listening to their conversation. Oh man, I'm so dead.

"You know what, dude? You rock! You know Janette Platt?"

Mitch nodded, totally unprepared for this but going with it. "Yeah, definitely. She's awesome!"

"I know. She's my mom," the surfer said proudly. "She's been following your health plan and everything. A couple of days ago, the doctor took her off her blood pressure medicine. Dude, you're the shit!"

Mitch felt a wave of relief wash over when the guy paddled in close and reached out to shake his hand.

"Thanks for helping her, bro. We've been trying to get her to take better care of herself for a long time. I'm Brian, by the way."

Just as Mitch opened his mouth to say, "Nice to meet you," Joe paddled by, returning to the lineup after catching a wave. He interrupted and said, "Dude, nice floater."

"Huh? Oh, thanks, man," Mitch said, just trying to keep up.

Then Jake and Ken both paddled by, flashing the shaka sign to Mitch as they took their places in the lineup. Where were you guys ten minutes ago? Mitch thought.

Brian invited Mitch to take his place among them, and from then on he was no longer an outsider. The crew embraced him as a member of the tribe. There was a special vibe in the water that day. For the rest of the day, everyone took turns catching waves and hooting for each other, surfing until the sun went down. Mitch had finally made it to the main peak.

***

At dusk, they all scurried out of the water, tired, hungry, happy, and stoked. Ken was the first to say good-bye. He toweled off and turned to carry his board back to his car.

Mitch called from behind him, "See you tomorrow!"

Ken turned and wagged his finger. He called back, "No, actually. Tomorrow I'm leaving for a three-week surf trip to the Maldives. Don't cause too much trouble while I'm gone, eh?"

All the other surfers ooh'ed, ah'd and oh man'd at the mention of the Maldives.

"You're stoked," said Joe.

"That's so rad," said Brian. "You had me at three-week surf vacation," Mitch said. He stood dripping wet on the sand but didn't even bother to towel off. His lip started to quiver in the cool evening air, but still he stood motionless. "Where are you staying?"

"We're starting at Sultans. We've chartered a yacht with a full crew and chef," Ken said casually. "Our captain knows all the spots. Three of my best friends from college are going island hopping, chasing the swells, with some fishing and diving in between. We do it once a year."

Mitch salivated as if Ken was describing an elaborate feast.

"Hey Ken," asked one of the other guys. "What's the gnarliest wave you've ever surfed?"

Ken grabbed the towel from around his neck and buried his face in it for a moment, drying the water that had dripped down from his wet brown hair.

"I'd have to say Teahupo'o. It's so intense, but what a perfect barrel!" Ken answered.

One of the other surfers nodded as he took off his leash. His name was José and at fifty-five years old, he was the oldest member of the group. The guys constantly referred to him as "the old timer," but showed him plenty of respect so he didn't mind. José referred to the guys in their twenties as "grommets," or "shredder gromms" if he wanted to pay a compliment.

"What about you, José? Where was the gnarliest wave you ever surfed?" Ken asked.

"Pipeline," he answered instantly.

"You surfed Pipeline?" Mitch said with childlike astonishment. He walked over to ask him. "What was it like?"

"I caught it one time," José said quietly. Mitch had to lean in close just to hear him. "Breaking on the second reef, offshore winds, just enough west in it so it was spitting on every wave. You could drive a truck through the barrel and not get wet. One of the most spiritual experiences of my life."

A new spark ignited inside of Mitch. He looked for his coach but found that Jake had already started walking up the beach and wasn't looking back. As the group said goodbye and dispersed, Mitch jogged to the parking lot. He felt a pang of longing. He wondered if he would ever be able to take a week-long surf vacation, let alone a three-week one. He wondered if he'd ever be able to afford to go someplace more exotic than Mexico, let alone a yacht with a personal chef in the Maldives. He wondered if he'd ever get to take a trip like Ken's even once in his life, let alone once a year.

He tried not to harp on it because it had been such a good day; he didn't want to ruin it by focusing on what he lacked. But as he loaded all his gear into the Jeep, an image of Pipeline entered his mind. Curiosity drove his steps around his vehicle and straight back to Jake's Surf Hut, where he found Jake sitting in a chair on the back patio, sipping an iced tea.

He looked just the same as he did about a year ago, when Mitch had asked him to be his surf coach. The sky even looked gray, as though it might rain.

Mitch took a seat in the empty chair next to Jake, who didn't appear surprised at all to see him. He put his iced tea down on the small table next to him and said, "Yes."

"How do you know what I was gonna say?" Mitch said.

"I don't. I'm guessing," Jake said. "Go ahead."

"Have you ever surfed Pipeline?"

"Yes," Jake said, in the exact same tone as the first time.

"No way!" Mitch exclaimed up to the ceiling, his feet rising up off the floor. He slapped his knees and said, "Why didn't you ever tell me?"

"You never asked," Jake said calmly. He dipped his fingers into a small jar of coconut oil and began to massage one of his thighs with his thumbs.

"Is it as gnarly as they say it is?" Mitch asked. "Do you think I could get good enough to surf Pipe? How do you prepare for something like that?"

Jake put out his hand for Mitch to settle down and resumed the massage on his leg. For a few long moments, the only sounds were the seagulls, the wind, and the waves.

"Why do you want to surf Pipeline?" asked Jake, not at all carelessly, and placing particular emphasis on the why.

"It's... " Mitch considered, "I don't know, it's the Mount Everest of surfing, right? Don't all surfers want to surf Pipeline?"

"No. Why do you want to surf Pipeline?" Jake repeated.

Mitch stammered and fidgeted. Somehow Jake's tone made him feel as though there was a right answer and a wrong answer, and he didn't want to get it wrong.

"Did you know more people have died at Pipeline than any other surf spot in the world?" Jake challenged. Mitch stopped fidgeting.

"How long can you hold your breath?" Jake continued. "Are you willing to take a fifteen- to twenty-foot bomb on the head? In three feet of water?"

Mitch recoiled as he envisioned what that would be like.

"If you thought breaking into this lineup was tough," Jake said, pointing out to the water, "Ha! A hundred people minimum. Seventy percent of them pros, all the rest hardcore locals. Oh and wait until you meet the Da Hui."

Mitch leaned back in the wooden chair. He thought Jake was done smacking him down, but he started up again.

"Do you know how much it costs to fly to Hawaii? And the oversized baggage fee?"

Mitch slouched in the chair like a rag doll, his head heavy with questions and doubts. "I guess," he mumbled, "I have some things to think about."

With the same intonation as when the conversation started, Jake went back to massaging his leg and said, "Yes."

CHAPTER 10

LEAN INTO YOUR FEAR

Never forget no matter how overwhelming life's
challenges and problems seem to be, that one person
can make a difference in the world. In fact,
it is always because of one person that all the changes that
matter in the world come about. So be that one person.

–R. Buckminster Fuller

Finding time to shoot Coco's yoga-for-surfers video was no easy task. Mitch and Coco kept agreeing they'd schedule it "when things settle down," "when we're both not so busy" and "when we get a chance," but somehow time never opened up. When September rolled by and the chilly mornings and gusty evenings of October set in, Coco put her foot down.

"Let's get relentless," she said, and they took out their day planners and cell phones. They slashed an entire week's worth of events and appointments, rescheduling where they could, flat-out cancelling when they couldn't, and by the end they managed to clear out a week to make the project happen.

The shoot went great—far better than Mitch had imagined it would. The beach at dawn felt harsh with the wind chill, but Coco never let it show. On camera, her strong, toned figure stood out perfectly against the scattered colors of the early morning light beyond the horizon, and with her black, shiny hair pulled tightly into a ponytail. She looked exotic and strong, feminine and natural—peacefully poised for an energizing yoga practice session on the sand.

Late in the afternoon on the last day of the shoot, they drove to a different location and set up at the top of a one-hundred-foot sandstone cliff with a golden tint, where Coco performed a series of balance poses with the ocean behind her. The only sounds were the waves and the caws of seagulls as they soared overhead. Perfectly timed with the orange and purple lighting of the setting sun, the resulting footage looked majestic.

"We got some great footage today!" Mitch said after watching the playback on camera. Coco put on a jacket and stared out at the horizon.

"Hey, are you all right?" he said, noticing her faraway gaze.

She turned her head to him slowly and said, "Have you ever seen the videos on YouTube with the huge amounts of plastic garbage floating out in the Pacific?"

Mitch sighed heavily and turned his camera off. "Yes. But I don't watch them anymore because they're too depressing."

"Sometimes when I look out at the Pacific I'm in awe of the beauty, but in the back of my mind I can see the giant plastic island. The gyre is a thousand miles off the coast of California, and twice as big as the state of Texas," she said.

"Yeah," Mitch said, folding up his camera. "I read an article about it on the Surf Rider Foundation website. They have a program called "Rise above Plastics" to show people how they can help solve the problem instead of watching helplessly."

"That's awesome. That gives me hope," Coco said, coming over to help Mitch pack up. "Part of why I love the surfing community is that so many surfers are also activists who are trying to make the world a better place. Have you heard of Jon Rose with Waves for Water? They bring clean drinking water to villages all over the world that don't have access. And Kyle Thierman founded Surfing for Change—he makes documentaries when he goes on surfing trips. There's one, called "Indonesian Trash Tubes" that's really good. It's upsetting, but the truth needs to get out there. Anyway, I like it when people put their gifts and talents in service of a good cause."

Mitch zipped up his camera bag and said, "Me too. I met Rob Machado at the US Open of surfing just this past July, and part of why I'm such a big fan is that he's huge on environmental projects. Now that I think about it, he's big on yoga, too. What do you think about the idea of asking him to collaborate with us somehow?"

"I love it," Coco said, astounded that Mitch knew Rob Machado. "Collaborate how? You mean like asking him to be in the video?"

"I don't know," Mitch said, "but yeah, maybe he can do a few poses, or maybe we can include some footage of his surfing, or maybe we can ask if he'll do a one-minute intro or endorsement. I'm not sure, I'm just thinking out loud here, but what if we donated one dollar from every video sale to the Rob Machado Foundation? That might be a win-win."

"Great idea," Coco said. She grabbed the tripod and collapsed it so Mitch could put it away. "I mean, if you think he would do it. How well do you know him? Are you friends, or...?"

Mitch grinned and held a black bag open while Coco slid the tripod inside. "No, I've only met him twice, but my company sponsored a booth at his surf contest fundraiser. I don't think you have to be best friends with someone in order to ask them to collaborate with you on a project though—not if you believe in the same causes. Anyway, there's no harm in asking, right?"

Coco agreed. "Definitely no harm in asking."

When the shoot was over and Mitch returned to business as usual, he found himself feeling more than a little unsettled. At first he didn't understand why, exactly, but the situation became clear over time. On one hand, everything was working out for him—he was in a healthy relationship with an amazing, beautiful woman. He had a job he liked and a boss he respected, he had a growing side business, he had time to surf, enough money to spend and save, and he was healthier than he'd been in years. For most people, this would be happily ever after. Mitch knew it too. But somehow, deep in the recesses of his consciousness, a germ of dissatisfaction had set in, and it was growing.

"Why'd you try to talk me out of surfing Pipeline?" Mitch blurted during a morning training session with Jake. "Do you think I'm not good enough?" The tide was low so they did a core workout on the beach. Mitch's question came during his second set of sit-ups.

Jake, holding Mitch's feet firmly in the sand, looked up at the clouds and said, "Ah, so that's what's been gnawing at you."

"No..." protested Mitch, pausing at the top of his sit-up. He looked away, then back at Jake and said, "...yes." He put his hands behind his head and continued the exercise.

"I wasn't trying to talk you out of it," Jake said kindly, "I just wanted you to think about it. Have you?"

Mitch spoke in short spurts, between reps, as sweat trickled down his torso. "Nonstop. I was even practicing...telling you...that if you wouldn't coach me...I was gonna have to find someone who would."

"You are really serious about this," Jake said. He held on to Mitch's feet until he finished the set, and then let go, allowing Mitch to stretch out on the cool, damp sand. Jake sat beside him and said, "Why do you want to surf Pipeline?"

Mitch stretched and breathed into the sky. "I want to see if I have what it takes to do it. I'll condition myself for a year, two years, whatever it takes to get good enough. I guess the challenge is part of what turns me on. To surf that perfect barrel...to surf Pipeline would be like...like a rite of passage."

"A rite of passage into what?" Jake pressed.

Mitch imagined himself taking off on a huge, perfect wave at Pipeline, getting barreled and becoming one with the ocean in its most dynamic state. He pictured it again and again in his mind and asked himself, What does it mean?

Then it hit him. "I guess," Mitch said calmly, "to prove to myself that I can achieve whatever I set out to."

Seeing that Mitch was intrinsically motivated, Jake said "We'll start your training next week."

Mitch sat up with a relieved smile upon hearing Jake's agreement to help him on his quest to surf Pipeline, and yet inside he felt a mix of excitement and a fear. There was still so much that remained unsettled. Once Mitch's ab-buster routine was finished, he stood, groaned, twisted back and forth, and looked fidgety, looking around in all directions like a small dog looking for a place to dig.

"What else is on your mind?" asked Jake, watching Mitch's dance in the sand.

Mitch grabbed his T-shirt and towel and sighed, "I don't know."

"Come on up to the hut for tea and let's have a talk," Jake said.

In Jake's office, surrounded by photos, surf memorabilia, and books, Mitch leaned against the doorframe drumming his fingers against the side of his cup of hot tea. Jake sank into the swivel chair near his desk and waited.

"I'm struggling with a decision," said Mitch. "I'm seriously considering leaving my job at Eco-Friendly Lighting."

Jake raised his eyebrows and rolled his chair a bit closer to his desk. "Is something wrong?"

"No, it's not like that," he said, staring at an autographed photo of Kelly Slater at the Pipe Masters. "I mean, I'm so grateful to you for helping me get the job in the first place, and I'm so grateful to Ken, I feel guilty even saying this. But I really wish I had more freedom and flexibility, more time with Coco, with you, and more time for my coaching business. I want to take long surf vacations like Ken does and travel to exotic places like all these on your walls, but I never have enough money and I never have enough vacation days. I just did a video shoot with Coco and it was almost impossible just to clear the schedule to create the time."

Jake sat back in his seat, allowing Mitch to vent.

"And what I really want," Mitch said, placing his cup on the desk, "I feel weird even saying this because it sounds so ungrateful, but... what I really want is to be the owner, like you and Ken. Not the employee who gets two to three weeks of vacation each year. Is that wrong?"

"No," Jake said, brushing a few stray strands of his silver hair off to the side. "It's not wrong to aspire for more, as long as you're willing to do the work and take the risk of starting a business."

Mitch sat on the small stool near the desk, but then quickly stood again. "But you know what image keeps playing itself over and over in my mind? The Monday morning meeting. It's one of my favorite parts of the week. I love how Ken leads it—he always teaches us something new and always makes it fun and collaborative. But sometimes when he's away on a surf trip and he teleconferences in to the meeting, I can see the waves behind him in the monitor. Whether he's on a luxurious yacht, a pristine beach, or a fancy hotel room, he's always just a step away from the ocean. And recently I've started to feel these, like, hunger pangs. I feel like I'm watching someone else live my dream while I sit in a conference room watching it on TV!"

Jake studied Mitch's face and then looked at his watch. "Do you have ten minutes to spare before leaving for work?" Mitch nodded, and Jake rose and pointed toward a framed photo on the back wall next to the bookcase. It showed Pipeline on Oahu's North Shore at sunset. The green glow of the lip of a twenty-foot wave and yellow sky made the photograph look almost three-dimensional.

"I know I said we'd start training next week, but I've changed my mind and we're going to start right now," Jake said. "Are you ready?"

At first, Mitch wanted to ask, "Hey, wait, what about everything I just said?" But then he let it go. He knew better by now when it came to Jake. There would never be a straight answer, but there would always be an answer. He scrambled for his notebook and a pen and took a seat.

Jake pointed to the top of the wave in the photo and said, "First lesson: Learning how to fall at Pipeline. Depending on where you are on the wave, there are a few ways to fall that can minimize your risk of injury. If you get bucked off on the take-off and you're on the outside, it's best to step off, get underneath the surface of the water, and let the wave go over you. If you're on the inside, the smartest way to fall is a belly flop, so you can stay on top of the water to avoid the shallow reef. And sometimes, if you're going over the falls, the only thing you can do is cover your head, hold your breath and ride it out."

As Jake lectured, he pointed out the most dangerous sections of the wave and what to do in certain conditions. He pulled out a chart that showed the bathymetry of where Pipe's three reefs were located, and how they affected the size of the swells in the progressively deeper water. He pointed out the shallow spots on the reef, where the rocks were on the inside, and told Mitch how to avoid getting injured if he fell there.

"If you're going to fall on the inside where it's shallow, put your arms over your head like this, to protect your head and face. If you're being dragged through the rinse cycle, like a rag doll, don't fight it. Resistance is futile. You have to wait it out, keep calm, and keep your heart rate down."

Then Jake stepped away from all the photos, maps, and charts, and spoke these final words, as if he were a Naval officer addressing a young sailor, "You're gonna fall, Mitch. It's not a question of 'if' but 'how often' and 'how hard.' So learning to fall is critical. At Pipe, people get caught underneath, the leash gets wrapped up on the rocks, and they get held down. And with all the water pulling on them they can't free themselves. The most important thing is to stay calm. You've got to coach yourself to be calm. Relax, stay alert and aware, and don't spaz out and burn your oxygen. When the turbulence starts to clear, start looking for which way is up, because your next goal will be to get to the surface."

Mitch scribbled furiously to record every word of the lesson. After a few minutes of writing in silence, Mitch looked up and around, but Jake wasn't there. Mitch stood and walked about the Surf Hut but found himself alone. Just before gathering his backpack and jacket to go, he glanced at the words scrawled into his notebook and these jumped out at him: "...they get held down and they can't free themselves." The words ran through his mind as he went home to change for work.

***

"Do you mind if I run something by you?" Mitch asked Coco at the end of Taco Tuesday dinner.

Coco leaned forward resting her elbows on the wooden table. "What's up?"

Mitch pushed his plate off to the side and stated, "I'm seriously considering leaving my job."

Coco's eyebrows went up in the exact same manner as Jake's, and also just like Jake, she said, "Is something wrong?"

Mitch grinned at the similarity and marveled at how cool and level-headed both Coco and Jake were at all times. He imagined running this issue by his father. In his mind he could already hear the explosion: What?! Leave the company? What are you gonna do about health insurance? How are you gonna pay your rent? You've finally got some stability in your life and now you're just gonna throw it all away? And didn't this Ken give you a chance when you didn't think anyone else would? Entitlement—that's what's wrong with your generation. No gratitude and no loyalty!

Coco placed her hand on top of Mitch's, snapping him out of his daydream. He looked at her and said, "No, nothing's wrong at Eco-Friendly. But I guess I've learned so much from Ken about how to run a business that now I want to run my own. I want his lifestyle. But I don't know, maybe..." he paused.

"Maybe what?" Coco asked.

"Maybe I'm being ungrateful even thinking about letting go of a steady, reliable income with a great company. I've heard 80% of entrepreneurs fail when starting a new business. Jake gave me a lesson about how to fall safely at Pipe, and said 'it is not if you will fall at Pipe, but how often and how hard. How do I make sure I'm being smart about this? What if I'm paddling out in waves bigger than I can handle?"

Coco straightened up as if she were about to teach one of her yoga classes. "I respect you for asking these tough questions. It is not always easy to hear that inner voice, let alone follow your heart into the unknown. You know I didn't always run my own studio. I worked at someone else's place for a long time before going out on my own. Would you like to hear the checklist I used before I left my job?"

"Yes. There's a checklist?" Mitch said, and pulled his chair in closer to the table.

"It's not an official checklist. Just some questions to consider before leaving your day job." Coco pulled up a list from her iPhone. "First question: What do you want to create and why? What kind of business, what kind of lifestyle, and what kind of schedule?

"Easy," Mitch answered. "I want to be my own boss. I want to have time to surf and travel like Ken and Jake. I love scheduling my own workload. It makes me feel like my work is a choice and not an obligation. I love coaching and want to do that full time. Watching my clients transform their health is the most rewarding work I've ever done. My ideal work schedule would be Monday through Friday, ten a.m. to four p.m., so I could surf mornings and exercise in the evenings. I want to take a three-day weekend the last week of every month. I also want to take a couple week-long surfing trips each year to killer tropical destinations! I used to think that was total fantasy, until I met Ken. Now I'm like, 'why not?'"

"Sounds amazing," she said, and paused while their waitress came to clear their plates. When they were alone again, she asked, "Question number two: Do you have reserves? That means an emergency fund, liquid capital, enough to cover your current expenses for the next twelve months."

"I've got nine months," Mitch had just reviewed his accounts the previous night, so he knew his numbers. "I've definitely paid down all my debt, so that's good."

"That's great," Coco agreed. "No debt is amazing. The third question: What percent of your income are you living off of?" Mitch said, "Seventy percent. Wait no, it's sixty percent, now that I've paid off my debt. I'm pretty stoked. I've gotten really lean and reduced so many of my expenses. Ten percent goes to retirement, ten percent to reserves, ten percent for my parents' retirement, and the ten percent that was going to debt reduction is now going into my Pipeline fund."

"Great! Next question," Coco said. "With your coaching business, how close are you to replacing your income from your day job?"

"I'm almost earning the same base salary from coaching ten hours per week as I do working thirty hours a week at Eco-Friendly," Mitch said, pleased to learn that he was ahead of the game on most of these questions. "If I had more time, I know I could add more clients and even exceed that."

"So..." Coco said, as the waitress brought hot water and a selection of herbal teas. "It sounds like you're only a few months away from being at choice. At least financially. Is there anything else stopping you from making the leap?"

Mitch smoothed his hair back while he thought about it. "Well, this is gonna sound so weird, but...it almost feels like a breakup."

Coco smirked and giggled. "Really?" she asked, tearing open a tea bag. "What do you mean?"

"Really," Mitch said, laughing now too, but only because Coco's was contagious. "I really love Eco-Friendly, and the mission, and the team, and Ken, and it kind of reminds me of one of my past relationships. I loved this girl, but I wasn't in love. Something was missing, even though it wasn't her fault. She didn't do anything wrong. I don't want Ken to think I was just using Eco-Friendly as a stepping stone, or that I think this job is 'not good enough' for me." Mitch drew quotes in the air with his fingers.

Coco said, "Well if that's how you truly feel, don't you think you owe it to her, er, to Eco-Friendly Lighting, to let them know? Sometimes you have to let go of something good to..."

"...to make room for something great," Mitch finished. All the pieces clicked and he knew what he had to do. He sat back, listened to the soft jazz coming through the speakers, and decided he would give Ken two months' notice on Friday.

***

Mitch walked into Ken's office at the end of the week and expressed gratitude and appreciation for all he'd learned. He offered to stay on at least a few months to give Ken enough time to replace him. Ken took it well and gave his blessing.

"I always knew you had an entrepreneur inside you!" he said. "Your personal training business is off to a great start. I can't wait to see what you do with it. If you ever decide to come back here, the door is open to you. You've been a great partner."

Eight weeks later, Mitch cleaned out his desk and left the building with his bobbleheads and other trinkets in a cardboard box. It did feel like a breakup, and he was definitely going to miss Eco-Friendly Lighting and all his coworkers, but he didn't feel at all guilty, confused, or conflicted about it. He knew he was taking a risk, but it wasn't a foolhardy one.

Mitch turned the key in the ignition of his Jeep and "Best Day of My Life," by the American Authors, blasted from the radio. Before pulling out of the parking lot, he sent Coco a text:

Big day. Last day as an employee and I'm finishing the video tonight. Here's a draft of the cover. What do you think?

The craziest part was—and Mitch still had to pinch himself to believe it—Rob Machado agreed to participate in the video! With a few hours of filming with Coco done, Mitch contacted the staff of the Rob Machado Foundation and made an appointment. When he met with Rob, he gave a brief overview of the video, explained that Coco wanted to donate one dollar from each sale to the foundation, and asked if Rob would be willing to give a thirty-second endorsement for the video. Not only did Rob agree, he gave Mitch some film footage from one of his recent surf sessions and allowed Jake to film him doing some yoga stretches on the beach before a session at Seaside Reef, his home break!

Mitch couldn't believe the generosity, and he couldn't wait to show Coco. He spent every night editing Coco's video, inserting Rob's surf footage to transition between sections. He put Rob's endorsement right up front, in which he thanked everyone for buying the video and explained how important yoga had been to his physical training as an elite surfer and his spiritual well-being. Then Rob reminded viewers that a portion of their money was going to help educate kids on how to care for the environment.

When the entire video was completed, Mitch found himself feeling more inspired by it than any of the dozens of surf videos he'd ever made before in his life. His eyes were bloodshot, he had a headache from staring at the computer monitor for so long, and his back ached from all the hours seated at his desk, but the misery paled in comparison to the overwhelming pride and fulfillment he felt inside. It was so well made. Mitch didn't cut any corners, and Coco gave it everything she had. He couldn't wait to get it into the market.

***

At first for Mitch, leaving his day job was like receiving a gift of nine extra hours a day to pursue what he loved. But those hours didn't remain "free" for long. He worked hard at growing his coaching business and started training for Pipeline. Before long, he was working just as many hours as he had at Eco-Friendly. It was simply a transition to a different type of employment—self-employment.

Not only that, but nothing Jake or anyone else could have said would have prepared Mitch for the level of difficulty and challenges he began to face. He and Jake upped their training schedule to two hours a day, three days a week; and then Mitch worked out with his clients all day after that and on the days in between. Physically, Mitch was asking more of himself now than at any other time in his life.

The workouts seemed more appropriate for a Navy Seal than a recreational surfer. Once, Jake dropped a weight into deep water, and Mitch had to swim down to it with a one-foot-long piece of cord and tie a square knot around it. Then he had to go back down, untie the square knot and tie a bowline. He had to dive down a third time, untie the bowline, and then finish by swimming around the pier for endurance.

On the shore, Jake had Mitch jump up onto a flat boulder, then jump back down. Up and down he jumped, again and again. Then he put his feet up on the rock and did push-ups into the sand. Next Mitch frog-hopped up a long set of stairs, skipping three stairs. "This works your core and it's great for getting you quickly to your feet, which is critical for Pipeline. Good work—just two more sets," Jake coached from the side.

Mitch could barely hear, let alone process, most of the encouragement Jake offered him during these workouts. All he could handle was the minimum sensory input necessary to stay alive.

After his workout sessions, Mitch hit the pavement with Coco, selling their video all over Southern California. They went to surf contests, community events, and surf shops with boxes full of DVDs, ready to sell. They posted flyers that said, "Free first-time trial for Yoga for Surfers class!" Virtually everyone who took one of Coco's free classes ended up buying the video to take home. They exceeded their sales goals and expanded their network to the point where Mitch had to invest in sophisticated customer relationship management software just to keep track of all the new people they were meeting. Sales really took off when they created a password protected digital download version.

Within a few weeks, Coco's yoga classes at the studio were full, with a waiting list for new memberships. Mitch increased his client base from ten to twenty, also with a waiting list. Coco started to become known in the local surf community, and every once in a while, people would recognize her and say, "Hey, I love your Yoga for Surfers video!" while she was out with Mitch, making him feel like the luckiest guy on the planet.

One unusually warm Saturday in November, Mitch and Coco relaxed on the beach for the first time in what felt like ages. They didn't talk for most of the afternoon—just experienced the silence and sounds of nature. When you're on the go 24-7, sometimes you just want to be.

The hours passed, and Mitch lifted handfuls of sand and let the grains run through his fingers. Occasionally, one of them stood to get a cold drink from their cooler, adjust their beach umbrella, or return a stray beach ball to the kids playing nearby. But for the most part, they lay still. It wasn't until the sun started to set that Coco sat up, cross-legged, and began to speak.

"I'm trying not to think about all the emails I've got to return, but they keep invading my mind."

Mitch propped himself up on his elbows. "I was thinking exactly the same thing. I was relaxed for most of the day, but then I looked at my watch and suddenly all the emails and appointments and reminders started to fill my brain."

"I wonder sometimes," Coco said, doodling in the sand with her index finger, "if I should hire a couple of yoga teachers to cover some of my classes so I can work on the business instead of in the business. I'm at a point where I can hardly keep up."

"Why don't you?" Mitch shrugged.

"I'm worried that if I give up some of my classes, my personal income will go down," she said, wiping away the sand doodle with the palm of her hand. Mitch rolled over and pulled a magazine out of his backpack. It was one of those local community guides filled with coupons and first-time client offers for businesses in Huntington Beach. He sat up and flipped to a page in the middle that featured an ad for a chiropractic office, an acupuncturist, and a physical therapist, all at the same address.

"Check out this ad. I just saw it this morning," Mitch said, handing the magazine over to Coco. "What if we found a building with office suites, and got together with other businesses that have synergy with us, and created a wellness center? We could have yoga, personal training, and what else, maybe massage or chiropractic?"

Coco studied the magazine ad. "If we had two yoga rooms, I

could have multiple classes going on at once. And you could have a training room so you can work with clients when it's too cold to meet at the beach."

"And we could also use the yoga room for events to build our community," Mitch said, sitting up now.

"What if we asked Nicole to rent one of the suites?" Coco said, smiling. Nicole was the massage therapist they both visited a couple of times per month. "Or maybe a chiropractor like Dr. Rick. I would be stoked to have them here."

"Yeah, we could leverage our marketing power and refer clients to each other," Mitch said, and quickly turned to get his journal and pen out of his backpack.

"So..." Coco said, starting to turn the pages of the magazine. She closed it without finding what she was looking for and tossed it back over toward Mitch's backpack. "How would this work? We would be the landlords and rent out the office suites, or...?" She squirmed and pushed her hair back behind her ears. "How much do office suites cost? Are we buying or renting? Do we need to hire a property manager? What kind of contracts do we need?" She took out her smartphone and opened a browser, then closed it. "I don't even know what to Google."

Mitch had been scribbling feverishly in his journal but stopped when he caught a glimpse of Coco. He realized her energy had gone from excitement to anxiety, so he closed his journal, put down the pen, and locked eyes with her. Together they took a long, deep breath.

"Maybe we should slow down," Mitch said. "No need to paddle out before we get to know the break."

Coco nodded and sat back on her elbows. "Agreed. Let's just let the idea germinate for a while," she said. The sun set, and the temperature dropped, so they went home.

***

"There's no growth in the comfort zone. Ready to get uncomfortable?" asked Jake at their next workout. He and Mitch stood at the water's edge at sunrise. Jake reached into his bag of gear and pulled out a rock. "Hold this." He gave it to Mitch, who almost dropped it because he wasn't expecting it to be so heavy. It weighed at least twenty pounds.

"Hold it like a football, with both arms folded around. Walk into the ocean. Don't swim. Walk on the ocean floor and hold your breath for as long as you can. When you can't hold it any longer, bend down, place the rock on the ocean floor and come up for air. I'll give you a fifteen-second break, then dive back down, grab the rock, walk, and repeat. I'll meet you halfway down the pier. Turn around there, then come back doing the same thing."

As per his usual style, Jake didn't stick around to listen to any whining or protest. He jogged up the pier to the halfway mark. He pulled a couple of items from his bag—a stopwatch and a lifeguard rescue buoy. Mitch even thought he saw an oxygen unit and mask up there. When Jake gave the signal that he was ready, Mitch lifted the rock and started to walk.

He managed about twenty steps per breath going out, holding his breath well over a minute at first, and then less and less with each dive. Mitch pushed his limits mentally and physically, especially during the last few seconds of each "rock walk." His lungs burning, light-headed, he felt his heart pounding. He also knew that once he reached his maximum hold length, he'd still have to hold on for a few more seconds in order to get to the surface. As he gasped for air on his fifteen-second break, he treaded water and tried to slow his breath and heart rate. But then Jake would yell, "Five! Four! Three! Two! One! Rock walk!"

The hardest part was at the middle of the pier, where the water really started to get deep. That was where Mitch thought Jake might need to use that rescue equipment. But even at twenty feet below, Mitch knew that he could reach the surface in just three to five seconds, so he stuck with it. He made it out in five dives, and made it back to the beach in seven dives.

Jake was waiting at the shoreline and took the rock from Mitch.

He leaned in and checked Mitch's eyes for signs of disorientation. Mitch worked to catch his breath and recover, walking slowly in a circle.

"Good work!" called Jake. "The first step to building a muscle is to break it down and stretch it beyond its current capacity. If you stay in your comfort zone, not only will you stop growing, but you'll atrophy and become fragile. I know your lungs are burning, but if you want to surf Pipeline you have to expand your capacity."

When Mitch was finally able to speak, he looked out at the pier—the second longest public pier on the west coast—and said softly, "I can't believe I did that. That was intense!"

"That's how you create growth," Jake said. "Break it down, fuel it, give it time to recover. Soon you'll be able to hold your breath for several minutes. Now, go fuel up with a healthy meal and take tomorrow off to recover."

***

Later that afternoon, Mitch called Coco and suggested they start looking at properties.

They met with a Realtor that Sunday. The sticker shock was real, as rent prices for office space in Huntington Beach were sky high. Mitch and Coco were both already paying $2,000 a month in rent for their apartments. Coco paid another $1,500 a month to rent her yoga studio. They were hoping that opening a wellness center together would enable them to make more money. If all that extra money had to go right back into rent, then what was the point?

Building after building they turned away, and Mitch started to wonder if they should just drop the idea. "And stay stuck?" Coco challenged. "No way. Somewhere out there is the perfect building for us. We will find it." Mitch appreciated Coco's attitude and dedication. Coco committed to looking harder by going out with the Realtor three days a week instead of just on Sundays.

One Saturday morning, Coco knocked loudly on Mitch's door.

Still in his bathrobe, he rubbed his eyes and plodded across the room to open it. "Dusty, how many times I gotta tell you not to forget your key...Coco!"

"You gotta come quick!" she said, grabbing Mitch's arms and bouncing with excitement. "Get dressed! Come on, let's go!"

Mitch guessed it had something to do with the wellness center, so he forced himself to wake up fast, clean himself up, and throw on a pair of jeans and a polo shirt. "Did you find a good place?" he called out from the bathroom while brushing his teeth.

"I did!" Coco called back. "But we've got to hurry because I don't want someone else to discover it. It just went on the market and the Realtor's waiting for us there."

They drove to a spot that could only be described as "the perfect location." Just off Main Street, about a mile and a half from the beach, stood a simple, white stucco building with a Starbucks nearby and a smoothie shop next door. Once Mitch stepped inside, though, he couldn't hear any of the traffic noise.

"Thick, concrete walls," said the Realtor—a heavy-set, fifty-something woman in a soft gray pantsuit. The way she spoke reminded Mitch of his father—a little gruff, and no-nonsense. "They keep outside noise out, and inside noise in. That's the advantage of an older building. Construction standards were different back then. In the newer buildings, you can hear everything." She slapped one of the walls with her hand, as if slapping the back of an old drinking buddy.

Mitch walked up the steep, concrete staircase to the second floor, and found himself delighted by what he saw—cream-colored walls, dark hardwood floors, a spacious kitchen with classic appliances, and a picture window that looked out on the main boulevard that went right into Huntington Pier.

"What a great loft!" he said to Coco as she stepped in from the staircase. "How would we use this? Like a kitchen to demo new recipes for healthy cooking classes? There's even a full bathroom and tons of closet space for storage. I like this as a sitting room, though. I can totally see the little Buddha statues over there and a couch."

"Mitch," Coco cut him off. "This is the part I have to explain. Maybe we better sit down." She led him to the picture window, where they both sat on the ledge. "The rent for this place is as high as all the others. The only difference is that this one comes with this upstairs loft included in the rental price. And yes, there's a kitchen, a living room, a full bathroom, lots of closet space ...and a bedroom."

Mitch took another look around while she spoke, and his eyebrows lifted.

"It's an apartment," Coco spelled out for him. "We could live here. And work downstairs. That's how we can afford it."

Mitch suddenly gasped, as he had forgotten to breathe for at least a minute after Coco spoke. He stood awkwardly and started to teeter. His head spun and faintly in the distance he could hear Coco say, "What do you think?"

Searching for an anchor, Mitch managed to walk across the floor to the stairwell. He leaned on the banister, and put one hand out behind him to assure Coco he was all right and just needed a minute. He stared down the steep, long stairwell, and suddenly had a flashback to the previous week...

It was another one of those mystery trips, where Jake told Mitch to get in the Jeep and drive with no mention of where they were headed or why. An hour later, Mitch found himself parked on a residential street in San Clemente. Jake led Mitch through the side gate of somebody's house, and in the backyard there appeared a massive, homemade wooden skateboard ramp.

"Don't worry. We're not trespassing," Jake said, noticing the look on Mitch's face. "They know we're coming."

The fact that they had just walked onto someone's property without even ringing the front doorbell worried Mitch somewhat, but what rendered him speechless was the sheer height of the ramp. Jake trotted right on over to the stairs leading up to the top, but Mitch didn't budge.

"I thought you liked to skateboard," Jake called out.

"Uh, yeah, to shoot down to the pier to grab a bite, but not this. I've never skated a half-pipe," Mitch explained.

"This isn't a half-pipe. It's a vert ramp," Jake corrected. "It's fifteen feet high with two feet of vertical on top. Bigger than the one at Vans." Jake was referring to Vans Off the Wall Skatepark—the enormous indoor/outdoor skate park up in Huntington Beach.

"Of course not," Mitch sighed. "That would have been much too easy."

He walked over to Jake, who pulled a skateboard from the Jeep. He gave it to Mitch. Then from a large duffle bag he pulled knee pads, elbow pads, and a helmet. Mitch put them on, but with his eyes he made it clear that he wasn't agreeing to anything. The drop on that ramp was intimidating from his vantage point on the ground—he couldn't imagine how much worse it would be from the top. Somehow, Jake got him to climb up.

"When you drop in on big waves, there's a feeling of weightlessness that you have to become familiar with," Jake instructed. "It's kind of like a controlled free-fall. When you feel gravity pulling you down the face, lean in. Don't pull back. If you do, the board will fly right out from under you and you'll eat it. Lean in and use gravity to help you feel the wall."

Mitch looked across the ramp and then down, and reeled from dizziness. He did everything he could to control his breathing and stay calm, but every time he opened his eyes, the view gave him a jolt.

"Breathe in through your nose and out through your mouth," Jake said gently. "You know what FEAR is? False Evidence Appearing Real. In reality, if you let go of the rail and drop in, what's the worst that can happen? You lose your balance, fall off, and slide down the ramp. You're so padded up though, that if you don't fight it, it's almost as safe as falling in water. Fear can lead to paralysis. But you can learn to harness it. Just think about how many things you've done that you didn't think you could do. You look at this vert ramp and you think it's your enemy, but it's not. Fear is your enemy. Once you overcome it, you're empowered to take on other fears."

Mitch looked at Jake to show he was okay and ready to go for it. He stood back from the edge about two feet. He blinked hard.

"You want to know the secret to conquering fear?" Jake whispered. He leaned in close, as if they were soldiers in a bunker together about to rush the hill. "You conquer the fear of doing something... by doing it. Action precedes courage—not the other way around. Lean in and let go."

Mitch placed the skateboard close to the edge of the ramp, and stepped up on it.

Lean in and let go!

Back at the loft, Mitch signed the lease to move in with Coco on the first of December.

CHAPTER 11:

LANDLOCKED BY NATURE

Nature is trying very hard to make us succeed, but nature does not depend on us. We are not the only experiment.

—R. Buckminster Fuller

Mitch dreaded having "the talk" with Dusty. He imagined Dusty's bummed expression hearing his bro was bailing him for a "Betty." But it actually worked out perfectly, because before Mitch could say a word, Dusty burst in their apartment with big news.

"Dude, you are never gonna believe it. I scored a gig as a guide at a killer surf camp in Indo! I get my own bungalow, free food, and get to surf my brains out all…day…long." He held up both his hands, flashing a double shaka. "How epic is that?"

After hearing all the details, Mitch congratulated him and gave him a bro hug.

"Well, send me some pictures, dude," Mitch said, trying not to feel jealous. "Maybe one day I'll get out there to visit you."

"That would be killer," said Dusty, and he stood and shouldered his backpack. "But you better get on it. It's just a temp gig and I don't know how long it'll last."

Mitch rose and opened the door for him. Dusty strode right through and headed for the stairs. "Guess what?" Mitch called. "Coco and I are moving in together and starting a wellness center!"

Dusty turned to say, "That's rad, congrats bro! You guys'll kill it!" Mitch watched as Dusty's head bobbed out of sight and his footsteps could no longer be heard.

"See you around, bro," he said, and went back inside to start deciding what to bring with him to the new place and what to donate to Goodwill.

***

Moving day went smoothly, and because Mitch and Coco were both so driven, they found their groove in the wellness center rather quickly. Financially, it was one of the best decisions they'd ever made, because their income more than doubled with all the opportunities and revenue streams the new building created.

First, they reduced expenses by dropping their individual rents ($1500 each) and sharing the cost of the upstairs loft, which was included in the cost of renting the center. Then there was the rental income. The wellness center had seven suites, and they rented out five for a competitive $500/month. The renters included an acupuncturist, two massage therapists, one naturopathic doctor, and one colon therapist. Mitch took one suite for himself, and Coco converted her suite, the largest suite, into a second yoga studio. The savings on rent and the income from the sub-leasing covered the entire studio cost, so everything after that was profit.

In addition, the renters agreed to a 70/30 split on event income, using the yoga studio as the venue. Whenever someone hosted a workshop in the wellness center, they'd sell tickets, and then Mitch and Coco would take 30 percent.

Mitch and Coco also made between 10 and 50 percent from all products sold through the center. They bought shelving and display cases to set up in the front reception area to create a small boutique selling yoga mats, an all-natural bamboo clothing line, and organic snacks and drinks. They also offered their tenants the opportunity to use the space to sell their products in exchange for a 10 percent cut. Most took advantage of the offer. Mitch and Coco hired a reception-ist to work for everyone, answering phones and greeting guests, and handling the sales transactions.

Revenue continued to stream in from Coco's Yoga for Surfers video as well. The profit per unit was only a few dollars, but they sold several hundred per month, so it created a nice passive residual income. But even more valuable was the exposure from the video and trailers featuring Rob Machado, which attracted so many new clients that she was able to hire two more yoga instructors and fill up their classes in addition to her own. So now Coco earned money from her own classes, and an additional 50 percent from her instruc-tors' classes.

Overhead costs included rent, the receptionist, a bookkeeper, banking fees, marketing and advertising, and their referral pro-grams. The monthly net seemed high, but in just a few months with the multiple revenue streams, they had solid cashflow and profit margin. Mitch and Coco's personal incomes ended up at around $8,600 per month, or just more than $100,000 per year, each.

Mitch still worked like a horse, but it was nice now to have the money to show for it. Six figures was a huge milestone for an entre-preneur. Not only that, but he had built up the knowledge, skills, and self-discipline to be able to manage that money so it wouldn't slip through his fingers. He went from spending more than he earned while working at Reynolds, to living off 60 percent of his income and saving 40 percent—also a huge milestone.

At the beginning of January, Mitch and Coco sat down to plan and budget their trip to Hawaii so Mitch could surf Pipeline. They both knew that the cost of the trip wasn't just airfare and accommo-dations; they would lose a large portion of their income, too. While away, they wouldn't be able to meet with clients or teach classes. They added up all the trip expenses, plus the amount of lost income, and calculated the trip's true cost.

"I don't think I can afford to go for more than seven days," Mitch said from the cinnamon-colored sofa in the loft's tiny living room. Coco made a smoothie in the kitchen while he reviewed his numbers once again.

"Well," she said, dropping some fresh blueberries and protein powder into the blender, "Seven days is enough time for you to surf Pipeline though, right?"

"You're right. We can make it work," Mitch agreed. He closed his journal and placed it gently on the reclaimed-wood coffee table. It belonged to Coco and had carved Indian panels on the sides. Mitch liked her eastern tantric décor, or at least the few pieces she brought into the cozy 800 square foot loft. She also left plenty of room for Mitch to bring in his surf and beach-themed pieces, which he appreciated. It helped him feel more at ease with the transition from "me" to "we."

Coco walked over with two smoothies, handed him one and nestled on the couch next to him. He put his arm around her and she said, "Next year we'll be able to take longer surf trips. I'm sure of it."

"Mm-hmm," he said, sipping the smoothie and relaxing back into the couch, "and we'll move out of this starter home into a nice big house or maybe a condo on the beach."

"Yes! I would love a place on the beach with lots of room for entertaining."

"And floor-to-ceiling windows so we can see the water."

"And a stone patio with a barbecue."

"And a hot tub!"

"And a reading nook."

They continued their pong-pong daydreaming and did so regularly as the weeks went by. They'd sit on the couch together, review their day, and then start upgrading their lives one detail at a time. Eventually, it became a ritual—one that had a shadow side. Happiness and fulfillment always seemed to lie in the next thing. Tomorrow. Someday in the distant future or someday soon, they thought, they'd get what they wanted and be happy, but someday was never today.

Despite the longing, they did have quite a lot of fun together, tackling the new challenges of building their business, celebrating the transformations and success of their clients. There were definitely aggravations and setbacks, but Coco was endlessly optimistic that everything would always work out for the best, and it usually did. Whenever Mitch lamented about a problem he didn't know what to do with, Coco always answered the same, "Well, honey, I don't know what you're going to do, but I know you're smart enough to figure it out."

As Coco's birthday approached at the end of January, Mitch began to brainstorm all the ways in which he could celebrate this amazing woman he had fallen in love with. When the day came, he left the wellness center early and called Coco, apologizing.

"Hey, I'm stuck in traffic. My meeting was late, then my whole day got thrown off—you know how it is. I'm really sorry but it looks like I'll be coming home late."

There was a pause. A long one.

Finally, she said, "You know it's my birthday, right?"

"Aw yeah, honey. I know, and that's why I really wanted to get home early, but I'm really stuck here. I'll make it up to you, I promise," he said, along with all the other things men say when they're screwing up. Coco mumbled something that sounded like, "It's okay," and they hung up.

When he got home, an hour and a half later than usual, the sun was still up but it was well past dinner time. Mitch found Coco seated on the couch, "reading" a book with her eyebrows raised high.

"Did you eat dinner yet?" he asked. She shook her head.

Mitch knew immediately that if he were to ask, "How are you?" right then, she'd say, "Fine." If he were to ask, "What's wrong?" she'd say, "Nothing." She was in that place.

He wasted no time in apologizing for his lateness and invited her to go out for some fresh air, a nice walk, and a late dinner. With a sigh, Coco tossed the book to the coffee table, got up, pulled a shawl around her shoulders, slipped on her shoes, allowed Mitch to link his arm with hers, and together they walked out the door.

The beach relaxed her, and after a few minutes Coco warmed up considerably. Soon they were talking freely again, sharing stories from the day as the water licked their heels. When they came upon the sand dunes, Mitch suggested they leave the shoreline and go exploring a little. They came upon a cave, and Mitch motioned for her to follow him inside.

Coco gasped when she saw it, stunned and delighted, and placed both hands over her mouth. A beautiful brand new Indian Mandala round blanket rested on the ground in brilliant reds, deep purples, apricot, and teal. Upon it lay two champagne glasses and a wicker picnic basket with her favorite Thai coconut chicken soup, green salad with peanut sauce, and a bottle of sparkling wine. Candles and tiki torches lit the entire area.

Then it dawned on her. She pieced together that Mitch had set up this scene the entire time he'd been pretending to be "stuck in traffic." The candles cast a golden glow. A gentle wind blew and created dancing shadows on the dunes. Mitch lit two aromatherapy warmers, and soon the aroma of plumeria reached Coco's senses. She breathed it in deeply.

Mitch pulled out his phone and connected it to the outdoor speaker he'd set up. Knowing he hit this one out of the park, he clicked "Play."

"You got a smile so bright, you know you coulda been a candle..." by UB40 whispered from the speaker. Coco stepped gingerly over to Mitch and reached up to kiss him.

"You're amazing," Coco said, cupping his face in her hands. "Thank you for making me feel so special. I have a surprise for you too. I've been learning some sensual tantra practices. Are you ready to take that advanced class we talked about?" she said with a wink. Time stopped for the two lovers, and they shared a magical evening of champagne, laughs, and passion under the stars.

***

Mitch had been watching the long-range forecast for North Shore. He saw a huge purple blob, indicating a big swell about two and a half weeks out. They bought their plane tickets and rented a midsize SUV, booked a North Shore vacation rental online, started to clear their calendars and let their clients know they were going to be gone for that entire week in February. They made sure to coach their staff and tenants about how to handle issues while they were gone, and after a few more weeks of waiting, Mitch and Coco finally headed for Hawaii.

Jake flew out with them. However, when they landed at the Honolulu airport, he checked his phone messages and suddenly told Mitch he had to leave in just four days for Saipan, a small island near Guam. Mitch couldn't imagine what sort of surfing emergency there could be in Saipan, but he didn't even ask because something far more important stole his attention.

While looking for the signs leading to baggage claim, Mitch noticed a thick, wool blanket of clouds move across the sky outside and cast a shadow across the entire terminal. Everyone looked up and out the walls of windows as heavy raindrops began to fall, pelting the runways, taxiways, and ramps. Then the sound of thunder rumbled through, as if the storm wanted to show it meant business. Mitch pulled out his phone to check the surf report and cursed out loud.

```
High surf advisory in effect starting 3
pm Saturday . . . heavy rain, gale-force
winds reaching 40-50 mph, strong break-
ing waves are expected, making all water
activities very dangerous . . .
```

Coco put her hand on Mitch's arm gently and said, "Hey, it'll be okay. These tropical storms usually pass right through."

Mitch tried. He really did. He was like a parent choosing to ignore his toddler's temper tantrum, thinking, Well, eventually this will stop. She can't scream and cry all day, can she? It dumped rain as they loaded their rental car, strapped their board bags on the roof rack, and jumped on the highway to the North Shore.

Waikiki and downtown Honolulu are concrete jungles, complete with high-rise apartments, professional buildings, endless rows of condos and fast food chains. Eight hundred thousand of Hawaii's 1.3 million people live and work there, and that number doesn't even include all the tourists. Mitch drove like a man on a mission, squinting for better visibility, stressed about the traffic, and the rain came down stronger and faster.

Once they drove out of town and entered the more rural parts, the tension in Mitch's shoulders eased a bit. They passed by the Dole plantation's lush fields of mineral rich red volcanic soil. Rows of pineapple, coffee beans, and sugar cane covered rolling hills with rugged mountains in the background.

As they drove up the last hill, Mitch felt a surge of optimism. He expected that at the top there'd be an unobstructed view of thousands of miles of blue Pacific Ocean, contrasted by tropical green coastline. He hoped to see the "Seven Mile Miracle" of the North Shore—the stretch of beach that boasts more world class surf spots than anywhere else on the globe, and which he'd only ever seen in photos and magazines.

But his optimism was crushed by the gray, ominous field of storm clouds rolling in like an endless set of giant waves, ready to crush anything in their path.

They arrived at their quaint, two-bedroom, oceanfront vacation rental right in front of a spot called "Log Cabins." As they unpacked their suitcases, the rain continued, and like every toddler's parent, Mitch learned that Yes, she really can cry all day. This storm was not going to quit.

Jake suggested they eat, get a good night's sleep, and wake up early to take a drive around the island.

"If it's still raining by the time I leave," he said, "I want to make sure you know where the best breaks are and you know their personalities." Mitch nodded and tossed his empty suitcase in a closet. Coco picked up the flyers and menus fanned out on the dining room table, hoping to find a good restaurant nearby.

Jake turned toward the door, threw them a shaka and said, "I'm going to visit some friends. Rest up, you guys. See you in the morning."

***

At 7 a.m. Mitch, Coco, and Jake hopped into the SUV and cruised the Seven Mile Miracle. The vacation rental included free use of beach cruisers, but because it was so miserable out, they decided they'd better drive. Regardless, Mitch took the bikes out of the small, single-car garage and chained them to the front porch. He wanted them ready for when the weather cleared and he could finally ride the half-mile down the bike path to Ehukai Beach (aka Pipeline).

The strong winds and showers continued, sometimes lighter, sometimes heavier, sometimes stopping for just a few minutes before starting right back up again. The skies remained an angry gray and all Mitch saw as they drove the "Kam Highway" were stormy, angry, unsurfable seas. The waves were big, but completely out of control.

As Jake gave them the tour of all the main breaks from Haleiwa to Turtle Bay, Mitch noticed quite a few locals loading dirt bikes into their trucks. He wondered aloud, "Why would anyone want to go for a ride in this weather?"

"Out here in the country," Coco answered, "when there is too much weather to surf, a lot of locals go dirt biking. These guys don't care about mud! You wanna go check it out?"

Mitch didn't answer—just shook his head, leaned his forehead against the window and sank into a deep, blue funk. "Let's just go back to the beach house and wait it out."

Jake dropped them off and said, "I'll be over at Uncle Brian's if you need anything. Tonight I'll check the buoys and wind forecast.

Maybe we can find some ride-able waves on the other side of the island. We might be able to find a protected area where the swell wraps in."

The next day, Mitch and Jake did, at least, "get wet." They paddled out at Diamond Head even though it was choppy side-shore and only chest high. Paddling around, duck diving, and catching even the smallest wave felt good, especially in 75-degree water. It was better than nothing.

After lunch, back on the north shore, the weather continued. Coco found a deck of cards in one of the drawers next to the TV, and they played Crazy Eights for hours. When that got old, they switched to Backgammon. In the evenings, the big-screen TV was loaded with satellite, cable, Netflix, and every other possible form of entertainment, so they took advantage of that.

They spent the next few days having "vacation sex", doing yoga, watching movies, eating, and playing games in the living room. Mitch stood next to the window every few hours and stared at the dark seas. Shoulders slouched, he moped around like a grounded 14-year-old.

Even Coco started to get irritable. Not that she had a surfing goal to tackle, but she was going stir-crazy, cooped up indoors.

"I think I want to just go for a walk. I don't care if I get soaking wet. It's not that cold," she said. She put on her shoes and opened the front door, but standing right there in the doorway was Jake, with his hand raised, about to knock. "Oh!" Coco said, startled. "Hi. Are you leaving for Saipan?"

"Not just yet. I'm taking the last flight out," Jake said. Coco invited him in, but Jake stayed in the doorway to avoid tracking water and mud on the floor. He noticed Mitch laid out catatonically on the couch and said in a loud voice, "Yo Mitch, get up! I have a surprise for you. We're going to a luau."

"A luau!" Coco instantly perked up.

"Yes. I want to introduce you to some of my ohana, and they're all gathering at my friend's house right at Lani's. It's close."

"I'll get ready! Five minutes!" Coco almost shouted and scurried into the bedroom.

Mitch lay like a beached whale and contemplated Jake's invitation. Hmm, luau or stare at the ceiling? Luau or stare at the ceiling?

With great effort, he log-rolled off the couch, picked himself up, and trudged over to the bedroom. Coco soon emerged wearing a floral-patterned dress with strappy sandals. She grabbed an umbrella from the open-weave basket near the door and practically leaped down the front steps and into the car. With his hands in his pockets, Mitch sluggishly followed in a simple pair of jeans, a sand-colored t-shirt, and hoodie. He closed the door behind him and looked out at the rain, still falling steadily. Jake patted him on the back in sympathy, and they went down to join Coco.

***

Jake pulled in a driveway and parked under a huge banyan tree. They all got out and walked along a row of 'ohi'a trees with full-bodied red flowers in bloom. They walked across the grass yard with four white canopies set up adjacent to the house. Under the tents Mitch saw a crowd of people—at least fifty—most colorfully dressed, talking and having fun.

What an epic backyard, Mitch thought. The space was fabulous— just the right size for a large party while also being secluded and intimate.

Three musicians—two guitarists and one on a ukulele—were jamming and singing in harmony under the middle canopy. The music was the perfect background for the adults' chatter and the children's laughter. Suddenly Mitch felt glad he went.

And when he saw the buffet of food, a big smile emerged—spinach salad, sweet potato salad, ambrosia, cucumber-carrot salad, an assortment of ripe fresh fruit, poi, grilled salmon, kalua pig, laulau, chicken long rice, purple taro rolls, and more. Mitch was about to take out his phone and snap pictures of the food when a heavyset woman approached.

She wore a white blouse with a green floral sarong and held her arms out as she walked through the crowd toward Jake. She hugged him like a mother whose son had just come home from college. Jake introduced her to Mitch and Coco as Auntie Lili. "Aloha," she said warmly as she hugged them both.

Then a child of about six ran up to Jake, bowed slightly, and raised a lei made of orchids in front of himself at heart level. Jake took the lei and placed it around his neck and smiled. Auntie Lili walked to the end of the buffet table while the child held up one lei each for Mitch and Coco. Once finished, he ran off happily to rejoin his friends, and Auntie Lili returned with a stack of three white plates. She thrust them toward Jake, Mitch, and Coco and said, "Mai! Mai e 'ai!" which means, "Come! Come eat!"

Jake clasped his hands around his plate, dropped his head obediently, and made a beeline for the buffet. He raised his head for a moment to say something to Mitch and Coco, but Auntie Lili said, "No. You eat. I take care of dem. Dey so skinny!" and Jake dropped his head back down.

Auntie led Mitch and Coco to the buffet and began to scoop food onto their plates. "You want lomilomi? Yes, you want." Scoop. "You want pipi kaula? Yes, you want." Scoop.

Carrying three mountains of food, Jake, Mitch, and Coco joined the other guests at the tables. Coco picked up on the positive vibes right away and fit right in, chatting away with the women, eating with gusto, so happy to be out in the fresh air with good people. Mitch ate as well, but a little less.

"Be careful that Auntie doesn't see you pushing that laulau around your plate," muttered Jake.

"What is she gonna do?" Mitch joked. "Hold me down and force feed me?"

"Yes" said Jake, straight-faced.

Just then a man with long, wavy hair, dark skin, and smiling eyes came over to their table and tapped Jake on the shoulder.

Jake turned and shouted, "Nassim!" Jake stood and gave the man a strong hug. Then he turned to Mitch and said, "This is Nassim Haramein. He's a great friend of mine going back...sheesh!...decades."

"Nice to meet you," said Mitch, extending his hand for a handshake, but instead Nassim pulled him in for a hug and said, "Aloha!"

Jake scooted down the bench so Nassim could join them, and then he said to Mitch, "Nassim actually lives on Kauai, but he had some business meetings so he flew in for a few days. He's an experienced surfer, a waterman, a deep-sea diver, and he knows a lot of the locals. I told him about your mission to surf Pipe and asked if he could show you around since I'm taking off."

"Wow, that is so cool of you," Mitch said sincerely to Nassim, who answered by placing his hand on Mitch's shoulder and saying, "Sure brah, if you're a friend of Jake's you're a friend of mine!"

"Nassim is a remarkable research physicist," Jake added. "You'll be blown away by his projects."

Nassim tugged on Jake's ponytail and muttered, "Don't tell him about the top-secret stuff." Jake retaliated with a light punch to Nassim's stomach. Mitch could see they were like brothers and enjoyed the antics. Seeing Jake in a playful, social environment was a nice change from the stoic, military-style training sessions Mitch had grown used to.

Looking around at all the canopies, Mitch found himself struck by the easy, laid-back, positive vibes of everyone at the party. They all seemed so happy, as though they had neither problems nor cares in the world. Over by the musicians, a group of women in traditional grass skirts taught hula dancing to the younger girls. Under another canopy, children sat on the ground and listened to an old man tell stories. A couple men sat at a table nearby playing what Mitch thought was checkers, but learned later it was called "konane." All these happy kids, he marveled, and not a video game in sight.

Just then, a little boy ran up to the table, calling, "Uncle Jake! Uncle Jake! Come look what I found!"

Jake matched the child's urgency and asked, "What is it?" But the child didn't answer—just frantically motioned for Jake to come.

"It's probably a green anole," said Jake over his shoulder.

"Well, that's important," Nassim nodded.

Jake got up from the table, paused to show Auntie his empty plate, and took his leave, trotting after the child out to the garden.

Nassim turned to Mitch and said, "So what do you think? Jake told me this is your first luau."

"Oh, this is amazing," Mitch replied, wiping his fingers with a napkin and pushing his plate off to the side. "This food is so fresh, everyone is happy. I've been to a lot of parties in my life, but the vibe here is different. I can't put my finger on it, but it just is."

"We call it the 'Aloha Spirit,'" said Nassim. "Most people think Aloha just means hello and goodbye. Alo means presence, and ha means breath. The literal meaning of Aloha is 'the presence of breath,' or 'the breath of life.' Another way to say it is being present with life, in an attitude of gratitude. That is one of the things I love about living in Hawaii."

"Yeah, you can really feel that energy," said Mitch. "Everyone seems stoked."

"Speaking of energy," Nassim continued, "tell me what's going on with Jake's project in Saipan. I was just about to ask him when he ran off."

Mitch shook his head. "Honestly, I don't know anything about it. I thought it was surf-related."

Nassim scooted closer to Mitch on the bench and explained, "Jake and I have the patent on a tide-and-solar-powered water de-salinization plant for islands that need fresh drinking water."

Nassim was soft-spoken, with a French-Moroccan accent, so

Mitch leaned in to make sure he heard correctly. "Jake's been working with the US government to get a contract to do a big installation on Saipan."

"What?!" yelped Mitch, trying to see if Nassim was putting him on. "Jake never mentioned anything about a desalinization project."

"Ah. Well, that sounds like Jake," said Nassim, reaching toward a fruit platter in the center of the table. He picked up a small bunch of grapes and said, "He never toots his own horn. Has he told you about all his businesses?"

Mitch stared blankly.

"He started nine different businesses and retired a multimillionaire about ten years ago," Nassim said, popping a grape in his mouth. "That's when he opened his tenth business—his surf school in Huntington Beach."

"What?? Dude. No. Way." He could tell by Nassim's expression that this was no joke.

Nassim continued filling in the blanks of Jake's past while Mitch listened with a mixture of fascination and disbelief. Jake started out in business thirty years ago as a roofer, built a solid reputation and great crew, then as an early adopter he started specializing in solar panels and made millions. Then he spun off and co-founded a business called Eco-Friendly Lighting with Ken (My Ken? My former boss Ken? Yes.) He had a couple failures but as he learned the core principles of sustainability, he built three more businesses and sold them. He is on a whole bunch of Boards of Directors, including my Resonance Science Foundation. A few years ago he decided to move on to desalinization plants. Have you been to any of his houses? Jake owns a beach house in Seal Beach, a beautiful house on Kauai, a bunch of rental properties, and a surf camp, yoga retreat in Costa Rica.

"Then why doesn't he have a car?" Mitch protested. "And why does he always make me pay for lunch??" Mitch looked at Nassim like he was a couch and wanted to shake him for loose change.

"There's too much traffic in So Cal. I don't want to own a car," said Jake behind them.

"And he's a cheap son of a gun," finished Nassim to which Jake responded with a "you got me" look.

"No, seriously—why didn't you ever tell me you're a...like a... business tycoon?" asked Mitch.

Jake shrugged as if nothing could matter less and said, "You never asked."

"Have I just been walking around with blinders on?" asked Mitch incredulously. "I mean, how did I not see this?"

That question really seemed to grab Nassim's attention, the way a detective might react when stumbling upon a clue. He glanced at Jake as if asking permission to investigate. Jake assented with his eyes and walked over to another table to join a group of men playing cards.

Nassim stood and invited Mitch to follow him to one of the other canopies. There were fewer people inside so it was easier to hear. Nassim motioned toward the rain and said, "Tell me. What do you see?"

Mitch put one hand on his hip and rubbed his neck with the other as all the frustration of the past three days came flooding back. "What do I see? Rainstorms. Strong winds and shitty weather. Pardon my language, but I can't help it." He started to fidget, shifting his weight back and forth from his left foot to his right and thrusting his hands in his pockets. "I'm sure Jake's already explained it to you. I've spent all this money and all this time and trained so hard just to get here, and now this rain is shutting me out. I'm super bummed."

"I get it brah," said Nassim, from one landlocked surfer to another.

"Yeah, it's happened before, too. In my old job where I was so close to a goal—I was about to win this huge bonus and take this killer surf trip, but then just at the last minute, everything fell apart. It's like the universe is conspiring against me or something. The timing of everything just sucks!" Mitch said, trying to contain his impulse to kick over a chair.

Nassim stood perfectly still, observing without judgment, and when Mitch finished, he considered his next words carefully.

"Have you ever stopped to consider the opposite? What if the universe is conspiring for you?" He observed how the raindrops dripped down from the awning to the ground, seeping into the earth below. "Sometimes it helps just to have faith."

Mitch looked at Nassim like he had nine heads. "I wouldn't expect to hear that from a scientist. I mean no disrespect whatsoever. I'm just saying, 'Have faith' isn't something scientists generally say. What do you research, exactly?"

"I study quantum gravity and its application to technology, new energy, applied resonance, life science, permaculture, ancient civilizations and consciousness."

"Ah," said Mitch, staring blankly.

"I study the nonlinear interconnectedness of all things. My foundation made a movie to help explain. It's called The Connected Universe."

"Uh-huh."

"I may be able to help you," Nassim offered humbly. "Are you open to some insights relating to your situation right now, or do you prefer to handle this on your own?"

Mitch unwound a bit. At Nassim's invitation, he sat down on a palm tree stump. Nassim sat opposite him. Mitch leaned forward and put his hands on his thighs.

"The first concept I would like you to entertain is that you did not create the universe and you are not in charge of it."

"I don't think I'm in charge..." Mitch protested.

"Don't you? Didn't you plan and train for this trip so you could come out here and surf Pipeline? Aren't you frustrated now because you feel like you did everything right, but the universe is letting you down?"

"Yes, that's exactly how I feel," said Mitch.

"Instead of control," Nassim related, "I like to think about life as if it's all about riding a wave. We have no control over the swell direction, winds, or tides, but if we pay attention to these things we can learn to align with them and go with the flow. It takes faith, but when you can do that, this anger you have and this stress you are carrying will start to melt away, and you'll be able to ride the wave of life!"

Mitch looked past Nassim at the stormy weather while he processed the idea. He took a deep breath of the dewy, tropical air, and looked back up at Nassim and nodded several times.

Nassim continued, "The second concept I would like you to entertain—and it's going to sound strange but just bear with me—is that the universe is not against you, and this storm is not against you. I've come to learn that everything happens for a reason, and it serves me."

Mitch raised one eyebrow, but then forced himself to relax it. He tossed out prejudgment and stayed focused.

"Your body is made up of one hundred trillion cells that are incredibly well organized," Nassim explained. "They're talking to themselves at incredible speed and duplicating, undergoing billions of chemical changes every second. If you were to take one of the cells from your body and put it under a microscope, you would think of the cell as a thing—a thing separate from you—but in fact, that cell is you, right?"

Mitch visualized a cell, one of his cells, under a microscope.

"And that cell is made up of organelles, each with different roles but talking to each other and collaborating on your behalf. And those organelles are made up of molecules, and molecules are made up of atoms. And all those atoms are all talking so they can conspire to make that cell. And this goes on and on inward. It also goes on and on outward. The universe is talking to itself, from infinitely big to infinitely small. Everything is intimately connected."

Mitch looked up after a moment and said, "And so...?"

"Everything happens for a reason, and it serves me. Everything is perfect, even when I don't understand it!"

Nassim rested for a moment in silence as Mitch tried to wrap his brain around the idea. "Okay, but how does that help anything in terms of my surf trip?" Mitch asked. "What's the practical application?"

"The answer to that must be experienced—not explained," replied Nassim. He turned his head and observed the raindrops gliding down one of the metal poles that held up the tent. A small drop journeyed down the pole and stopped midway, but then another drop came along and touched it. They combined to form one larger drop and continued all the way down the pole toward the grass.

Nassim turned back to Mitch and said, "Why don't you come back with me to Kauai? I would like you to meet a special person—a wise man who holds sacred knowledge and has totally transformed my life and many others. He's a Hawaiian healer who holds the teachings from the great elders, and I think what you really need lies in an experience only he can provide. Getting there is an adventure, but if you like hiking you'll enjoy it, and the trip will be well worth it."

Mitch looked over at the other canopies to find Coco, and finally spotted her hula dancing with some other women. If he told her they would be spending another day indoors tomorrow, she'd be so disappointed. She was made for adventure. Maybe a day trip would be a good idea.

"By coincidence," Nassim said, looking at his watch, "Jake has to leave for the airport. But there's enough time to pack an overnight bag, and then we can all just go to the airport together. Jake will be off to Saipan and us to Kauai. What-a-ya-say?"

"Looks like surfing is out, so why not? Just let me make sure Coco is on board." Mitch said.

Nassim reached his palm outside the tent to feel the rain and said, "Let's grab Jake, say Aloha and get going."

***

Coco needed no convincing—they were on a plane that night. The flight from Oahu was a little bumpy and nerve-wracking for Mitch because of the wind and rain, but Nassim and Jake assured him that because visibility was okay, and there was no lightning, it was safe enough to fly. They arrived on Kauai in about twenty minutes. Mitch and Coco spent the rest of the night in the guest house at Nassim's ranch, and woke up at 5 a.m. for the hike.

They were instructed to leave their cell phones, pagers, watches, and any other electronic devices at the guest house. In explanation, all Nassim said was, "Energies."

With a yawn and few words, Mitch and Coco climbed into Nassim's Nissan Pathfinder and drove out to the backcountry, silhouetted against the pink morning sky.

They went through some residential neighborhoods, over some mountains, into a valley, and past a farm. Soon they were driving on dirt roads, and Mitch noticed fewer and fewer houses outside until there were none. Eventually, they entered an overgrown, thick forest and Mitch wondered if there was even still a road at all. But Nassim kept going until they reached the end of an overlook and parked in a little roundabout about thirty feet from the edge.

"From here we hike the rest of the way in."

Coco loved every moment of hiking through the forest with its canopy of moss-covered trees and ferns. "Everything is so alive!" she exclaimed. "If you watch closely, everything is moving."

Mitch could see the awe in her eyes, and it made him glad. He was enjoying the journey, but was still a bit disconnected. He appreciated the beauty around him, but part of his awareness was on the surf he was missing out on, whereas Coco was 100 percent present. She was a literal 'tree hugger,' stopping to pet and hug several trees as if they were big, snuggly Hawaiian friends.

Soon they came upon a river and followed it until the water spilled over a cliff, creating a waterfall into the valley below. Nassim told them that once they hiked down the side of the waterfall, they would arrive at their destination.

"Finally," muttered Mitch as he took a swig of water from his water bottle.

"Sacredly," corrected Nassim.

Then Nassim led them in a zigzag path down the mountain until they reached the bottom.

***

They came upon a clearing where you could see rock terraces built by ancient Hawaiians over 1,000 years ago. The rocks were black lava with moss greener and thicker than Mitch had ever seen. Coco knelt down and touched the moss, petting it gently. Up ahead there appeared three circular structures. The first was a large round canopy with no walls—just six large, round tree trunks holding up a palm thatched roof. The second structure looked like a turtle shell low to the ground, which Nassim informed them was a sweat lodge. The third was a cabin with a roof made of palm fronds, woven branches and mud packed walls. Each structure was encircled by a low retaining wall made of black lava stones, with interconnected circles and a big fire pit in the middle.

Mitch couldn't believe his eyes. It seemed everywhere he looked he saw the trilogy symbol.

A large, muscular man, built like a WWE wrestler, emerged from the cabin. He was wearing a white robe with big wooden beads and a green ceremonial shawl over his shoulders. He spotted the three travelers and threw his hands up in delight, the same way Mitch's grandmother used to throw her hands up for hugs when they drove to her house for a holiday visit.

The man came closer and spread his arms out wide toward Nassim, whose slim frame almost disappeared inside the giant teddy-bear hug. Mitch tried to guess the man's age. Maybe sixty? He had no wrinkles, though, and his hair was as dark and shiny as a horse's mane.

"You've brought some new friends!" said the man, releasing Nassim.

"Yes, Kimo, I'd like you to meet Mitch and Coco, travelers from California. They're friends of Uncle Jake," said Nassim. "Mitch, Coco, I'd like to introduce you to this man whose traditional Hawaiian name I cannot pronounce, so we all call him Kimo for short."

Kimo giggled and shook Nassim's shoulder playfully. Nassim continued, "Kimo comes from a long line of Kapuna, wisdom-keepers—his mother, his grandmother, his great-grandfather, and beyond. His ancestry can be traced all the way back to ancient Hawaiian royalty."

"Are you a kahuna?" asked Mitch.

"If that word helps your understanding," Kimo replied, "I would simply say that my calling is to keep alive and share the teachings of the ancient ones."

"Any chance you have a prayer to make this rain go away so I can surf?" asked Mitch, and then immediately regretted it. He was trying to be funny, but it came out a bit flippant. Coco frowned.

Kimo paused then broke out in laughter. His booming, playful laugh broke the ice.

"Come," said Kimo, putting his arm around Mitch to walk toward the three structures. "The ancient ones have a special message for you."

CHAPTER 12

GETTING BARRELED

Unity is plural... at minimum two.

—R. Buckminster Fuller

Kimo invited Mitch, Coco, and Nassim first to the cabin to rest, drink water, and take off their shoes. The cabin was simple, clean, and made using the traditional ways. To the left there was a small stone stove with a fire inside, and Kimo said they could sit to dry their hands and feet. In the middle of the room was a long table made of koa wood, with thick-cut rounds of palm tree trunks placed as stools. The scent was of soil—rich and alive with minerals.

All around the room were shelves containing spices, bunches of herbs, both fresh and dried, crystals, minerals, feathers, seashells, clay pots, mortars and pestles, tiny dropper bottles filled with liquid, and other foreign items. Mitch resisted the urge to touch them, finding himself both fascinated and uncomfortable at the same time. *I hope we're not going to make a sacrifice or drink chicken blood,* he thought. *What does a kahuna do anyway? Is he a witch doctor?*

They dried off quickly and Nassim suggested they take out some of the fruit and nuts they had brought along in their backpacks. Everyone took a seat on a tree stump and quietly ate. Soon they felt rested and refreshed.

"So, bruddah Mitch," said Kimo from his seat at the head of the table. "Why are you here?"

Mitch finished the last few sunflower seeds from his trail mix and said, "Well, it's pretty simple. I've been learning about big wave surfing with Jake, who I guess you know." Kimo nodded. "Eighteen months ago I set a goal to come to Hawaii and surf Pipeline, so I've been training and preparing for this trip, and now...here I am."

"I see," said Kimo, the way a doctor might respond while interviewing a patient. "Tell me about your training."

"First, there's the physical training," Mitch explained. "Jake helped me get to a healthy weight, and then I started exercising intensely, building up strength and endurance. I've built up my lung capacity to be able to hold my breath for more than two minutes under water. I even skated a vert ramp to get a feel for what it's like to drop in on a really steep vertical wave, and you know, other stuff like that."

Kimo rocked back and forth as he took in the information and then came back for more. Mitch continued, "Then there's the mental training. I studied the bathymetry and best swell directions for Pipeline. I learned where the rocks are, where to paddle out and how the currents work. I learned a true respect for the power of the ocean. I know how to time the sets, what to do if I fall, basically everything a surfer needs to know in order to surf Pipeline safely."

Again, Kimo rocked back and leaned forward. He waited to hear more, but Mitch didn't have much more to add. "I guess that's it," Mitch said, replacing the lids on his reusable food containers.

Nassim took the containers, as well as Coco's, and silently placed them back into their backpacks so Mitch and Kimo could continue their discussion. Kimo sat back on his tree stump to think. His face went blank for a moment, as if he were transported somewhere from within, but then his expression returned.

"Have you ever heard about aumakua?" he asked. Mitch noticed that Kimo's tone had become more serious—not in a scolding way, but in a way that showed deep concern, as if Mitch's very life depended on the answer.

"Um...uh no...?" Mitch replied. Kimo retreated once again into his own thoughts, taking deep breaths and closing his eyes. Eventually, his happy expression returned and he placed his hand on the thick table, as if the doctor had arrived at his diagnosis and was now closing the patient interview.

"We start now," he said, and stood up to grab a dual-colored stick from one of the shelves behind him.

"What's that?" Mitch said with alarm.

Kimo held up the stick with his pinky sticking out and said, "Incense."

"Oh," Mitch relaxed. "Um, can I ask, how does all this work exactly?"

Kimo chuckled again. "Brudda Mitch, you ask many questions. It's good to be curious. And sometimes it's best just to be. The process is simple. We drink tea, we sweat, we talk story and then let the forest teach us what we need to learn."

With that, he left Mitch and Coco to exchange a glance of befuddlement, and Nassim to prepare them for the next step.

Nassim instructed Mitch and Coco to leave their socks and shoes in the cabin, along with their backpacks and other belongings. They would now move to the sweat lodge carrying nothing and wearing only loose, breathable clothes. Barefoot, they stepped out onto the soft blanket of lush, green grass. Mitch thought it should feel muddier somehow, with all the rainfall, but the ground yielded only mildly beneath his feet. They walked clockwise across the clearing toward the hut, following the pathway through the knee-high black Tahitian stone retaining wall.

The doorway was covered by two criss-crossing flaps. Just outside on the ground was a bucket full of water and half coconut shell scooper. Each person stopped and received a blessing from Kimo while being smudged by incense in an abalone shell.

The hot 105-degree dry air engulfed them as they stepped inside the sweat lodge. Inside were four bamboo mats on the ground, and Nassim motioned for Mitch and Coco to take one. In the very middle was the fire pit. It was not a fire with wood and smoke but instead red-hot volcano rocks piled on each other. Mitch slowed his breathing because his nostrils burned with every inhale. Man it is hot in here.

Kimo was the last to come in. He walked around the circle, chanted some words in Hawaiian, dropped some herbs and poured water on the pile of rocks, which sent a plume of steam, infused with a sweet minty smell throughout the lodge. Kimo sat in the center opposite the door. Behind him a table made of three large rocks—two vertical and one across, like the rocks at Stonehenge. Mitch wondered if it was an altar. ...and if it's an altar, what does he offer as a sacrifice?

He sat on his mat, facing everyone, and for the first few minutes he said nothing. Then he looked into each person's eyes and said "ALOHA." They could feel the love beaming through his eyes. He took a few deep, long breaths, and instinctively Mitch, Coco, and Nassim did the same thing.

"Aloha...is the most Hawaiian word," he began slowly. "Its true meaning goes beyond what is found in dictionaries. We use it to greet each other and to say goodbye. We use it to show love and affection, a way to show respect for others. For those who follow the path of Huna," he continued, "Aloha means even more. It is a spiritual path. A way of life. My teacher used to say 'Aloha' is a value, one of unconditional love."

Kimo reached over and handed Coco his treasured, personally signed, framed picture of legendary surfer Duke Kahanamoku. He nodded, indicating she should read it for all to hear:

```
"In Hawaii, we greet friends, loved ones
or strangers with Aloha, which means
love. Aloha is the key word to the uni-
versal spirit of real hospitality, which
```

makes Hawaii renowned as the world's center of understanding and fellowship. Try meeting or leaving people with Aloha. You'll be surprised by their reaction. I believe it and it is my creed. Aloha to you."

—Duke Kahanamoku

Kimo paused, looked down, closed his eyes and took a deep breath, looked up again then continued. "Has Jake taught you how to quiet your mind so you can hear your inner voice of truth?"

"Uh, no, not really, but he did teach me Wim Hof breathing exercises, and Coco and I do yoga breathing," said Mitch.

Holding a teapot, Kimo leaned forward. "This tea will help quiet what some call 'monkey-mind,' The ego, the chatter that distracts us from Spirit. Tell me more about your breathing and meditation practice," asked Kimo as he handed them each a cup of tea. After they finished sharing, Kimo sat up and said, "Perfect! Use your breathing practice. The more we clear the mind, the more open we are to receive guidance from Spirit and the ancestors."

"Your goal to surf Pipeline is what got you here, but your true purpose is yet to reveal itself until you are ready to receive it. There is knowledge that exists beyond your five senses. It cannot be broken down, defined, or taught. I will not attempt to explain this to you. Instead, I invite you to experience it for yourself."

Kimo gestured toward the exit. Mitch did a double-take as he tried to figure out what he wanted them to do. Coco and Nassim rose to their feet.

"Where are we supposed to go?" Mitch asked, wondering why he was the only one who appeared to have any trepidation about wandering off in the middle of a rainforest with no map, cell phone, or compass.

"This valley is one of the most sacred places in Hawaii," Kimo explained. "In this place you can connect with the wisdom of our ancestors. The mana is very strong here. Your task is simply to go by yourself and be. Clear your mind and let nature and the Great Spirit speak to you."

"For how long?" Mitch asked. Coco and Nassim had already left the hut, each walking in different directions. "Wait, I don't have a watch. How will I know when to come back?"

"Nature will speak to you," Kimo said, as he folded his arms, lowered his head, and closed his eyes. His face went blank in the same way it had when they were in the cabin. It was as if he was no longer in the room.

Mitch stepped outside the hut and slowly turned 360 degrees, trying to decide which way to go. He heard the sound of the waterfall in the distance—the same one they saw when they hiked down that morning. He felt an impulse to go there and followed it.

It was drizzling, so visibility wasn't bad. As he got closer, the sound of the crashing water grew louder. Mitch gazed in awe at the power of the water cascading down the steep wall. When he stepped up onto the rocks at the edge of the plunge pool, the roar drowned out almost all other sounds. It was a force of nature, both beautiful and brutal. He knew that the basin was probably very deep, and the adventurer in him imagined jumping off the four-story ledge.

He worked his way across the black and gray mossy rocks, which felt wet, smooth yet sticky, like the back of a dolphin. The air was warm, but the light rain was nature's perfect air conditioning. He stopped on one especially large rock, angled in such a way that he could lay back on it. From this reclined position, he looked up at the canopy and took in the trees, bamboo, 'ohi'a, and koa, and the green, near-fluorescent moss growing everywhere. He inhaled the vapor that rose from the falls and tasted its freshness and minerals. His focus naturally turned toward the cascade of water, which conjured a cascade of equally powerful emotions. Awe, gratitude, appreciation. A feeling of love and connectedness he'd only felt while surfing or making love. It literally took his breath away. He remembered Kimo's recommendation to use his breathing practice. As he followed the rhythm of his breath, he noticed the ripples of water circling out in the plunge pool—miniature waves pulsing out toward the rocks.

His eyes became unfocused and began to look at all things, in all directions at once. He saw such beauty in the trees that they seemed to glow. He saw what looked like spider webs, connecting everything. He breathed in the mana.

He thought about how sound also traveled in waves, and how light traveled in waves. Every color in the rainbow was determined, simply by the distance from one wave crest to the next. He thought about how the rain fell from the sky, fed the trees, then collected in rivers and streams, flowed down the waterfall, and continued out to the Pacific Ocean. Then, warmed by the sun, it evaporated returning back to the sky, where it cooled down and became rain again, starting a new cycle. He thought, What if that was the cycle of life a soul goes through?

He became aware of himself and his own energy bundle. Not as separate from but rather interacting and collaborating with nature. It felt like he was exchanging energy, receiving and sending ripples outward with every heartbeat, every breath, every thought and every action. Mitch began to breathe in sync with everything around him. When he breathed, the forest breathed at the same time. He felt a deep interconnectedness to the plants and trees realizing as he breathed in the oxygen they exhaled, they breathed in the CO_2 he exhaled. He felt a deep sense of peace. Aloha.

"Everything is connected. Everything is a wave," he heard a voice say with clarity and conviction. "Even time moves in waves." He saw the cycles of the seasons—summer followed by autumn, followed by winter and then spring again as it repeated forever. He saw life cycles—leaves growing on trees, falling off, being used by ants for food, reabsorbing into the soil, then growing back again. The tide came in, and the tide rolled out. There were no wasted parts, no accidental missteps—just perfect patterns...everywhere.

"Everything is perfect," the voice said calmly, causing Mitch to snap out of his blissful meditation and look around. Is someone there? he thought. He looked left and right but saw no one.

Suddenly feeling very thirsty, and like he needed to share his experience he slowly and intentionally walked across the rocks, stepped down back onto the grass, and headed back to the huts.

When he arrived, neither Coco nor Nassim had yet returned, but Kimo was there, busily working at the altar. Mitch noticed a black cast-iron pot suspended over the fire pit, and the moment he stepped into the hut he realized the scent of the incense had grown faint. How long was I gone? he wondered.

Kimo saw Mitch and picked up a dried gourd from the table. He beckoned for Mitch to come take it. Seeing that there was fresh water inside, Mitch drank in silence savoring each drop.

He glanced down at the array of herbs, spices, and tools on the table. He pointed to some small brown sticks that looked like miniature rolled-up cigars and asked, "What are those?"

"Cinnamon sticks!" Kimo answered cheerfully. "I thought everyone might like some hot tea. I have mint, jasmine, and ginger too. What do you like?"

Mitch chuckled and shook his head. "You're a trip, dude." He chose one with ginger.

"Speaking of trips," Kimo said while putting Mitch's tea into a pot, "would you like to tell me anything about your nature walk?"

"I had an amazing experience," Mitch paused, searching for the right words as he took another sip of fresh water. "I totally get what Nassim was trying to explain. Everything is connected. I experienced all of nature working in harmony with itself, one being, even me. It was...amazing. I can't even describe it to be honest with you."

"Good," said Kimo, as if Mitch's answer was correct. He tended the fire warming the tea.

"I also heard a voice." Mitch added. Kimo stopped. "Well, I think I heard it. No, I'm sure I heard it. But when I looked around no one was there. Was I tripping?"

"Yes," Kimo answered, and gently pulled the black pot from the fire. He tilted it to pour Mitch his tea. He put the pot back on the warmer and led Mitch back over to the bamboo mats on the floor. Just as he sat down, Nassim and Coco returned, warm, happy, and sprinkled with raindrops. Kimo offered them tea and gestured for them to sit on their mats.

"Ancient Hawaiians," Kimo began, "became aware of a personal, supernatural essence. A spirit or life force, that was connected to the body but also separate from the body. During your journey out into nature, did you ever experience yourself as energy? An energy that was inside you, and was you, and was separate from you, all at once?"

Mitch sat up tall and said, "Wow, yes. I can't believe how easily you just described that, but yeah."

"The ancient ones taught us that everything is alive. This essence, or 'life spirit,' infuses all of nature. Everything—not just human beings, but also animals, plants, rocks, rainbows, stars, and everything else—has its own spirit, or soul."

After the experience Mitch just had out in the rainforest, his heart and mind were completely open, he put forth no argument.

"The ancients believed that human beings have three souls." Kimo held up three fingers and said, "Unihipili, a lower soul of the physical body; Uhane, a soul of the conscious mind; and 'Aumaka, a higher soul—our personal, cosmic oversoul."

"That's the word you asked me about in the cabin," said Mitch.

"Yes. Makua means parent, and au means time. Our parent in time. Many perceive the oversoul as a guardian angel, some simply as their higher self. The oversoul is always in contact with us and communicates best through the medium of inspiration, sending us ideas, messages, hunches, dreams, and visions. It is always trying to guide us. It is our primary spiritual teacher, if we have the courage to listen. When we meditate or sit in silence and tranquility, sometimes the answer to a dilemma just comes to us."

"Whoa," said Mitch. "So you think the voice I heard was my 'aumaka?"

"It is possible," said Kimo, folding his arms, "that you were visited by the menehune playing hide-and-seek. But my hunch is that the voice probably came from within you."

Mitch brought his knees to his chest. He wasn't aware of it, but he started to rock back and forth a bit, just like Kimo did when he processed information.

"The Hawaiians of old thought of the self as a trilogy," said Kimo. "Three soul aspects that function separately and in harmony—mind, body, and spirit. To them, Aloha meant 'God or spirit within us.' The way of the Huna is to move constantly toward unity and harmony with your real self, God, and mankind. To be respectful, honest, patient, kind to all life forms, and to be grateful and humble."

Struck by the trilogy reference, Mitch used his fingers to draw the three interconnecting circles on the ground. Just looking at it, gave him a sense of comfort and balance. A longtime mystery revealed.

He rose out of contemplation and glanced over at Coco. Her clothes were soaked and stuck to her body. She looked as though she found the fountain of youth—like a kid who had just spent a summer afternoon running through sprinklers. He felt so much love for her he almost cried.

With Nassim and Kimo he felt an indescribable connection. Everyone sat together drinking tea and sharing their experiences in the rainforest.

***

Mitch, Nassim, and Coco left before sunset and hiked back up to Nassim's van. The long drive back to the ranch left them weary. Mitch and Coco showered at the guest house and after a quick bite to eat, Nassim drove them to the airport. There were some rain delays in the flight schedule, so they didn't actually get back to Oahu until late that evening, but they didn't mind. They were still glowing from their retreat in the valley.

On the morning of their sixth day, the sky still groaned with mild thunder and clouds. Mitch and Coco spent the morning at a Ted's Bakery, then walked in the rain back to their rental. They saw a couple of local boys along the way lighting firecrackers in the street, drinking beer, and making lots of noise. Coco covered her ears and said she would never understand the appeal of beer and firecrackers.

"Eh, they're just bored," Mitch said, fondly remembering his own mischievous youth. "Surfers tend to get antsy if they don't get their fix after a few days."

By 10 a.m., Mitch completely wrote off surfing, packed up his boards and got ready for the flight home. Coco asked if he wanted to check out the Pearl Harbor museum and have lunch there, so they went.

At around 2:00, the rain softened to a drizzle. Mitch and Coco visited the Battleship Missouri Memorial and the USS Bowfin Submarine Museum. Mitch made sure to take a lot of pictures. His father would be happy to know he took some time out of his surf trip to visit the memorial. He decided that when he got home, he'd go to his parents' for a visit and show them the pictures.

Back at the rental at 4 p.m., Coco nestled into Mitch's arm on the couch, just like she always did during their daydreaming sessions back in California.

"I'm sorry you didn't get to surf Pipeline," she said gently while she caressed the hair on the back of his neck.

"I guess it wasn't meant to be. But we had a great time, didn't we? We'll have to plan another trip out here," he said with a devilish grin.

"Are you ready to go back to work?" she asked.

"Yeah, I am, actually," replied Mitch. "I miss everyone."

"I was thinking," she said, clasping her fingers over his. "I really love our loft. I know it's smallish, but I think it's cozy."

"I love it too," Mitch said.

"And we got to come to Hawaii for a whole week, when two years ago you couldn't even get away for a weekend."

"That's true," he agreed, leaning his cheek against her hair. "Thanks for the reminder."

"I don't want to go back to our 'starter home,'" said Coco, closing her eyes. "I just want to go back there and call it 'home,' and just be."

Mitch held her tight. He made an agreement with himself to stop striving so hard to be like his former boss, Ken, and start appreciating and enjoying his own life as it was. He had come so far and built so much. He had more than enough in order to be happy—it was really just a question of waking up and being fully present to enjoy it.

Just then, he noticed a curious silence. The sound of the wind that had been howling through the living room wasn't there. The sound of the raindrops tap-dancing up on the roof wasn't there. He gently slid out from behind Coco and got up to look out the window.

"Hey," he said, gesturing for her to get up and come see. "Honey...it finally stopped raining. I know you're tired, but I want to go check Pipe. This is probably my last chance to see it before we leave for California. Do you want to check it with me?"

"Yeah, sure, let's go," she said, and went to the bedroom to slip on her shoes.

They hopped on the two bicycles that had been locked on the front patio ever since their arrival and headed up the bike path. At the end of the small sandy walkway between houses, the view opened up, and Mitch's heart stopped.

"Oh my God!" he exclaimed. "It's cleaned up! It's off shore...and it's peaky!"

Coco stopped beside him and noted, "Look—there are only a handful of surfers in the water."

"And half are on boogie boards!"

Usually, there are fifty to one hundred surfers in the lineup at

Pipeline, but Mitch guessed that most of them had already written the day off. His heart pumping, he raced back to the rental. Coco called out not to wait for her; she'd catch up. Mitch unpacked his surfboard and frantically screwed in his fins. He threw on his rash guard, grabbed his leash and wax, and jumped back on the bike calling out, "Banzai!" as he passed Coco at lightning speed on the way out the door.

He locked the bike to a tree and walked down to the shoreline, heart pumping. The sun began its descent behind the rugged mountains of Mokoleia. He waxed his board while looking at Pipeline—how beautiful and intimidating it was! He felt like a horse at the starting gates, holding himself back, breathing deeply, slowing his heart rate while he studied the line-up and the currents.

Knowing he needed to be at his physical best, he ran through Coco's "Five Minute Surfer Warm-up." He looked up to see her set down her beach towel, and she ran up to give him a good-luck kiss. He took one moment away from the ocean to gently touch his forehead to hers. Looking deep into her eyes, he smiled and said, "Everything is perfect!" They drank in the moment in silence, exchanging breaths and expanding the feeling of Aloha.

Suddenly they heard a thunderous boom and felt the sand shake. Mitch's attention instantly turned back to the ocean. The last wave of the set rolled through, and he thought, Now's the time to hit it! He ran down the steep sandy beach, jumped into the water and landed midair on his board, catching the back current out, right in front of the rock Jake told him to line up with.

There was no shock upon entry—the water was just as warm as the air. Mitch felt the rush of a river as Pipeline's ten-mile-per-hour current pulled him out and to the right. He paddled steadily, riding the current all the way out and into to the channel. He punched through a few medium-sized waves and then began the two-hundred-yard paddle back to the left and out to the peak.

Mitch made it out relatively easily because he was in prime condition. He felt strong. But even so, he balked when he suddenly realized how big the waves really were. Waves were always much bigger than they appeared from the shore.

A chill ran down Mitch's spine. He slowly paddled into the pit where a small group of surfers waited. As one of the locals dropped in he could tell these waves were 20 to 25 foot faces!

The thickness was like nothing he had ever seen. These waves were huge mountains of water that had travelled thousands of miles, finally reaching their destination from all the way across the Pacific Ocean. And when they reached this perfectly designed reef, they hit with godlike force, lifting everything in their path.

By now the offshore winds blew steadily. Green and yellow shimmers lit up the glassy water. As the lines rolled in, Mitch could feel the surge of the ocean lifting then dropping him, like there was a power underneath that wanted to make its presence known. As he paddled out, he watched a small group of super-stoked locals trading waves, making gnarly vertical drops, and getting slotted on every wave. The five-wave sets were only a few minutes apart, and very consistent.

Finally, Mitch reached the lineup. He was last in line.

While he waited for his turn, two medium-sized waves rolled in. A bunch of the other guys paddled for them, but Mitch let them go by. He had noticed the third and fourth waves were bigger and had better form.

Instinctively he began to paddle out to the deeper water to get in position. He looked over to another surfer who had priority, but he wasn't going for it, so Mitch said to himself, This bad boy is all mine!

Mitch paddled with intention to get into position. He wanted to go deep, but not too deep. He turned his board around and paddled like his life depended on it. It did.

The mountain of water caught him and lifted him up. There was that strange sensation—a feeling of weightlessness and falling upwards. Without hesitation, Mitch popped up, leaned forward and dropped down the twenty-foot face.

But as soon as Mitch made a big sweeping bottom turn, he looked down the line and saw that fifty yards ahead it was already starting to close out. Shit. There's no way I can make this section, he thought.

Thinking fast, he decided his best escape would be to straighten out, go toward the shore, and try to outrun the whitewater. So he crouched low for stability, but there was no way to outrun this freight train. The whitewater quickly overtook him and gobbled him up. Then it spun him around, took him under, and rolled him over.

Mitch didn't know which way was up at first, but he knew about the rinse cycle—Jake taught him—so he held his breath, stayed calm, and covered his head. Once he felt the tug of his leash, he slowly floated to the surface.

He grabbed his board and immediately had to duck-dive under the next wave. Luckily, he made it out of the impact zone just in time. No harm done, he thought. He felt a little winded, but also excited— like a boxer at the end of round one.

As Mitch turned to paddle back out to the peak, he remembered one practice session when Jake had said, "Some waves just weren't meant to be ridden!" He thought to himself, Okay, next time, a little more patience and better wave selection.

He paddled back out into the lineup. After a nice five-wave set cleared the lineup, it was his turn again. This time he caught a smaller wave, double overhead plus, with a fifteen-foot face. This wave had a nice shoulder, good form, and it was coming right to Mitch as if it was made for him.

He turned around and paddled. The wave lifted him up, and he leaned forward and dropped in. Right after his first bottom turn, he did a high carve and stalled just enough to let the tube catch up. In perfect position, the wave opened up. The lip threw over his head for a few seconds and then shot him out.

The inside section was faster, and Mitch had to race the lip to get to the channel. He won this race, popping into the channel at twenty miles per hour, and settled back onto his board, feeling confident. It was only a medium-sized wave, but he rode it well.

He paddled back out and waited his turn. Mitch noticed the swell building, and the sky glowed a fiery orange. Some of the giant walls of water were so big they completely blocked out the setting sun. From the surfer's perspective, the whole world went from being totally sunny to totally shadowed and dark in a matter of seconds.

Not only that, but the waves were starting to break on the second reef, so all the guys had to paddle farther out for the sets.

Mitch spotted three big lines on the outer reef. He looked over at the guy on the outside as they both scrambled to get out far enough not to get caught inside. They both barely made it over the first wave, then the other surfer turned around and went for the second wave. So Mitch was left all alone to pick up the third wave. The winds were blowing hard offshore. He could feel the headwind pushing him back, so he paddled his heart out.

Suddenly, the wave lifted him up. Mitch rose with it, still paddling, but somehow he didn't feel like he was moving forward. He felt a flutter in his chest as an image of the worst-case scenario flashed through his mind—getting stuck at the top—and this moment of fear caused him to pop up just a split second too early. The wind got under his board and the wave kept lifting him up. He was in the worst case scenario. He didn't have enough forward momentum to drop in.

The lip heaved, and Mitch and his board were airborne. "Over the falls," as if the ocean just picked him up and threw him like a basketball. The next thing he knew, he was free-falling next to his board down the twenty-five-foot monster. As he fell, in midair he thought, Oh shit—the reef is so shallow. He took the biggest gulp of breath he could and waited for the impact.

As soon as he hit the water, the entire weight of the ocean slammed right down on top of him and forced him down to the bottom. In fetal position, he covered his head, hoping not to hit the reef. The water rolled him, and spun him, and rolled him again—this was no ordinary rinse cycle. Just as he felt he was rising to the top, the turbulence sucked him right back down. His right shoulder blade bounced firmly off the reef, and fortunately his one-millimeter rash guard kept him from getting scratched or cut.

In surf lingo this is called, "getting ragdolled" or "getting pounded"—the ocean has its way with you, like a pit bull mercilessly tearing apart a limp ragdoll.

The key to survival, and the hardest part, is to stay calm and conserve your breath as you're held under. For more than forty-five seconds Mitch fought the urge to thrash about and scratch his way to the surface. But once he started running low on air, he began to panic. How long can this wave hold me down? he thought, and opened his eyes to see which way was up.

In a complete whiteout, he reached a point where he started to reconcile the possibility that this could be it. Images of all the people in his life that were closest to him rippled across his consciousness. Coco, Jake, Dusty, his mother and father, and Ken. Finally, he stopped struggling.

A voice whispered, "Just stay calm...Everything is perfect."

Mitch made the decision to hold on just a little longer. His lungs burned, but they'd burned before in training, and he knew he had a few more seconds of air left.

Suddenly he felt the tug of his leash, telling him which way was up. Feeling the turbulence fading, he started swimming to the surface just in time to take a gulp of life-saving air.

Within seconds, a huge wall of whitewater forced him to grab a quick breath as he took another one on the head. It mowed over him, holding him down for only fifteen or twenty seconds, dragging him further toward the shore. Eventually, it spit him out gently into the channel, and Mitch grabbed his board and clung to it like a lifeboat.

Clumsily he climbed onto his board and tried to catch his breath. Now in the calm water of the channel, he said a prayer of gratitude. Mitch was not a religious person, but realizing what a close call that was and that life and love was so precious, he would never take them for granted again.

Mitch thought about paddling in and admitting defeat. Pipeline was the deadliest wave on the planet—a wild beast. His adrenaline-induced survival instincts told him it's only thirty yards to the shore and the safety of solid ground.

But then a series of images started running through his mind like video clips—clips of him training with Jake and Coco, surfing with Dusty as a kid—and he heard that voice, "You can't give up! This is why you're here. You've trained over a year for this. No—you've trained your whole life for this."

Feeling more focused and determined than ever, Mitch paddled out again.

It was nearly dark. The water shimmered with a slightly green tint from the edge of the sun, almost ready to set. The scene was both beautiful and ominous.

Only three surfers remained in the water, and when Mitch joined them, they welcomed him with a nod. They were so stoked to have the peak all to themselves that it didn't even matter that Mitch was a haole. Besides, he had just looked death in the face and come back for more. If there was one way to earn instant respect, that was it.

"Nice wipeout. Hit the bottom?"

Mitch nodded.

"Gotta finish on a good one, bro. Here comes another set," said one of the surfers as he gave him the shaka sign and began paddling out with a smile and chin-lift of respect.

They all paddled out as another big set came in on the second reef. Mitch had learned that the first few waves of the set, if they were big, could be closeouts. The third and fourth had better form and clean barrel sections. He patiently let the first few waves go and let the other guys catch them.

His wave, the fourth wave, was at least four times overhead. As he paddled out to get into position, he could feel the entire ocean sucking off the reef. He felt the ocean lift him up, and he stayed in it and kept stroking and stroking until he felt his board release and start sliding down the face. Just as the ocean heaved he snapped to his feet. He stuck the take off and he felt it. He leaned into his front side rail and started his turn as he dropped in.

The first fifteen feet were so vertical that it was literally a free-fall, with only his tail and one fin skimming the face of the wave. As he hit the bottom, his other fins grabbed as he set his rail for a full G-force bottom turn.

He felt a surge of speed as he slingshot past the first section. He gently turned up the face and snapped a carve under the lip about halfway up, stalled for an instant, then immediately shifted his weight to his front foot and front side rail. The wave surged, and the huge, thick lip started to throw over his head.

Inside the barrel, he stood slightly crouched, dragging his left hand along the face of the wave. He was in the sweet spot on his board, his rail and fins cut like a hot blade through butter. Unconsciously he made micro-shifts of his weight, adjusting his line, his speed, and he felt totally in control—total balance, and a total connection with the wave and the entire ocean.

Even though he was flying down the line at twenty miles per hour, he felt motionless. Time stood still. The sound he heard in the tube was the same as a sound he'd heard only twice before—like the inside a seashell or the soft hush of catching air on his snowboard. It was the sound of the earth breathing—a slow deliberate exhale.

All of a sudden, that breath became a spray and Mitch shot out like a bullet from the barrel of a gun. The speed rush launched him out to the shoulder, so he leaned back and did a huge front-side cutback, sending a giant spray off the back. As he completed the turn he grabbed his rail and pulled his nose back into the pocket. Extending his legs, he pumped a few times generating enough speed to make the next section. He turned up the face again and cracked the lip, floating down with it. He pulled around the whitewater just in time to tuck into the inside barrel section for another cover up.

Mitch made it out of the second tube just as the wave finally closed out. With his speed and momentum, he launched off the top of the wave, holding his board with both hands, flying ten feet in the air.

"Woo-hoo!" he shouted as he and his surfboard splashed into the water. He came up smiling from ear to ear.

He couldn't have ridden that wave any better. I can go in on that wave, he thought.

It was dark, he was alive—so alive—and all he could do now was hope somebody saw it.

Coco and Jake started walking down the beach towards Mitch as he belly-boarded in, picked up his board, and jogged up the beach. He beamed with pride, panted with exhaustion, and gaped at Jake in confusion.

"What are you doing here?" Mitch asked between breaths. "I thought you were in Saipan."

"I went, took care of business, and came back," Jake said matter-of-factly. "Soon as the rain stopped I knew where to find you."

Coco put a towel around Mitch's shoulders and gave him a kiss, and Jake took his surfboard. All at once they turned to look back at the break. In one final heave, the ocean swallowed up the last of the sun.

"Mahalo!" Mitch called out, with his arms outstretched to the horizon. He threw one arm around Coco's neck and one arm around Jake's, like Kimo's giant teddy bear hug.

"My ohana!" he said in a surprisingly accurate imitation of Kimo's voice. "We go home now, I make hot tea, and we talk story!"

Laughing, all three walked up the beach, stepping over the cracked coconut shells and loose palm fronds blown over from the storm.

CONCLUSION

You never change things by fighting
the existing reality. To change something,
build a new model that makes
the existing model obsolete.

—R. Buckminster Fuller

Mitch journaled while Coco napped, curled up in a blue travel blanket in the window seat, fully reclined. Jake sat across the narrow aisle reading a book. Mitch wrote Jake's name across the smooth paper with his weighted metal pen, and then drew a Venn diagram, labeling each circle: "Mind," "Body," and "Finances."

He wrote "Coco," then drew three circles and labeled each circle: "Mind," "Body," "Spirit."

Finally, he wrote "Me." He drew three circles, and paused to think.

Just then, a flight attendant stopped in the aisle to ask if anyone would like a drink, causing Jake to look up. He rubbed his eyes, closed his book, looked across the aisle at Mitch and then back to the flight attendant.

"Two sparkling waters, please," he said. "We're celebrating." Mitch closed his journal. He turned to wake Coco to see if she wanted anything, but she looked so peaceful and serene in her blanketed cocoon that he just let her be.

The flight attendant set the cups and napkins on their tray tables and moved to the next row. Jake lifted his cup to Mitch and said, "To your successful journey!"

Mitch shook his head and said, "Nah, to our successful journey. I couldn't have done it without you."

Jake hesitated. "That's not true." he said, "You did this. For me, it was simply a pleasure to watch and observe." Then he took a sip and placed the cup on his tray table.

Mitch squirmed, "I don't think so. You taught me everything I know."

"Nope, this was all you."

"How can you say that?" Mitch asked. "I'm trying to show gratitude and you're not..."

"Listen," Jake interrupted. "Do you know how many students said they wanted to surf Pipe but were not willing to pay the price? There's only so much a mentor can do. A mentor can't learn for you. Sure I taught you the principles and pointed you in the right direction. But the hard work of taking those principles and mastering them... You put in the hours and hours of practice, waking up at crack of dawn every day. You showed up on time. You paddled out. You faced your fears. I'm proud of you for busting your ass and for not giving up. Where'd you get that persistence, discipline, and courage from? I can't take credit for that."

Mitch looked away for a moment, stunned. A strong sense of pride and ownership rushed over him like a waterfall. Suddenly an image of his parents flashed across his mind.

"I guess...you're right in that I did it myself. Just now I realized where my determination and work ethic come from: My parents. I remember my dad saying, 'If you work hard and follow your heart, you will be successful at whatever you do!' And that belief has been with me my entire life. And my mom is an eternal optimist. She always sees the glass as half-full and believes everything will work out for the best. I never realized it but the main reason I've been able to take risks and take action in spite of my fears was because deep down, I always believed everything is perfect, everything happens for a reason, and there is a higher plan, even if I don't see it at the time. She planted that belief deep inside me."

"What a blessing to have that kind of upbringing," said Jake. "A foundation for success." Mitch raised his cup silently to his parents and drank. He couldn't wait to visit them when he got home.

"Sometimes it's not easy to have faith everything will work out. When that rainstorm wouldn't let up, I thought for sure the trip was a write off and all that hard work and training was out the window. But in the end it worked out perfectly. I got to surf near-perfect Pipe, with only a few guys in the water—better than anything I ever could have planned myself."

Mitch's positive energy rippled outward from a smile so wide that Jake wondered if the flight attendant spiked his drink.

"I'll toast to that," Jake responded and raised his cup. "Everything is perfect!"

"Everything is perfect!" Mitch answered, and they drank.

"That's how the law of precession works." Jake commented. Mitch raised his eyebrow and cocked his head. The flight attendant came by to take away trash, and Jake asked if they could each have another can of "sparkling."

"The law of precession," Jake began, "Is one of Bucky's generalized principles. It's an immutable law of universe, with no exception."

"Who's Bucky?"

"Buckminster Fuller," Jake clarified. "Remember Marshall Thurber? He's one of Bucky's disciples, he's also one of my heroes. Bucky was a genius, a philosopher, comprehensive anticipatory design engineer trying to save humanity from ourselves. He talked about this universal law called "precession", and it works like this...."

Jake took the square paper napkin out from under his drink and clicked open a pen. He drew a flower on the right, and a honeybee on the left, and said, "This honeybee here has a goal and wants to get to this flower to get what?"

"Nectar to make honey."

"That's right. He's gonna take that nectar home to feed his family," said Jake, and then he wrote, "#1" at the top of the napkin. "Rule number one. For the law of precession to be in effect, you have to be 'In motion'. The real power of a goal is that it gets you in motion. Not the goal itself, but that it gets you into forward action."

Mitch nodded and said, "Got it."

Jake drew a spiral vertical arrow from the bee to the flower.

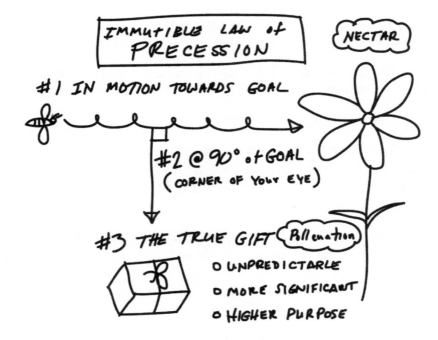

"Number two. The second principle," he said, "is that the 'true gift' of any goal lies at ninety degrees from the direction of your goal." He drew a box with a bow on it. "The true gift will be predictably unpredictable, have higher significance, and will always be at ninety degrees."

Mitch put his drink down and shook his head, but before he could say, "Huh?" Jake elaborated.

"In this case," Jake said with the tip of his pen on the honeybee, "The honeybee goes and collects his nectar—carbs—and along the way some pollen—protein—as he moves from flower to flower. Simultaneously at ninety degrees, something more significant is happening. That bee is pollinating the great botanicals that enable our entire planet's breath. That is the 'true gift.'"

"On my journey with Kimo I saw how the plants absorb our 'wasted' CO_2, absorb sunlight, and release oxygen, which is what keeps us alive," Mitch added.

"Exactly. Without honeybees, vegetation would die in a matter of months, and our planet wouldn't be able to sustain life as we know it. And the bee is thinking, 'Here I go, collecting food for the kids.' But by pursuing that goal, and using his unique gifts and talents, he's in perfect harmony and flow with all of nature and playing a much bigger role on Spaceship Earth. Precession is always there, but you can miss it if you only look straight ahead. Remember, it will be out of the corner of your eye at ninety degrees."

Jake paused and let Mitch absorb the lesson. Once Mitch began to nod slowly, Jake took out another napkin, drew a stick figure and labeled it, "Mitch."

"So what was your nectar?" he asked.

"I wanted to learn how to surf Pipe," answered Mitch.

"Yes." Jake drew a surfboard on the napkin, with a spiral arrow pointing to it from the stick figure. "Surf pipe. Surf pipe. Surf pipe," Jake joked. "So you took action. You got into motion. And what happened at ninety degrees that wasn't predictable?"

Humans are "honey, money seeking bees".

—R. Buckminster Fuller

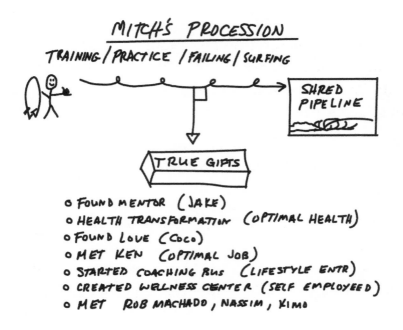

"Well first," Mitch said, leaning back and looking up, trying to remember back to when this whole journey started. "First I met you. You've been my mentor, my coach, and a great friend. One of the biggest gifts of my entire life!"

Jake said, and wrote "found mentor" on the napkin, with an arrow pointing to it at 90 degrees.

"Then I met Coco, totally unexpected, I mean, I was actively avoiding women at the time! I tried everything in my power not to fall in love, but it happened, and I've never been happier."

Jake wrote, "Found love" on the napkin.

"I got in shape too," Mitch said, remembering how his pants fit better and better with each passing month.

"Got healthy!" wrote Jake.

"Then I met Ken, through you, and he gave me the job at Eco-Friendly Lighting, and I learned so much I was inspired to start my own business."

"Mm-hmm, keep going," said Jake, scribbling on the napkin as Mitch spoke.

"Then I started helping my clients transform through my coaching business...and as I became a better surfer I got accepted by the locals at our home break...I moved in with Coco, and Oh! I met Rob Machado, I met Nassim and Kimo who helped me discover Aumaka, my spirit voice...What else? I surfed Pipeline."

"That's a lot of precession" Jake said with a grin. "Found mentor, found love, restored your health, became an elite athlete, got a job you loved, started your own business, met and collaborated with a surf hero, connected with your spirit. You sure have come a long way for someone who spent all his time thinking, 'Surf Pipeline."

Mitch marveled at seeing it all on paper. "I'm so lucky. So lucky."

Jake took his pen and drew some arcs on the napkin, like ripples of water circling outward from the stick figure on the surfboard. "Didn't you tell me," he asked, "about how one of your clients got off her medication because you helped her lose weight? And she turned out to be the mother of one of the local surfers you had issues with?"

Mitch nodded.

"You were just doing your job, right? You weren't out to rescue entire families. You were just out to coach your client," Jake explained. "Coach the client. Coach the client. Coach the client. Look at the precessional effect there. That guy is stoked to have his mother healthy and so is his entire family. We can't even predict the ripple effect that will have. Small world, right?"

"Pretty cool," Mitch agreed.

"And what about the money you and Coco donated to Waves for Water and the Rob Machado Foundation from your Yoga for Surfers video? There are children in dozens of countries with clean drinking water and hundreds of little environmental activists out there you may never meet because of the precession of your actions. Your goal to surf Pipeline is now literally helping to save our planet," Jake said. "Law of precession." He clicked his pen closed and put it away in his shirt pocket.

Mitch leaned back and closed his eyes to soak it all in. When he opened his eyes he glanced down at his magazine and saw a full spread on tow-in surfing. The caption said,

`A Perfect Day at Peahi (Jaws) - Maui.`

"Jake, check this out," Mitch said, but Jake was busy clearing off his tray table and gathering the trash to take to the flight attendants' station at the rear of the plane.

As he stood, he merely glanced at the magazine, patted Mitch's shoulder and said, "That's the next level." Then he picked up Mitch's empty cup and took off down the aisle. When he returned and took his seat, he added, "I'm actually going on a trip with a couple of Australian friends who are tow-in maniacs. I might not see you for three or four weeks, depending on how the swells stack up."

"Aw man," Mitch said, clenching the sides of the magazine, "I wish I could take a month off like that. I'm already gonna have to work my tail off just to catch up at the wellness center and I've only been gone a week!"

"Yes, that's the next level," said Jake, pulling a book out of the carry-on bag at his feet: Cash Flow Quadrant, by Robert Kiyosaki and Sharon Lecter. He placed it on top of Mitch's surf magazine and said, "Read this and when I get back we'll talk about how to get from a self-employed entrepreneur to a business owner."

While Mitch examined the book, Jake made himself comfortable for an in-flight nap. He took out a travel blanket, covered himself, and pushed the button to recline.

As Jake dozed off, Mitch opened his journal, careful not to disturb Coco, still sleeping soundly. The journal was full, except for a few blank pages at the end, which he planned to use to chronicle his experience of surfing Pipeline for the very first time. He couldn't wait to fill those pages with memories of facing the awesome power of Mother Nature at Pipeline.

He looked at the three blank circles he drew earlier, and then carefully added a fourth. He labeled each circle, "Mind," "Body," "Finances," and "Spirit."

He began to write.

I now realize that this journey was not about surfing Pipeline. It was about finding myself. Changing my entire view of the world and my place in it.

Looking back, I realize it's not about the BMW, or the high-paying corporate job, it's not about the $50,000 bonus check, the trophy girlfriend, or the luxury apartment or Top Producer awards.

It's about being a learner, being humble, and having a mentor. It's about understanding everything is energy, moving in waves and patterns. Some patterns are universal, immutable laws and like strong currents, if you align with them you can literally ride the waves of the universe.

It's about carving my own path, following my heart, and doing work I'm passionate about. It's about taking responsibility for the creative power I have to organize my life around what matters most.

So 'now what do I do?' I set a next-level goal, stay in motion, and wake up every day with gratitude and curiosity about the work and precession that's ahead.

INSERT IMAGE [Four circles labeled Mind, Body, Finances, Spirit, and the name "Mitch Springer: The Wave Hunter" over all.]

RECOMMENDED READING

<u>Referenced in the book</u>

Dr. A's Habits of Health, by Dr. Wayne Scott Andersen

The Richest Man in Babylon, by George Samuel Clason

Unlimited Wealth, by Paul Pilzer

The New Wellness Revolution, by Paul Pilzer

The Next Millionaires, by Paul Pilzer

Rich Dad, Poor Dad, by Robert Kiyosaki and Sharon Letcher

Cashflow Quadrant, by Robert Kiyosaki and Sharon Letcher

Antifragile: Things that Gain from Disorder, by Nassim Nicholas Taleb

Good to Great: Why Some Companies Make the Leap... And Others Don't, by Jim Collins

Conscious Capitalism: Liberating the Heroic Spirit of Business, by John Mackey, Rajendra Sisodia, and Bill George

Operators Manual for Spaceship Earth, by Buckminster Fuller

Other Recommended Reading

Money and You, by Bill Allen and Marshall Thurber

The Accounting Game, by Judith Orloff and Darrell Mullis

Wooden: A Lifetime of Observations and Reflections On and Off the Court, by John Wooden and Steve Jamison

Coach Wooden's Pyramid of Success: Building Blocks for a Better Life, by John Wooden and Jay Carty

The Celestine Prophecy, by James Redfield

The Alchemist, by Paulo Coelho

The Way of the Peaceful Warrior, by Dan Millman

Jonathan Livingston Seagull, by Richard Bach and Russell Munson

Your Life as Art, by Robert Fritz

The Four Agreements: A Practical Guide to Personal Freedom, by Don Miguel Ruiz and Janet Mills

Emotional Intelligence 2.0, by Travis Bradberry, Jean Greaves, and Patrick Lencioni

Outliers: The Story of Success, by Malcolm Gladwell

The War of Art, by Steven Pressfield and Shawn Coyne

Turning Pro, by Steven Pressfield

Self Reliance, an Essay by Ralph Waldo Emerson

ABOUT THE AUTHOR

Greg Rex has started and help built 10 different companies. In 2002, burnt out on the corporate grind, Greg decided to simplify his life and become a health coach. Partnering with co-founder Dr. Wayne Andersen they pioneered and built what has become Optavia Inc., one of America's largest and successful transformational coaching companies. Optavia was named one of the fastest growing companies in America by Fortune and Forbes, and one of the Most Trusted Companies in America by Forbes in 2016 and 2017. Greg has trained over 10,000 health professionals and health coaches and has helped over 150,000 people improve their health and well being.

Greg lives in both San Diego and in Lake Tahoe and travels internationally to share his insights and principles on how to become a lifestyle entrepreneur and to organize your career and life around what matters most to you.

CPSIA information can be obtained
at www.ICGtesting.com
Printed in the USA
FSHW022101060819
60781FS